# The Road to Damascus ...
## and Beyond

# The Road to Damascus ... and Beyond

## A reawakening of the spirit by thru-hiking the Appalachian Trail

George "Ole Smoky Lonesome" Sandul

Note: For purposes of respect and protecting privacy, permission has been obtained
for all actual trail names shown. However, it is hard to locate people knowing only
their trail names. So, numerous changes have been made. But, it is difficult to retain
originality without duplication, with so many trail names having already been used. Such
duplication to actual trail names is merely coincidence. Some of the character names
have been changed to protect their anonymity.

Profits from the sale of this book are earmarked for donations to the Appalachian Trail
Conservancy and the preservation of the Appalachian Trail.

The author's stories and experiences related in this book are strictly in his opinion.
Concepts and ideas also are in the opinion of the author.

This book was printed in the United States of America.

**To order additional copies of this book, contact:**
Xlibris Corporation
1-888-795-4274
www.Xlibris.com
Orders@Xlibris.com
57576

Mt. Katahdin
Millinocket
CANADA
Caratunk
Maine
Gorham
VT
Glencliff
Hanover
NH
New York
Dalton
MA
CT
Bear
Mt
Kent
Delaware Water Gap
Port Clinton
Duncannon
PA
NJ
Boiling Springs
MD
Harpers Ferry
West Virginia
Waynesboro
Pearisburg
Virginia
Daleville
Damascus
Erwin
North Carolina
Hot Springs
Tennessee
Wesser
Springer Mountain
Georgia

Appalachian

Trail

50 days on trail—near Catawba, VA—mile 700(about)—May 24

# Contents

Petites Gap, VA
View from tent
May 29
Day 55—mile 759

To Kris

# Acknowledgements

Numerous people who were involved are not mentioned in the story just simply because there are too many. A sincere thanks to all of you, with the hikers being first and foremost for without them, there would be no story. Thanks to my family. Especially to my wife, Kris, who religiously sent out the twenty-one mail drop boxes and dealt with the disinterest of the post office man and was always there for my phone calls, listening with rapt interest to my tales of woe.

Thanks to our middle kid, oldest son, Curt. He was there to see me off with his family (the surprise visitors coming all the way from Missouri) and seemed to buoy the spirits of his mother, almost to a state of elation, leading me to believe that she was happiest when I was going someplace for a long time. Curt, who does not march to anybody's drummer, seems to have a special ability to do good when it is least expected. Thanks to our youngest son, Will, he made Katahdin a truly meaningful experience. Thanks to our daughter, Tammy, our oldest, for the telephone calls to her always gave me impetus to continue. She, much in the fashion of Corsican, kept telling me not to quit. And thanks to my dear friend back in Ocala, Christine, she was my advisor and my inspiration when no others would do and provided candid critique when necessary. And thanks to another dear friend, Bob Dillon, the world-class finger-style guitarist, who was kind enough to send me CARE packages of extra food and other unexpected goodies. And thanks to my friend, Ellen, who supported my efforts so well when I was carrying that forty-pound bag of sand up and down the streets of Ocala. And thanks to my boss, Carlos Silvestre, for letting me have six months off when the surveying season was at its peak. And a sincere thanks to yet another dear friend, Lee Perry. His intense interest in this venture might have been the difference, giving me inspiration to actually complete the hike.

And my most sincere thanks to my dear cousin Doris, who listened to my stories as I proceeded north and documented such progress on her map of the Appalachian Trail that is framed and adorns a special place in her home.

And finally, thanks to my Canadian cousins Patricia and Marion, who always have encouraged and inspired me.

My most sincere thanks to the crew at Xlibris who dealt with my last minutes changes with patience and understanding. Kyla Solaiman was outstanding in her encouragement and just would not let me quit. And, to Kevin Burton my heart felt thanks for not allowing me to cancel my contract after getting discouraged.

And, how could I have contacted so many of the important people in this story without the professional and expert help of Laurie Potteiger at the Appalachian Trail Conservancy headquarters—thank you so much.

# Preface

This is the story of one person's dream to accomplish what was thought to be impossible. An assumption that was truly conjecture, for only by trying could the true answer be resolved. However, accomplishments in our human voyage should not be the standard by which we are measured and then judged. Of more importance is that we tried and failed when that is compared to having not tried at all. Thru-hiking the Appalachian Trail is a manifestation of the human struggle—a microcosm of a life well lived, a life of questing and not merely existing. And for this endeavor to truly have meaning, the hike has to be on the Trail's terms as originally intended.

The Trail's nature is such that accomplishing a thru-hike required one element more than any other—deep commitment.

This is not a story about adventure or derring-do or unbelievable feats of strength and stamina. A person can prepare for hiking the Appalachian Trail by strengthening their bodies, by educating themselves about hiking and backpacking and dealing with the rigors of the Trail and learning about ways of adjusting for weather and what to avoid, and by adjusting their attitudes for dealing without amenities.

However, if there is no commitment then it is all for naught.

Yes, a potential thru-hiker could possibly, but not very probably, complete a thru-hike having embarked on the hike with no particular purpose in mind. It is possible. However, for this writer/hiker, it would not have been possible. Week 3 would have found me back home eating pancakes and ice cream whenever I wanted, watching TV whenever I wanted, and enjoying the amenities that are my God-given right.

Commitment can come in various forms. If you only tell yourself what you are going to do then you have nothing to lose. With that clandestine approach if you decide along about week 5 that this is just not for you, well, hey folks, just wanted to give it a try. Wasn't for me. Just too boring. Just too much time involved for the return. Can't dance, too wet to plow, so got better things to do. Just about anything will suffice as an excuse. The end result: a tiny return on very little investment.

However, if you start telling people—relatives, neighbors, friends—then the thing takes on an entirely new meaning. With these announcements and promises, of course, come the doubts: your abilities, your stamina, your strength, your perseverance. However, those conditions exist for all aspects of life. For the Appalachian Trail is abstract for now, but life is there staring us in the face every day. And hiking the AT in some ways is life in microcosm.

Commitment also comes from the various forms of preparation for the hike. If you chose to use mail drops that have to be prepared ahead of time, that certainly is more binding than saying that you are going to just procure supplies along the way. Yes, some supplementing will have to be done to the mail drops, but if they are there all ready to be sent out then you are more likely to continue. It would be kind of awkward to return home to eat humble pie while tearing open a box marked for, say, Bear Mountain, New York, right there in your living room.

Or the maps. Not essential for a thru-hike but so very nice to have. Buy the whole set ahead of time, and the preparation process is more complete. However, more importantly, it is a commitment. You might still be able to use camping gear on other less-ambitious hikes, but the AT maps pretty well spell it out as to its intended use. Buy all of them, and you are more likely to do the entire thing. Sure, you might sell them. Maybe. Better to keep them and confirm that what the maps have printed on them is really out there.

Commitment will not come easy for it has become a rather old-fashioned term. Couples prefer to live together to see "if things will work out." And every couple on earth could find a reason, or rather an excuse, for ending a relationship. Dedication toward a company that provides employment is viewed on an interim basis, waiting for greener pastures and something that looks more promising on the other side of the fence. The world of sports is probably the saddest indication of this relatively new trend. The term *team* really does not mean too much for there may not be even one member included from the year before. The old concept of bringing together the talent on hand and utilizing the resources to place people in positions where their talents can best be utilized give way to simply replacement with a "better coach" and "better players" as the stakes go up and money seems to be no object or deterrent to who or what is available.

A rather meaningless approach to life. Anything worth anything must have commitment. It's doubtful that the human race would have progressed much past the stone ages without the resolve to improve, to get smarter, and to find better ways without commitment. Everybody has a potential to be anything even if that anything is somewhat limited by his or her abilities. However, that concept runs totally contrary to our throwaway society where husbands, wives, coworkers are discarded with hardly a second thought.

Discarded without being given a second chance! Way before one was placed in a position to have to dig deep into one's own potential and capabilities. Way before there was development of the raw materials of which one is comprised to start revealing everybody's basic composition of being a diamond in the rough. Way before it became necessary to become innovative and to learn. Most sadly, way before some semblance of self-assurance could be developed and those miraculous hidden traits would appear as the mother of necessity.

The hiking of the Appalachian Trail is a very personal thing. And with that comes the decisions as to what you want it to be. If within the psyche exists that deep desire to make that something a thru-hike then slowly a sense of commitment starts to take place. It was interesting to watch some of the groups that were hiking or attempting to thru-hike for invariably there was one person that didn't quite measure up to expectations, either his/her own or the group as an entity. And the result was to then just simply quit, to drop off the Trail.

However, if a hiker makes that commitment to him/herself, the strength to continue does not come from a support group but simply from within to stay the course and gut it out. To dig deep, to go beyond what you thought you could do. Within the makeup of the human spirit, there exists in most of us a will not to give up easily whether this comes from past experiences, past disappointments, environment or heredity. For most of us, we would have to draw from all of our composition of genes and experience to make such a commitment to spend almost half a year in a single endeavor where one encountered the spectrum of physical and mental and, in some cases, financial demands. When day 117 was still about the same as day 4 and ahead lay the same types of demands that just did not go away, it soon becomes much easier to start the rationalization process.

Yes, this story is about commitment. Not really anything else. The rest of it is window dressing or the red herring. Commitment. Or as Corsican so aptly advised, "Whatever you do, don't quit. Don't quit." Only through commitment can that mantra be answered to and a thru-hike completed.

# Prologue

*Your path is arduous but will be amply rewarding.*
*—in the fortune cookie in my Chinese take-out meal sometime before*
*leaving for Atlanta for the start of my hike of the Appalachian Trail*

*May 30, 2003—Day 56—Mile 777—(Journal entry)—finally got out of there
by 7:11 a.m. (nice to have a watch )—the 700' climb was rocky but went pretty
good—from Hitchcock Knob, the rest of the way was great—met Outlaw in that
stretch*

The Appalachian Trail experience never quite seems to follow a
pattern, and the human aspects never cease to amaze in scope and variety.
This day proved to epitomize what continued to prove and reprove itself as
the hike progressed north. I had spent a large part of the morning going
downhill, was in good spirits, and had arrived along the south bank of the
James River, looking forward to getting to the other side and hitching a
ride to town with the magic of resupply beckoning with its promise. And
of course, looking forward to the gluttony that naturally came with trips to
town, visions of ice cream bars permeated my brain, culinary delights—even
if not usually thought of as such—danced about the perimeter of my
imagination, the ultimate kid in a candy store turned loose within its
confines. Store, even the generic term, juiced up the psyche to levels of
exaltation and celebration. And having already covered almost 10 miles, and
it not being noon yet, elevated spirits that were already floating quite high.

I was also looking forward with anticipation to the crossing of the
James River as this was accomplished by walking over one of the longest

footbridges on the Trail, and certainly one of the best designs, good solid construction, and yes, beautiful. The Foot Bridge. An amusing twist as this footbridge was actually a proper noun, the Foot Bridge, named after Bill Foot, a thru-hiker that had completed the hike in 1987. It turned out to be quite an engineering marvel that any bridge builder would have been proud of as the photo album will attest to for it took about a half-dozen shots to satisfy the documentation process. The structure had been well planned and well placed somewhat in juxtaposition with the railroad bridge that ran askew and crosses it at the north end.

I slowly crossed the bridge, admiring the construction and enjoying walking on a level and even surface, always a treat for any thru-hiker that has been stumbling along on the Trail, tripping over rocks, and avoiding tree roots and other obstacles. I noted that there were a number of cars at the trailhead parking lot. It looked promising for getting a ride to town. Glasgow, Virginia, in comparison with other Trail towns, probably didn't quite meet the stereotypical image of idealism. However, thru-hikers learn early that ideals are merely a form of false optimism and better set aside, no place for such in this masochistic endeavor.

Ornery, a thru-hiker that I had seen before, was waiting for a trail angel; and we acknowledged each other as I approached the edge of the parking lot and unloaded my pack. He told me that a man named Jim was on a run to town and would be right back. So instead of putting myself in the uncomfortable position of sticking out my thumb hoping to save time, I thought it better to take my chances with this unknown purveyor of good arriving back shortly.

The wait proved to be advantageous. He was back in just a few minutes. We loaded our packs and were heading to the glitter of town. As we rode, which was always a wonder and pleasure, the conversation somehow turned to snakes, a topic not lacking in opinions and ideas, usually quite strongly stated. A hiker earlier had mentioned that he had been "struck at" by a copperhead. I mentioned the eastern diamondback that I encountered back in Florida in November while out on a surveying job and elaborated on the beauty of the large and very active snake. The trail angel seemed to lack appreciation for this type of beauty. He said something to the effect that "the only kind of beautiful rattlesnake is a dead one." I pretty much let it go at that. I had learned a long time ago that too many people have such fear of snakes that convincing them of their beauty and usefulness in nature was futile.

The ride proved uneventful and soon the Glasgow, Virginia, sign appeared as thoughts strayed from conversation about hikers to the real matter at hand, food. However as we approached town, I noted the junction with another highway to get into Glasgow, a left on Virginia Route

130 off Highway 501. Highway junctions present a problem getting back to the Trail as your hitch back might not be going the same way at the junction and it could mean that a prospective ride back might not work out. However, I would deal with that later.

I soon found myself in front of the Glasgow Food Mart lying in the grass in a gluttonous state of ecstasy. However, three ice creams bars didn't do much for my inner gnawing; so I wandered across the highway to the Grocery Express, drawn there by the smell of frying chicken. The offering of such came with potato wedges all severely drowned in old grease, just what a thru-hiker was looking for. I ordered what I knew wouldn't be enough but would at least satiate the immediate animalistic urges, hoping the pangs would abate enough to deal with the business at hand.

Now I was ready for resupply. A thru-hiker eventually learns that to attempt stocking up while in such a ravenous state before somewhat tempering that out-of-control appetite would end up with twenty-seven pounds of food to add to an already-overstuffed backpack. Now, back to the food mart.

I was soon waiting for my turn at check-out, cradling the usual fare of granola bars, peanut butter, bagels—trail food. I hadn't located a shopping basket and maybe that was by design, again regarding the weight of the backpack. My arms could only hold so much and was usually enough.

The man in front of me was huge and hard not to notice. As the check-out lady hit the total button, he handed her a ten-dollar bill and said, "Tell me it's not over ten bucks."

She curtly replied, "It's $14.92."

They stood staring at each other—she upward, he downward—in a sort of attitude of Mexican standoff. He asked her if possibly he could charge the remainder and to make up a tab for him. Nothing was said for some long moments. She regarded him as if he couldn't be recognized, or trusted; and being from this very rural area, he finally noted, "Come on, I'm the only white guy over seven feet tall in the county."

Silence. Long silence. I could stand it no longer and finally offered a solution to the problem, "Shoot, buddy, I'll give you the five bucks."

The store went deadly silent. For all within earshot, the world temporarily stopped. All attention turned to me, this rather deplorable and smelly apparition that maybe others were trying to ignore suddenly came into focus. It became obvious that some sort of local protocol might have been broken. Actually I find myself doing this in shopping lines fairly often. And thru-hikers usually aren't intimidated by too much, and I had found it necessary to support my supposed breech of custom by adding, "If nothing else, I won't have to stand here holding all of this stuff."

The big man was incredulous and continued to look down at me. Finally he had overcome his disbelief and, in a downward spiraling tone of voice, said, "You're . . . not . . . from . . . around . . . here, are . . . you." A statement, not a question.

My confidence from a few moments hence had more or less dissipated; however, a statement had been made from which there was no turning back. I eased my stuff onto the end of the counter, sliding his fourteen dollars and ninety-two cents worth somewhat out of the way and reached into my fanny pack and got the plastic-encased five-dollar bill out and handed it to the lady. He continued to look down at me as if he were observing possibly a UFO, something much too much for the mind to comprehend. I was amused when the lady handed him the eight cents and how he obliviously slid it into his jeans pocket. However, by this time, it had become very evident that this clearly was a case of serendipity, a ride back to the Trail.

"You're not heading back to the trail, are you?"

"The what?"

"The Trail, you know, the Appalachian Trail."

This required some explanation as he wasn't totally familiar with the location being only somewhat aware of its existence, not too unusual along the AT in a lot of the communities. He listened carefully to my story and then offered an again—downward spiraling tone of voice reply, "Yaaaaa . . . yaaaa, we are." It was evident that he had had no intention of going that way out of town, but my five dollars had made a lasting impression.

He headed out the door, and I still wasn't totally sure he would be there when I stepped outside. However, when I came around the side of the building, my backpack was gone. A glance over to a black Bronco-type vehicle parked nearby revealed its location. He had already loaded it along with the walking stick. I was invited to my place in the backseat.

His grandmother was driving. I suppose the likeliness of her having the five dollars occurred to me; however, this had long become a moot point—a ride back to the Trail always was of utmost precedence in orders of business. Shoot, it was turning out to be the best five-dollar investment I had ever made.

As we headed back east out of town, we talked of the significance of the Appalachian Trail and the gutsy-ness of the people that hiked it. We wound our way back to the Trail on the very crooked highway as the conversation turned to the goodness of people and how the AT seemed to bring out the best. A warm and fuzzy feeling permeated the friendly interior of the Bronco as we became slowly aware of what was happening. The good-byes were warm as we wished each other good luck in our endeavors and wished each other a good life. The likeliness of ever seeing each other again, we all knew, was quite slim.

Having been preoccupied at the time that I paid my bill for my groceries, the amount hadn't really registered. Now that amount took on meaning, more like a manifestation or possibly an epiphany. I stood in awe and looked at my total, having clearly remembered his total. Maybe something had happened here that wasn't totally happenstance. I stared at the receipt as I packed the groceries into my pack.

It was $17.76.

I thought, 1492 . . . 1776. American history in microcosm. Too profound for coincidence. Too evident to kiss off to happenstance. No, something greater had taken place, of that I was sure.

Numbers. Just numbers. However . . .

The hiking of the Trail is all about numbers. Miles to the next town, the time of day, the amount of food in days left in the pack, the weight of the pack, miles from the start, miles to Maine, miles covered that day, and so on. So numbers were an integral part of a life in this artificial world of super accomplishment where comparison was used daily to tabulate on a day-to-day basis, and virtually, everything was hinged to some quantity. I smiled as I looked upward with the usual utterance in these now-frequently-occurring instances.

"Thank you, Lord."

So it goes. Trail magic, I suppose. Or just another case of "amply rewarding." It doesn't take too much of this kind of stuff to more than offset the "arduous" part.

# *Chapter* 1

## Reasons

The mantra about hiking the Trail is, "You don't do it just to say that you did it."

You have got to be kidding!

If I ever meet the hiker that did it and then went home, put away the gear and never told anybody, I will be looking at either the most confident, unthreatened, stoic, and pardon the redundancy, taciturn of rock-solid-silent-type-citizens since the Duke went to that last pilgrim-age in the sky or somebody that just did not get it. I hiked the Trail to tell people about it. I did it because I am not that sure of myself. I did it because, quite frankly, I needed to feel that I had accomplished something! I did it because I reeked of insecurity. I did it because I wanted and needed some attention and wanted to tell people about it afterward. I did it for the mano a mano, that quest for derring-do that so gnaws at masculinity. I did it because it appealed to the threatened part of me that yearned for adoration; and I just did it wondering if something, just anything, could appease this sense of having accomplished so little in my life.

Working for the U.S. Geological Survey for thirty-five years of my life, twenty-four of those in the field, should have provided enough adventure to fill at least a couple of books. After "retirement," I dabbled with the subject content that experience had provided. To my surprise, it seemed that there wasn't that much of a demand for the musings and bitching of an ex-government man. All submittals resulted in rejection slips. Rejection is so hard. But with rejection, after one rebounds from that state of denial, comes new feelings—introspection, revelation. Aha, there has to be something viable out there that I can write about. The search began.

I am a writer first. A hiker—well, somewhere down the list you may find "hiker." And with that somewhat oxymoronic state of things, to say that you had hiked the entire Appalachian Trail—well, just maybe somebody out there might want to read about it. And since Mom is now long gone, it had to be somebody other than her.

The books that I read about the AT before doing it always were satisfying but left a vacuum in the psyche, thinking that there had to be something more to it. Some hiked for nature. Some hiked for the peace that it would provide. Some hiked in quest of the geologic wonder of the configuration of this most unique of old mountains and thusly could fill volumes on cartographic and geographic anomalies. Some hiked to "get away from the house." The younger set hiked it, if they could afford it, as the *last hurrah* before entering that labyrinth of the working world. Some just hiked it for no reason at all, maybe sort of a George W. Bush approach to life. As the old cliché goes, "Can't dance, too wet to plow," might as well hike the Appalachian Trail.

If you are planning on hiking the Trail, do not—I repeat—do not read this book! Yes, it will be full of information for that is its purpose. Oh, and entertainment too, for that probably is the main point. However, it will try to talk you out of hiking the Appalachian Trail. Unless you are an absolute glutton for punishment and like to abuse yourself, this just may not be what you are looking for. The year that I hiked it, only 8 percent of us masochists finished. Eight percent! The odds are not too good, huh?

Some of the photos tell the gruesome tale. Abuse. Total manifestation of abuse! My body screamed every day, "Quit doing this to me! Quit this thing!" Over and over. Somehow though, each morning, the tent got slogged into the already-slogged tent bag; and that got slogged into the already-slogged backpack. Then I ravenously devoured what little pittance of breakfast was allotted for that meal for that day for that segment of the Trail and somehow managed to hoist that black yoke upon my back and somehow managed to get the feet moving in that ever-north direction, even if that happened to be south for that particular segment, and started the first quarter mile and the wheezing and straining and fighting the laconic lactic acid overload, managed that first 1,320 feet and then told myself, "Well, you only have to do that fifty-nine more times today and then you are done."

And that is just today. Tomorrow morning at about four it starts all over again. And the next day until "the green tunnel" is about as inviting as a gang flogging at high noon. What and where in the heaven's name did all of this start! Good god, man (or woman), is that what you really want to do for five months of your life?!

Consider all of the options! Five months! One could paint the Sistine Chapel in five months, or certainly get a darn good start. Remember the to-do list that is way hidden back there somewhere. If you can't find the old list, come up with a new one. Or simply kick back and do nothing for five months. Five months (I know that you know this) is only thirty days short of half a year.

Or if that nagging feeling is still there, well, an option would be to go to the Great Smoky Mountains area and hike a little of the Trail. Two to three days or to the first main road that will take you back to civilization and amenities and sanity. A little makes so much more sense. Then maybe you could slowly evolve into a section-hiker and do a little more the next year.

With little pieces, one can kick back in the middle of the day and say such things as "I'm only going about 4 miles today." That boils down to, after that first quarter mile, only having to do it fifteen more times today. Doesn't that sound nice? Go a little ways and then eat something, watch the birds for a while and take some photos. Who cares? If you only make 3 miles, who cares? That's only a meagerly eleven more times.

A message is taped inside the front cover of my first journal reading, "Your path is arduous but will be amply rewarding." The fortune cookie message had appeared magically just when needed the most and became my own mantra. The word *arduous* became the byword of the hike. Repeated over and over, often facetiously. How arduous this section of the Trail is. How very arduous this mountain is. How arduous this rainy day is. Arduous. A fun word to say. The epitome of understatement when something a little more commanding, which would grab our attention a little more harsher, was needed. At times. Most of the time.

James River Face Wilderness
Near Glasgow, VA
May 30—Day 56
Mile 765 (about)

# Chapter 2

## First Steps: Insecurity

Day 1—April 5
Springer Mtn—Georgia
Mile 8.5

*April 5—Day 1—Mile 0—(Journal entry)—D-Day—up at 6:00-ish—showered—
dressed in trail clothes very emotional good-byes—left about 9:30 a.m.*

"Only 2,108.3 miles to go!"

I hadn't gone much more than two hundred yards! I was overdressed having donned my rain gear; experience hadn't taught me otherwise. Yet. I was dripping with sweat, my breath was laboring, my mind was troubled. The pack felt so heavy. My mind toyed with my subconscious that this was just a temporary thing. That the pack really didn't have to be there, and in a little while, I would be able to lay it down and continue without it.

My son Will was there with the entourage, watching my slow and painful first steps. I could clearly envision the smirk on his face as he hollered out my progress so far. They were standing close to the arch where the hiker enters into the land of the forbidding, the start of an adventure that might as well be to the moon. The sign just to the left of the arch reads, "Appalachian Trail Approach—Springer Mountain, Georgia, 8.5 miles—Mount Katahdin, Maine, 2,108.5 miles."

Two thousand one hundred and eight point five miles! The theories on the amount of steps vary. Walking along a smooth surface, a hiker should be able to cover a mile with about 1,700 steps. Hiking along the Appalachian Trail, it would take considerably more most of the time. Rocks and boulders—there is a definite difference and both are encountered—limit or impede the length of steps, and numerous times, backward steps are necessary to adjust for stepping in the correct places to avoid stumbling and slipping and falling. And a lot of times, one just has to backtrack to facilitate getting around the best way. And as one progresses farther north, more and more exposed tree roots become the obstacles along with the rocks.

There is just no way that the 1,700 steps to a mile could apply. One thousand eight hundred to 2,000 would not be too extreme an adjustment. So let's give it the benefit of the doubt—1,850 would not be unrealistic. So let's do the math. But first let's consider that posted mileage at the arch. And that seems to be supported by the signs posted along the Trail. Mileage is one of those debatable topics for which there is really no solution with all of the route changes and the simple fact that measuring the trail with any degree of accuracy would be virtually impossible.

So let's again take an average and just call it an even 2,150 miles. It would be close enough, and really, what difference does it make. So we come up with a total of just under four million steps. A number of past books on the subject have used five million steps as the magic number. So let's just say somewhere between four and five million steps.

And that morning, if that sign had read a million miles, it would not have seemed any more difficult! What had I gotten myself into?! What was I thinking?! And how could I just think of this as one step at a time instead of thinking of the entire impossible journey, all weighing down as this became my yoke to bear. I continued to struggle and knew that, eventually, some time in this wet morning and in this state of trepidation, things would eventually seem better.

The Approach Trail. Just 8 1/2 miles. It had a reputation all of its own. And that is before the actual Appalachian Trail starts, which doesn't happen until the top of Springer Mountain. Lots of folks love to tell of this stretch, and that if the wannabe thru-hiker can complete this that there is a very good chance that he or she will complete the total AT. All hikers seem to have their own ways of embarking on this journey for there are many ways. The preferred way is to get a ride to the parking lot on National Forest Road 42 at Big Stamp Gap and then hike backward for 0.9 mile on the Appalachian Trail to the top of Springer Mountain and then say a little prayer and declarations of hope and promise, get your picture taken, and then turn around to start the hike.

That just seemed sacrilegious to me. The first step on the Appalachian Trail in my way of thinking should be in the direction that you are hiking it, and that is north. My first step on the AT was going to be heading north! And anything other than the entire Approach Trail would also seem sacrilegious. So even though there are other embarkation points closer than Amicalola Falls State Park Visitor Center, the Approach Trail, the entire length of it, it would be.

The elevation at the visitor center is 1,705 feet above sea level. The elevation of Springer Mountain is 3,782 feet. That pretty much boils down to a 2,000-foot climb right out of the starting blocks. So it would be. About forty-five pounds of backpack, a lot of doubts and fears, and a heart that just will not stop pounding, up, up, up we go. Rest. Hike. Rest. Walk. Water break. Walk. Hike. Sweat. Katahdin seemed like an impossible dream.

Of course the first day on the Trail will always be remembered. Almost every detail. I had rehearsed this part so many times. My intentions were to make it to Stover Creek Shelter. Not that I had intentions of staying in the shelter. Common sense told me that starting out, I had better educate myself, be observant—learn how to hike and camp and be a thru-hiker. So even if I wasn't staying in a shelter, there was a need to be with people that were. I had no idea just how far I could make it in a day; however, having read a number of first person accounts of thru-hikes, I had a very good idea what was expected or what one had to do to be able to even consider the thought of making it all the way. So the first day was set in stone as being a 12-mile day whether I was up to it or not.

With seven people to talk to and say good-bye to and with a lot of questions and with all of the emotion that permeated the air, an early good-bye was pretty much out of the question. I was awake in our bedroom at Will and Jill's house in Mableton, a suburb of Atlanta, very early. I lay there and contemplated what was going to happen over the next months and wondered if I would be on the Trail even next week. It was quite disconcerting—while taking a walk around the neighborhood with my daughter-in-law, Jill, the night before leaving—to note that she was gliding along effortlessly while I was struggling up and down the hilly streets, trying not to huff and puff, futilely trying to save face in front of this gracious lady. Reminding myself that I wasn't even carrying a backpack provided very little to my already-shaky confidence level.

Every aspect caused anxiety. I worried about everything. I showered, knowing that it was my last in I did not know how long. I was ready early. Very early. My body was pulsing. My mind was racing. My emotions surged from very high to very low. I would miss my wife very much and couldn't imagine just how I would deal with being away from her for the entire five months should I be able to continue.

It seemed forever getting going. Of course, to the others, the day didn't necessitate urgency though there was a certain amount of utility of preparation. We had to have breakfast and go through a certain amount of an imagined protocol. Nothing preceded such a venture before, so we improvised what we thought should be done. Breakfast, of course, was a must. We did, however, keep it simple and light and, for me, as filling as possible.

We finally left the house about six forty-five. The drive to Amicalola Falls State Park would take about an hour and a half. The rain set in about halfway there, and everybody became very quiet. I'm sure that their thinking ran a lot of the same courses that mine was doing. Why did it have to rain on the very first day? Couldn't there be at least some comfort in having a nice day to begin; a sort of breaking-in period to adjust to all of the other inconveniences and lack of amenities in this sudden change of lifestyle. However, dealing with rain this early could work positively in that either I would have already been there, done that, or it could start to break my spirit. I chose the first alternative, and that more or less was the over-riding mode of operations.

Safety and the unknown factors kept rattling around. Could I hitchhike when the time came? It certainly was not a thought that I relished. I myself hadn't picked up a hitchhiker in years as that was just so discouraged anymore with this national paranoia of human perverts and weirdoes seemingly crowding our space. The idea of being in the clutches of some maniac and having to squeal like a pig certainly had crossed my mind a number of times, and people asking about such things just helped to fuel those internal imaginary fires.

Mostly, could I do it? It seemed now that so much was expected of me. Could I actually hike 15 miles a day for weeks on end? Did I have the strength and the perseverance? Was I plain physically able to do it?

A disconcerting thought occurred to me. Once when I was a substitute delivering papers (the *Fargo Forum*) for my brother and on an especially prolific day for the ads section, I just simply could not lift the bag of newspapers. His route was uptown where the apartments were above places of business, requiring a lot of stair climbing. The bag was just too heavy. I managed to make it through the day; but there was a period when I just gave up and succumbed to the burden and was found by some kindly man lying in my crumbled state of humanity, sobbing in a heartrending, pathetic way until he gave me some encouragement and inspiration. Would the hiking of the Trail result in a reenactment of that deplorable scene?

There were eight of us all together: My wife, Kris; our son Will and his wife, Jill; our son Curt and his wife, Marlo, and their two kids, Ta'lor and Rigdn. It was a royal send-off. The night before had been a feast of kingly proportions with all of the major food groups being covered, and the steak and shrimp, spinach salad and fruits had more than satiated my hunger and prepared me for what lay ahead. There is just so much excess that can be built up, and the hopes of taking on extra nutrition could only justify grossly overeating and really not accomplishing any other purpose. At least it was an easy task at hand. I ate and ate and ate. And that would become a way of life, the mode of operation for the next five months, whenever the opportunity would avail itself.

The next town wasn't thought of in terms of miles accomplished or what there was to see, for every day was another adventure and gorgeous sights eventually became commonplace. No, the next town would provide opportunity to eat and trips to the stores, trying to decipher my way through the myriad of precious food offered there.

The obsession became ice cream. I dreamed of making it to the halfway point and being a part of the celebration, a part of tradition. Pine Grove Furnace State Park did not seem possible in those early days. It was just a dream; something that I had read about in all of the books. It really didn't apply to my life. In the early days, I tried not to think about it, but goals were all there was. Today was nothing, tomorrow was fifteen more miles, hopefully, and with that came a sense of accomplishment. However, a projection of expectations too far in advance was just too much to comprehend and actually was more detrimental. As we are all taught from early in life, set goals but make them realistic, for trying to accomplish beyond your capabilities can only lead to discouragement. Looking as far ahead as Pennsylvania worked that way for me on the Appalachian Trail, just too much to handle.

Early in the procurement process of this grand adventure, I bought a poster map of the entire Appalachian Trail. The map is about a foot wide and four feet high. I proudly displayed this map and brought it to the attention of anybody that was willing to hear my story. A day's hiking on the map would amount to about the width a small button. It was quite disheartening to think that all of the toil of hiking for one day amounted to so very little in map measurement.

As I progressed north, it became evident that this map was on display in numerous public buildings along the Trail corridor. I was probably in Pennsylvania someplace before finally developing enough courage to actually take a peek. Of course, the more map that was below my present location made it easier to subject myself to this assessment process. By the time New Hampshire was reached, I went out of my way to seek out the infamous map and marvel at my accomplishment.

So inspiration had to come in other ways. Mine was ice cream. Visions of ice cream floated in my brain constantly. Leading me ever north, leading me to the next town. Another 15 miles out of the way and at the end of the metaphoric rainbow lay ice cream. Ice cream bars, ice cream cones, ice cream sundaes, and various concoctions that were made of this wondrous combination of frozen milk and cream and flavoring. And the epitome—the half gallon.

Throughout the hike, day 1 was replayed. What would be the most remembered of the events that took place on that most important day? The succession of good-byes to my wife, my two sons, my two daughters-in-law, my grandchildren? The tears? The hugs at the visitor center at Amicalola Falls State Park? One of the lady employees even joined in the hugging. Something similar to an official hugger, akin to the official greeter at Wal-Mart. All of these, of course, were well remembered and served me well as one draws deep for motivation and energy. However, the most remembered was making a friend. A good friend. A good friend for four days, but in my heart, he is a good friend forever.

The first day of a thru-hike on the Trail is a frightening experience. Not because of tangibles, but because of the intangibles. There is not a precedent for anything that you are doing. Should I do 15 miles? Should I just get to the first shelter? Should I work my way into this thing or try for big mileage right out of the starting gate? Questions that beg answers with no past experience to draw from to come to intelligent conclusions. The consensus from previous thru-hikers in the many books that I had read in my planning stages all agree that the biggest mistake is to do too much too soon before the body has had a chance to adapt. Also, the natural conditioning of the mental aspects seemed to be better not forced, allowing the mind and body to fall into a rhythm and daily mileage without making unreasonable demands. A certain amount of mandating is necessary, or a thru-hike is not possible. However, the mind and body have to be tricked into something similar to a transition, a sort of easing into the rigors of such an undertaking.

Still there is the constant mental gnawing at the fringes of common sense that reiterate that if a thru-hike was what the intent was, one is better off getting as much done early as possible. With a good start, there was encouragement and a base to build on. The pros and cons of either approach were at odds with each other. The internal debate went on.

My first day's intended destination of merely reaching Stover Creek Shelter meant that the first day would be 11 miles, including the 8.5-mile Approach Trail and then 2.5 to the shelter. Was that too much? It would be tragic to stick to a destination and then feel worn-out the second day, and dealing with that might be more destructive than just easing out the first day. Also plenty of time should be allowed to go through the neophyte business of getting setup and meal preparation and journal entry and all the chores that seem to loom; the one rehearsal way back in Florida hadn't provided enough experience to know just how all of this would go.

The Approach Trail is a rude wake-up call! It is quite appropriate when one starts at Amicalola Falls State Park that the first steps of an Appalachian Trail thru-hike are uphill. Two thousand vertical feet right from the start. Most people that agree, or at least want to believe, that if one can make the Approach Trail, one should be able to complete a thru-hike.

It should be added, however, that if one is convinced that completing the Approach Trail is a good indication that a thru-hike was probably going to happen, that feeling is quickly dispelled along about the third or fourth day or third or fourth week when one comes to a fairly intelligent conclusion that day 1 is a lot like day 4 or day 13 or day 72. The early conquest really doesn't prove too much at all. However, one can still feel that way for anything positive with regard to a thru-hike is the mood that has to prevail. It always amused me when a young hiker was asked where he—for female hikers were usually more dignified and realistic—was hiking to, and he said unequivocally, "Mount Katahdin, Maine."

I reached the top of Springer Mountain by midafternoon feeling good about myself and, for the first time, met Gizmo. He had thru-hiked twice, in 1990 and 2000, and now was employed as one of the "ridge runners" by the ATC and was one of the most helpful and encouraging hikers I encountered on the Trail. He was there to give us a short seminar on Leave No Trace procedures for hiking and camping. His information was helpful and received well by this hiker. He offered to take my picture at the first blaze for the Appalachian Trail. It was quite an honor to be so treated by a two-time previous thru-hiker.

We talked for a while about different aspects of thru-hiking. Shortly two other hikers appeared. The most talkative didn't have a trail name but kept telling us that he had ten pounds of moonshine in his very full backpack. Pounds and not quarts for on the Trail things are measured by weight and not volume. He and I exchanged personal information and instantly became friends. He was so full of life. The remainder of the hike to Stover we saw each other a number of times. He caught me after I left the summit, and then later, I passed him and beat him to the shelter. At these places of reuniting, we usually went into the bent-over-hands-on-the-knees football huddle position style, sucking cotton for additional air.

By this time, I started calling him the most obvious of trail names, he just became Shine, and not another thought was given to options. The potent diversion in his backpack was reason enough for the name; however, his other traits leaned the same direction. The world shone when he was around; he radiated good feelings similar to sunshine, or was merely a shining example of youth and exuberance and the good life. Shine followed me into the Stover Creek Shelter. He told me then that he was from Louisville, Kentucky, and had at times taught rock climbing and that his interests were primarily outdoor activities.

Also, in his much-too-heavy pack were a plethora of herbs and spices for he was quite a gourmet cook. It wasn't long before others were taking a liking to this kid from Kentucky with the ready smile and infectious enthusiasm. Also, we were much in awe for he was carrying about sixty pounds and seemed to be handling it okay; only time would tell whether he was capable of carrying such a load. As with the majority of us, he too was experimenting with the early aspects and his capabilities.

It turned out that Shine answered many of the questions about the Trail just by being there and doing what he thought was right for he had no precedent for what to do and how to do it. The same things that were haunting all of us.

The last time that I saw Shine was at Neels Gap. It was much too soon to be dropping off the Trail. We talked briefly. He told me that he was getting a ride to a doctor's office in a nearby town. He had a badly swollen and painful knee, a persistent thing that just would not go away. I never saw him again, and as he was the first friend on the Trail, I missed him for the entire hike and never did stop asking about him. Not one hiker had heard of him, and I knew that Neels Gap had probably been the end of Shine's thru-hike attempt. Since he may not have used Shine as his trail name, I do not know if he completed the hike or not.

Shine was the kind of hiker and fellow companion that the Trail was all about. But he had come out of the starting blocks much too hard and was carrying too much weight. So there was my first answer. If a young man of about twenty-five had problems with his legs, it was quite obvious that a man of sixty-two was going to have more problems. However, my pains all moved around; and usually, that is a good sign.

My pack weight was no longer an issue, even if too many hikers made comments that I was too heavy. Every item in the pack would eventually be used, and the actually final paring down would come. But not right away. That would have to wait until Fontana Dam. Pack weight, as mentioned so many times, is a matter of mental adjustment. The body will adapt, and as long as there are no frivolous items, things would work out. And at least for the early part of the hike, it worked out okay.

Shine has been there in the memory bank on and off. With no way to contact him, he will always be the first very good feelings about the Trail. He contributed to my experience immensely and will always be remembered. He was a friend for four days that had more influence than others that I have known for years. Shine, if for some reason you find yourself reading this book, please contact me. I'm in the Wausau, Wisconsin, phone directory and would love to hear from you.

# Chapter 3

## No Pain, No Gain

*April 12—Day 8—Mile 99—(Journal entry)—16.6 miles—too far!—easy to tear down all dried out—got going by 8:00 a.m.(or so)—seemed like tough going all day but made good time—intended to only go to Standing Indian Mountain (no good place to camp), kept going to Beech Gap—right heel started hurting up SI Mountain*

I was going to have to abandon the hike! My heels were on fire. My heels! What hiker anywhere would ever say, "Well, I had to quit, my heels just gave out on me." All the planning, all of those twenty-one boxes sitting there in my bedroom at home addressed to progressively farther places along the Trail, all of the training, all of the intrusion into Kris's life and sacrifices that she had made. All for naught. Heels! Who would have ever thunk it! Heels. It was only day 8, and it was all coming to an end. Having summitted my first really high peak, Standing Indian Mountain at 5,500 feet, and making 16.6 miles on that day, meant nothing now that it was over.

I lay in the tent and could think of nothing else, and with that intensive train of negative concentrated thought processes, the heels just kept getting worse. The entire gamut of the "for want of a nail a shoe was lost, for want of a shoe a horse was lost" routine kept going through my head. For want of heels that didn't hurt a hike was lost.

However, I wasn't going to be denied quite this easily. I wrestled with it the entire night and, the next morning, ignored the heels as well as I could and continued. The first steps were rather gingerly taken as weight was transferred to other places in a sort of tip-top fashion. And a slowly evolving aura of self-denial peeked through and presented another approach to the hiking of the Trail. Concentrating on other things, hunger and mileage for the day, and soon the heels were forgotten. In two days, the pain was gone and seemed like it had never been there.

I soon ascertained that pain that traveled was a good thing. A body that was being abused just has to let you know things; a little pain there, a little pain here. Moving around but not settling into one problematic location. Just aches and pains and the way of the life of a thru-hiker. Let it get you down for too long, and soon you are down to stay. No pain, no gain. It wasn't supposed to be easy. In about three days, the pain had moved to the knees then to the hips and then to the back and so on.

The worst thing to deal with was the sternum thing. For some reason, the backpack had ridden in a different place; and before long, there was a throbbing raw area right there where back becomes butt and just would not heal. The pack was adjusted and readjusted, and other techniques were employed. Nothing seemed to work. Eventually I bought some sponges that were packed inside the shirt in a plastic bag in hopes of merely padding the discomfort away, riding between the pack and injury. With little success.

About this same time, a pain developed in the right shoulder that just would not go away. It might have been in conjunction with the sternum thing as adjustments and weight transfer maneuvers were tried and retried. The shoulder thing would come on later in the day usually and just ache and throb. Not a moving pain there. It just stayed there. And late in the day, it was hard to imagine your way out of it. Gnawing at you when you were tired and just did not want to deal with it, hoping so much for some unbridled hiking with the sunshine on your face, the wind at your back, life being good, and idealism all around. Let's face it, pain sucks!

It was interesting observing other hikers in these early days. Also, it was hard not to notice that complaining was quite rare. For some. For others it just did not seem to stop. These hikers either were looking for excuses or just had a low threshold for discomfort, and it did not take long to realize that the complainers were probably not going to make it too far. Complaining can be constructive, serving the purpose of venting, or it can take the route of obsession. The obsessors were quickly recognized. It was the main topic of discussion somehow circumventing everything else that was being talked about. Neophytes that had not or were not going to accept pain as part of the process. Novices that could not or were not going to accept that bodies were being abused and that the natural result was pain as a reminder of that abuse, the informing barometer for this complex machine of letting the mind know that some massive changes had taken place in standard operating procedure. Pain was going to be a way of life for as long as these unreasonable demands were being made.

And with those observations came analysis, and usually, the conclusions that were drawn were that the essence of the hike was not about ideals. Those early dreams of a stroll in the woods, drinking water pure, communing with nature in this, the ultimate religious experience of peace and hope and love—there was going to be a lot of pain accompanying this Pollyanna romp surrounded by the best that God had to offer.

The gripers were not going far for they couldn't put aside the idealism; this thing was going to be enjoyable, nothing else mattered.

I didn't know early on just where I fit in. Was Sandul a good bloodline? Were there influences in life that would provide the strength needed, were those past experiences the stuff that was needed to provide the character to deal with it? Or would I just plain quit? Or as the saying goes on the Trail, would I "get off the Trail"? *Quit* was not an acceptable word. Getting off the trail was simply euphemism for failure, for not being able to do it, for quitting.

# Chapter 4

## Ukrainian

*April 9—Day 5—Mile 62—(Journal entry)—very difficult breaking camp—wet—everything is wet!—probably got out by 8:30-ish—energy level low (probably from no pasta last night)*

The blood of Sam Badiuk surged in my veins and arteries. And hopefully there was enough of it to take me up the next mountain and endure the next night and go on. I was reasonably sure that I could never have worked all day as he had and lifted hay bales into a hayloft as he had, slinging them effortlessly all day long or working the fields behind a team of oxen or horses or enduring the harsh winters. However, just possibly I could hike the Appalachian Trail in its entirety, a small task in comparison to his life of constant labor and hardship. If there were just a few ounces of his blood and an iota of his contrariness within this body of the same origin, it might be enough . . . maybe.

It was the fifth day of the hike; another day of rain which was really no different than any of the other four days. My routine was far from set, and drinking water and other logistics issues hadn't become a set of rules or procedures. I was experimenting for the most part and making some mistakes along the way. At Unicoi Gap, there didn't seem to be enough time to reach a place where I could camp for the night, but this conclusion was drawn on very little information for there was no precedent to draw from. I was very low on water, and a young couple that was just getting into their vehicle at the road looked like they wouldn't be needing theirs, if they had any. I started to ask but changed my mind in midsentence, preferring to work these things out for myself. Hiking the Trail, after all, was an effort to be as close to self-sufficient as one can be; it was too early to start developing bad habits. And as it ended up, water was not a problem at all as a source popped up right along the trail about halfway up the mountain. Also, a flat spot availed itself near the top of Rocky Mountain while there was still plenty of light and time; and soon pasta was cooking, fortified with a can of sardines. I had survived the scare, and life was again good. My thoughts turned to Sam Badiuk; I thought of his influence.

I am a full-blooded Ukrainian; a fact that you learn soon after meeting me. So this story will be no different. The reader has only made his way through the first few pages of this book to find out what is considered an important fact. An important part of taking on something as huge as hiking the Trail. This disclosure, however, runs quite contrary to my childhood way of thinking for then I hid my heritage, was ashamed of it during my formative years. As a new kid in town and especially after coming from the backwoods of Northern Minnesota to the city life of Fargo, North Dakota, I so ached to be accepted. I reeked of insecurity, was timid as a mouse; and anything that drew unwanted attention to me was avoided at all costs.

It was a cause for embarrassment when friends were at the house where my brother and I lived with my mother; always an aunt's house in those early years of having taken refuge from the North backwoods for Mom couldn't afford her own home. My mother and aunts usually talked Ukrainian, a natural regression when other non-Ukrainian adults weren't around. And when my friends gave me questioning looks, it made me feel quite uncomfortable. My thinking was that my peer group would see me as an oddball. Even if a light dusting of hayseeds already attested to that, I pretended that everything was just normal and my friends would just never notice that something here was different. Possibly there never was a conscious acceptance of me, and possibly as kids being different just wasn't too important anyway. However, feeling different was important to me in my quest for acceptance; and insecurity only fed those conceptions, real or imagined.

However, my ideas eventually changed. With time came a certain amount of self-esteem and wisdom and maturity and the realization that, indeed, my Ukrainian roots were something to be proud of, that I came from good stock and could almost be considered something special. By the time that I reached young adulthood, my mother had grown in stature in my mind, seeing her now as the powerful and influential matriarch that she was and that being Ukrainian to her was an extreme source of pride as she hung on to her traditions and foods and ways of life. She assumed her natural progression gracefully and accepted her role and responsibilities very seriously. To her, being Ukrainian held a certain purity, possibly feeling somewhat condescending toward lesser human beings with lesser mettle, a somewhat maligned though understandable attitude. Life had been hard, and she had to use the strengths that came from her ancestors to survive. By thirty years of age, I was no longer ashamed of my background.

The information about my Ukrainian heritage was somewhat nebulous in those early years. And as time went along, our people started realizing the importance of our historical background. It was in danger of being lost, and it was becoming harder and harder to retain as relatives were dying much too fast and vital facts would soon be gone forever. Our posterity would be without meaning if this past was lost forever. The thinking was that should this extreme source of pride, our lineage, be lost, our quality of life and sense of purpose would be diminished.

A cousin on my grandmother's side took the initiative to do something about it and started creating forms to send to relatives to gather the necessary information. But she didn't stop with just that for she also delved into public records and found vast amounts of pertinent information in provincial offices; she was pleasantly surprised to find the types of information that was recorded. Her work evolved to be a labor of love, took a number of years to complete; and finally, she put the thing together and it has become a fine reference; invaluable as time goes on and a book that retains a rather regal space on the family bookshelf. A source of information, of pride, and a sense of the importance of these roots that should not, could not, be forgotten. It was hard to remember what we did to remember past family things before this wonderful book came along.

My maternal grandfather came to the North American continent in 1900. If there are records as to just how he came here, that information has been lost; however, it is rather a moot point. The masses as a whole came on the same ship route and ended up in Eastern Canada and worked their way inland. The general consensus is that most Ukrainians that immigrated to Canada during this period were farmers, were considered peasants, and usually came from small villages and rural areas. My grandfather was no exception, having come from a region of Ukraine known as Bukovyna. He would have come by ship, about a three-week passage, and most likely arrived in Eastern Canada (possibly Montreal).

Enough is known about those early days to emphasize the hardship that he experienced and just how difficult it was to get established here. He came alone. To have brought his bride-to-be would have been premature or more accurately almost impossible, and possibly, he wanted to provide for her before she came—to create something, building enough where she could arrive and feel like she was at a place that could be called home. For she too had to survive the uprooting and performing the astounding task of coming to another country on a different continent very far away. At least some creature comforts should have to be expected even for these pioneers.

It is hard to imagine with today's guarantees what this massive undertaking must have felt like. Yes, there was a lot of so-called support in the mass exodus to Canada and Northern United States during this period. The very early ones were the ones that set the status quo, and others followed. However, coming to an alien country so far away having virtually nothing would have been daunting at the very least.

He came from a small village called Lukivtsi. It would have to be conjectured that he chose to be in a similar type of country with comparable weather and farm country where he could grow crops that he knew something about. So he chose the cold north where he could raise his cows and grow flax and grain crops such as barley and wheat and oats. He chose Canada because this was a land of promise where the country was begging to be settled with programs of land giveaway to attain that purpose.

He homesteaded 160 acres in Southern Manitoba. Possibly he got more than he bargained for with bitter winters of blizzards and forty below and with one hundred inches of seasonal snow. A country harsh enough to make this business of farming quite difficult. The records show that he began his labors shortly after arriving.

Sam Badiuk. My grandfather. I simply called him Gedo or sometimes Geed.

A man that in my childhood was mostly a source of awe for I deeply respected this man. Not that I knew much about him then. He was short and stocky and powerful. His hands were like vise grips. As a child, we would play games and gleefully try to escape that grip, but it was in vain. His was the strength that came from hard work and work he did for that was all he knew and only with physical work could he attain anything that even vaguely resembled wealth. However, his strength went much deeper for his lineage only knew hard physical labor and bodies had to become hard and tough to survive. No, there was no escaping that grip.

His attire rarely changed. Bib overalls with a long-sleeved shirt. I don't remember him ever wearing gloves in the summer. Photos of Sam Badiuk depict a man who was easy to laugh for his sense of humor rarely escaped him in spite of the life of hardship and endless labor. I remember that when he laughed, it was a contagious sort of uncontrolled release of unpretentious proportions. If there was no reason to laugh, he didn't; but usually, he couldn't contain himself anyway. Sam Badiuk was very real, life was real, and thus no needs for pretense.

He managed to improve the land enough to maintain his contract with the Canadian government. After attaining the land through the Homestead Act, there were requirements to keep it. *Improvements* may have been a rather-nebulous term. It meant removing rocks and clearing the land enough to be able to plant crops and to keep livestock, but that was all necessary anyway to maintain the minimalist livelihood which was his way of life.

Upon arriving, he had to construct a house of some sort for shelter from the harsh climate. He was acclimated to this harsh climate for it was not unlike where he had come from in Ukraine; the difference now was that he had control over his destiny. He could work all day long and really needed few creature *comforts*, a term that he probably would not have known anyway.

The house that he built was a basic building constructed of locally available materials of pine and aspen trees and mud. The construction was simple for there was no need for much more than shelter. Time was of essence for so much time was required to accomplish all that was needed to be done that there just was no time or reason or need for frivolous things. There was so little time, so little money, and so very much to do.

In three years, he had made enough improvements to the homestead that his thoughts turned to his companion. Mary Kosowan, my maternal grandmother, also came from the same village in Ukraine. I never called her anything other than Baba. I hardly knew her for we could never converse as she never did learn English, but I loved her deeply. I have often thought about that reunion. For her and Geed after three years of absolute solitary living and an entire ocean apart, it must have been quite a moment for joy and celebration.

Baba and Geed. They had known each other before he had left for Canada, and they had laid their plans well. After this long period of total denial and loneliness, they were finally reunited. She came from Ukraine in the early part of 1903; and on January 30, they were married in Gardenton, Manitoba, Canada, at the Ukrainian Orthodox Church to be partners for life.

My grandparents and I never had a real conversation in our lives. My childhood shame had taken its toll, and if I had known the Ukrainian language in my very early years, I had subconsciously driven it out of my thought processes. My knowledge of the language was limited to just a few words, phonetically shown in parenthesis, such as *beer* (peva), *whiskey* (howvleoka), and *son-of-a-bitch* (schlackveatvlafa) and a few numbers and a limited few other words. Not enough to carry on a conversation in a dialect that varied from the original Ukrainian, a language noted for having multiple pronunciations of words. Also, rolling of the tongue is necessary for proper emphasis and elaboration. Not an easy language to learn and a harder language to retain.

Those childhood visits to the old homestead were cherished moments. Entire summers were spent there. It was a time for motivation and influence. A time for molding and inspiration. A time to observe what true country life was like and a time for learning of my heritage. It was also a time for developing a deep respect for the environment and an appreciation of wildlife and animals and birds and trees and flowers and the ways of the natural world. A seed was being planted within my soul. I could never anticipate or know at that time just where this mentoring would lead me or the deep respect that I would develop for nature and the great outdoors.

Sam Badiuk became a local legend and a man that was held in high esteem by the peer group that was much like him, having come to Canada for much the same reasons and in much the same way. His prowess and his work ethic were second to none, and he was an innovator. He was an inventor of sorts; his most auspicious invention being his wood-splitting machine. His creation was quite simple, direct, and to the point; but it got the job done. Basically, it was an axe head welded to a flywheel powered by a two-stroke engine. It took a Jack Be Nimble character to set a log down for splitting quickly enough to allow time, for getting body appendages out of the way before the lumbering wheel with the viscous axe head came spinning around and down through the log. But Sam Badiuk was a determined man, and split logs he did and somehow survived the many hours that he spent with this unwieldy and ruthless piece of equipment.

Somewhere in the family archives is a faded black-and-white photo of him with his log-splitting machine. Sam Badiuk was proud of his creation. It saved him a lot of backbreaking labor and provided firewood for the cold and harsh winters with a minimum of physical labor. Heaven knows there was enough work to be done, and anything that could ease the load was a blessing.

Neighbors quickly learned of this new device and came to take advantage of this machine as a camaraderie slowly evolved. The legendary whiskey jar made the rounds. Clandestine, almost childlike, swigs of glee, much-needed diversion from the labor and drudgery. The jar never stayed in one place too long for fear of losing it. It strayed from hayloft to cow stall to machinery shed. An elusive game played with Baba. Too much good whiskey had been lost for she viewed this activity with a much-different opinion. When the guard became a little loose, the hallowed drink had found the ground when Baba carried on her own mini prohibition to try keep her man somewhat in line. Baba thought that a man should have a certain amount of pleasure in life, but whiskey wasn't one of them, preferring to please her husband more with culinary delights. Food that we just called Ukrainian cooking. She believed that sacrifice was the ways of the Ukrainian immigrant, and there should be no indulgence in activities that bordered on sin and hedonism. At least not where one could see you doing something not completely acceptable.

With all of the work with machinery, a homesteader eventually was the victim of the laws of averages. Some errant machinery caught him off guard one day and crushed two fingers of his left hand, one finger was left hanging. One has to wonder just what he was thinking at the time, the story being that he "calmly cut off the hanging finger and threw it away," wrapping the hand up as well as he could and went about the business of catching the horses and harnessing them to the wagon. He then drove into the nearby village of Vita, a horse trip of 11 miles, to have the hand attended to. One wonders what the good doctor had to say about the missing finger. The story is lacking in details; however, supposedly Baba chased a chicken that had gotten the finger in its beak. It is not known whether she ever caught the chicken, and one wonders what the chicken was going to do with the finger, a thought that only lingers momentarily and is better to dismiss from one's mind.

As a child, I do remember the disfigured left hand. If he ever told me what happened, those memories are long gone. We rarely talked; and when we did, it was usually a highly animated conversation of sorts with a lot of gesturing and innuendo—his in Ukrainian, mine in English—to make up for the language barrier.

In spite of this life of extreme deprivation and grueling physical labor, Sam Badiuk lived long enough to have been married to his wife, my grandmother, for fifty years. A huge celebration was held in their honor on that day. These two people were examples to the close-knit community of life being lived as it should be. A union of such length attributed to that fact.

Semeon "Sam" Badiuk. A man's man. Honest and hardworking. Tough and independent.

I humbly make my claim to be a part of this person and hang to the premise that some of his toughness and his determination made its way into my genes and gave me the qualities and the strength to help me hike the Appalachian Trail. A lot of this book is dedicated to him, for I have a lot of heroes, and so other parts of the book commemorate those persons. But my grandfather was first to influence my life. His spirit and tenacity, his values for the earth and his recognition of life being good because of the things that it gave him were the base upon which my psyche rested. For all that he owned came from natural things. He didn't know anything else. And to natural things did we pay homage in one way or another, whether by working the land or seeing as much of it as possible in this short time that we have on earth or by hiking through some of its most pristine creations.

So the hiking of the Appalachian Trail had to have come from this background for such desires cannot be attributed to other less-obvious reasons. And the desire to do such a thing was already forming when I was a young boy being influenced by this awesome person as traits started to take form deep within my soul. Just the desire to hike the Trail in its entirety has to come from deep inside and with reasons that aren't easily explained. A desire that has been explained in various ways in books about the Appalachian Trail, reasons that seem reasonable at times and at other times quite unreasonable.

My wife has always told me that a Ukrainian is not truly happy unless he or she is miserable. Probably one of those characteristics that evolved from dealing with harshness through the millennium, a testing of capabilities before a need even arose; a subconscious tempering of this steel of life. It proved to be the best trait for hiking the Appalachian Trail.

# Chapter 5

## The First Hundred Miles

*April 16—Day 12—Mile 160—(Journal entry)—good day—worked on technique a lot today—improved a lot—The old woods road at Stecoah Gap was blocked by logs and a new cut road—managed to get by—went about 3/4 mile past on ridge*

Points of reference had to be determined early to gage what was going to happen. An arena was being entered without precedence, reeking of the unknown, every aspect was foreign territory. Any previous hiking activities had been strictly day hikes with the exception of the overnight experiment as training for this venture. A hundred miles seem to be a good yardstick. What happened in that first 100 miles could possibly indicate what was going to happen in the subsequent months or weeks or if there even would be subsequent months or weeks. So the events of those first days and those first hundred miles were of intense interest. In retrospect, there was some similarity beyond that point; however, there were factors early on that later either could be disregarded or just no longer applied: lack of experience; lack of technique; preferences with regard to shelter, hiking partners, and the desire to have such; food; and so on. Also the first hundred miles had to be taken slowly; later, possibly, those precautions could be thrown to the wind. The first 100 miles also presented situations that would not occur until very late in the hike but not to the extent of early on, that being cold weather, including some snow and my ability to deal with it having become pretty much a full-blown

Floridian. So the first 100 miles was intensely monitored and conclusions were drawn from those records and comparisons were made as the hike progressed. Mostly, however, the milestone of a hundred miles brought a sense of accomplishment and satisfaction. How many people had went out and hiked a hundred miles?

The first day's distance read 11 miles. However, whether it was exhilaration and excitement that were carrying me along or other factors, I was not one bit tired. There were no physical ailments that couldn't be dealt with. All systems seemed to indicate go. It was a good start; however, the realization that averaging the necessary mileage to accomplish a thru-hike would be difficult. But most importantly, it was nice knowing that the task was not impossible. I had hiked for about seven hours, some of that in the rain and a very great deal of it uphill for I had gained two thousand feet in the first 8.5 miles, the Approach Trail and the climb to Springer Mountain.

The second day with an early start was a little better, not having to say family good-byes, as early-bird starts became standard operating procedure. By the end of day 3, I had covered 37 miles. However, the math was not working out as planned to make the mileage necessary. To complete a thru-hike on the AT required, in my estimation, an average of about 13 miles a day. The nature of the beast. One really couldn't start too early, and my starting day of April 5 seemed to be working out well. Then the weather at the other end became the issue for one just had to be done before October if at all possible. A sense of urgency was setting in early.

However, at the start, other factors were being taken into account, drawing on what I had read concerning not coming out of the starting blocks too hard and burning up in the process. The third night on Blood Mountain, seeing a sunset privy to few, provided inspiration as the process of setting in and making adjustments started taking place. Coming out of the tent to pee at about 8:00 p.m., I suddenly realized that the mountain was surrounded by clouds all lower than the peak. The mountain was bathed in color. Looking to the west revealed the purest red, a color that bled through the mist and haze to envelope the setting with a subtle pink to the east. A scene that made 37 miles of hiking for this prize seems like nothing.

The fourth day provided the first real accomplishment as Neels Gap evolved out of the mist and meant my first trail shower and some resupply. Neels Gap has the distinction of having the only building *on* the Trail, Walasi-Yi Center. It was exciting to have reached this first of goals and know that a phone call to Kris was my first priority. There was only one phone, and as I waited my turn, it became evident that I was in the company of a unique woman, Jojo Smiley. A thru-hiker with accomplishments of massive proportions, she had done what others could only envy and certainly too ambitious for most to try emulate. The previous year, she had hiked the ultimate, the Eastern Continental Trail. Starting in the Florida Keys, she had worked her way north, hiking roads and trails and into Alabama. Then she hiked the Alabama Pinhoti Trail, the Georgia Pinhoti Trail and the Benton MacKaye Trail that led her to the Appalachian Trail. Then she hiked the entire AT to Mt. Katahdin, continuing from there on roads and the International Trail and finally ended her journey on Belle Isle, Newfoundland. Her odyssey took her eleven months and four days. In my neophyte state of my fourth day on the Trail, I was humbled. Her name was well suited for she seemed always to be smiling. This year, she was doing short hops and trail magic on the AT with her partner, Nomad98, and seemed to be enjoying herself to the utmost.

My first call to Kris! From the Trail. What a rush! Emotion simply would not leave me alone as I choked and stammered my way through telling her what I had done, and she just listened. Having survived these first days with all of the doubts and fears, with all of the feelings of inadequacy, I had reached a place where I could finally talk with a little more authority. I could breach the subject that there was room for the possibility that the dream could become reality. I told her about how hard it was, that ups just simply were grinding ordeals and these sixty-two-year-old legs were not doing what they were being asked to do. At least not very well.

As usual, she was supportive and listened to my tales of woe with her usual patience. A pattern even at this early stage was starting to develop for these phone calls always resulted in my body and mind responding, kind of like taking a performance-enhancing drug. Our forty years together were the rudder for this mission for without her strength and character, her optimism and commitment, a thru-hike was not possible. My Swede with her quiet ways and unique sense of humor provided strength that only comes from another human being that has shared just about everything that life can throw at you. Without getting too far out on the limb of slobbering romantic idealism only she and our very long time together could lend sense to the different nuances to life and its complexities. We said good-byes reluctantly and the I-love-yous held meaning like never before and the treasure of our relationship had never been so evident.

By the end of the fourth day, a tally of 49 miles meant actually being halfway to a hundred miles and also meant having made it through the rain and mist and clouds and having been "lost" for the first time. That night was the first of many wet nights in the tent, and with that the harsh reality of this business of thru-hiking. Weather could only be taken in stride, not like choosing good days for a nice weekend jaunt. Thru-hiking meant taking what Mother Nature threw at you. Day after day.

Day 5 resulted in another 13 miles, and sitting in the tent that night, a realization set in that 100 miles of hiking was in itself a major accomplishment and would never happen in the first week with the average to this point being a mere 12.4 miles per day. A subtle form of panic started to prevail that soon became a way of life. And day 6 was not going to provide respite from this subpar performance with another 12 miles; however, I could enjoy the fact that 75 miles lay under my belt. Ending week 1 with a resupply run into Hiawassee meant that day 7 only garnered 8 miles. A week on the Trail! The panic was setting in a little stronger. At this rate, I wouldn't reach Katahdin until well into October. My mind raced through the plethora of misinformation about Baxter State Park that I had read. All of it confusing for the novice, pondering such things such as the closing of the park on a whim of bad weather, a lot of times closing before October even had come.

And I hadn't even taken a zero day!

Then came day 8, and some promise of longer mileages and some ray of sunshine of hope peaked through the doom. The distance "16.6 miles" was entered in the journal with the note "too far"; but the dramatic event on this day was that I was in another state, North Carolina. The tally was now 99 miles! That's close enough to a hundred to just consider it having been done. In reality, however, it wasn't until day 9 that 100 miles of hiking had finally been accomplished. I wryly noted to myself that I only had to do that twenty-one more times, have my picture taken at the top of Katahdin, and I was done. Day 9 however was uplifting in that again an impressive mileage was logged, 16 miles; and with that back-to-back performance came knowledge, experience, and a rising swell of possibility reared within. Thru-hiking the Appalachian Trail may, just may, be possible. And so it remained. A possibility, yes. A probability would only have been a misconception, something that one said reluctantly, that commitment to the entire 2,175 miles would have to come in other forms.

Water source—Proximity of Albert Mountain—North
Carolina—April 13

# Chapter 6

## Uncertainties

*April 11—Day 7—Mile 82—(Journal entry)—To 76 by 11:00-ish (3.5 miles)— fourth vehicle picked me up (odd guy—drove like a maniac—gave him $5)—went to Ingles*

When the initial plans were being made, my son Curt was concerned about my safety and well-being in my anticipated venture and asked about being scared of "things." I asked him what things he was referring to and received a rather-nebulous reply; something about animals and snakes and insects such as ticks and bees and those sorts of things. Curt is not one who lacks foresight, or insight, usually having a deeper understanding of situations than do most people. He could possibly see or anticipate dangers that would not have even occurred to me. Curt, after all, had a number of guns in his home; and though some of that was his usual love for the workmanship and beauty of man-made instruments, including precision weapons, his ownership of such probably stemmed mainly under the guise of "protection."

My own particular slant on these sorts of things was somewhat different. And even though I had hunted some with a friend in North Dakota in my early teen years, there was no way that I could ever kill anything, let alone shoot at a human being. I had never owned a gun in my life other than a speargun. The speargun dates back to those reckless teen years. Back to the weekend skin-diving (and scuba diving) trips to

Bad Medicine Lake in Northern Minnesota when all we took, in addition to a vast supply of beer, was salt and pepper, peanut butter and bread. The major food source being blue gills that were speared and, in short order, were cleaned and turned pleasantly brown in an iron skillet over a wood fire. The speargun served a purpose, was quick and severe (the fish didn't have a chance), and was illegal. As a teen, I could justify my crime by stating unequivocally that I didn't waste anything. That the fish were taken as food and nothing was wasted. And I suppose there was the belief that fish don't feel anything.

I would later reflect on those times and think that there would be no way that I could now spear a fish. It just would not happen. Ideas change, and yes, I do think that fish feel things; otherwise, why do they fight so hard when caught, or speared, though that was rather short-lived for the poor thing couldn't last long with a metal rod shot through its body? I am one of those rather wishy-washy people that can eat the flesh of animals, including fish, if somebody else does the dirty work. So possibly I speak with forked tongue. However, my use of such, as a feeble excuse or justification, is that my meat and fish eating is somewhat far between. But that is actually for health reasons more than feeling a kindred spirit with these wondrous beings, a form of pure rationale; indeed, creatures of the wild fascinate me more than anything. So if Native Americans could coexist with the animals and still use them for food and about everything else, I too can relate to that line of thought.

Curt envisioned bear and wolves and other woolly creatures being a force that had to be reckoned with, and in such a long endeavor such as thru-hiking the Appalachian Trail, it would seem almost impossible to avoid confrontations. I assured him that from the accounts that I had read, animals were not much of a problem and most hikers welcomed seeing various species as part of the experience and if that certain rules were followed, nothing would happen. Everything was under control. Bears, of course, are part of the AT experience, but wolves no longer live in that part of the world, man's imposition having long ago taken its effect as they took refuge farther and farther north.

However, the dangers of the creatures of the Trail had been grossly underestimated, and my first hitchhike proved me wrong. For I had failed to take into account the most dangerous of all species, the human beast. In considering the Trail experience, this much-too-prevalent creature is not considered as one anticipated for observation. Yes, of course, in a mall when doing people watching, but not on the Trail for that is one of the drawing points in doing this thing in the first place—to get away from people and commune with nature in its pure form.

As I approached the highway at Dicks Creek Gap and prepared for my first hitchhiking experience, the thoughts that this had been a source of trepidation during the planning stages of the hike slowly crept into consciousness. I tried to make myself a little more presentable, concentrating on straightening my hiking shorts and hat while making my way to the shoulder of U.S. Highway 76 before reluctantly sticking out my thumb in hopes of comfortably riding into Hiawassee, Georgia. Still lacking confidence, I felt more comfortable walking instead of just setting the pack down and sticking my thumb out. The necessary chutzpah just was not there to boldly and brazenly set down the pack and truly hitchhike in the stereotypical slouchy manner. A number of cars went by, and it appeared that the little pickup was doing the same when suddenly it stopped and backed up ever so slightly.

I ran as best as I could with the pack encumbrance. I managed to heft it over the side of the tailgate and somewhat hesitantly climbed into the cab. The man seemed cordial enough and did acknowledge my hello before turning the radio to a level that would have been outlawed in most mall parking lots as being an infringement on other person's rights.

Either he was legally deaf or just liked his music very loud. We couldn't talk, at least not at a comfortable level. And maybe that was his intention. And the bedlam inside the confines of the cab coming from the radio must have brought out the Dale Earnheart—wannabe urges. We approached the first curve—the first of a series of curves, after all this was mountain country—high and hard. The tires squalled, and my sideways glances at this man that I had known now for about two minutes revealed little to nothing. Much too soon, the thoughts of Curt and his concerns came back to me. To myself, I mused in a manner as if talking to my son—yes, there are dangers in hiking the Trail.

The little truck tires squalled right and left as he rode the curves with a vengeance. Hiawassee seemed a hundred miles away. Possibly the thought of stopping him and getting out occurred; however, discretion intervened with the decision that it would be wise not to piss him off. I slowly became conscious of being hot and realized that the truck interior felt like an oven. I was no longer accustomed to being inside, and additional heat was generated from my overactive adrenaline gland triggered by the terse atmosphere while riding with this lunatic. I was simply just happy getting a ride; and this being my first hitchhike, it went as just part of the hazards, for hitchhiking is one of the things that we are taught in our society not to do. Accepted merely as the risks one takes when taking a carnival ride or some sort of convoluted reasoning such as that. If the warnings about the dangers of hitchhiking were meant to be construed in this context then so be it.

He eventually turned the radio down just a little, and somehow through the racket, he asked where I wanted to be dropped off. I told him that the Ingles Store would be just fine. We pulled into the parking lot as a sense of overwhelming joy overcame my entire still-alive being; and subconsciously, I found myself reaching for my wallet and, in surreal state, was handing him five dollars, not totally in control of my reasoning and common sense. What little conversation we did have, more like hollering, had given him opportunity to convey what a hardship it was for him to exist on the annuity of a disabled veteran. Five dollars seemed like small stipend to pay for having my life spared. I walked toward my first AT resupply trip a liberated man, having stared death in the face and survived.

Yes, Curt, there are definitely dangers encountered while thru-hiking the Appalachian Trail.

I staggered into the store. Within minutes, surrounded by this plethora of goods, I was again facing real trauma. One that no amount of preparation could have manifested what I was in for. However, of all the AT literature, AT Web sites, talking with people about the AT, absolutely nothing addressed the situation. There were no instructions beforehand in dealing with this most basic of problems. In this neophyte role of Appalachian Trail thru-hiker, I had been caught totally unaware.

The cornucopia of food in all of its various forms with the irresistible displays was mind-boggling. I managed to make it through some aisles and had added more things than I could have used in a week before realizing that this wasn't working very well. The cheese section alone totally engrossed my attention for about five minutes. I finally settled on a mild cheddar, wishing that I could have taken about three or four other packages. Next were the luncheon meats and pepperoni and the deli section. I could pass by the ice cream. Supermarkets rarely have individual items in frozen foods, thus only present the problem of wanting, as buying such for the Trail was rather futile. My ice cream—buying skills were yet to be honed, and this first trip was confusing enough without dealing with that at this early stage. Little was I to know then just what ice cream would eventually mean to me on this AT expedition.

The simplicity of merely stopping to resupply had become a jumble of information and misinformation in my mind. Needing and wanting became synonymous and one thought. The plethora of just the cookies aisle left me dazed. I wandered through the store and realized that I had a lot of goods in the cart and really hadn't made a decision on anything yet. The shopping cart had been a mistake. I went back through the same aisles, returning a number of items, and then would go back in after weighing the alternatives. The cereals section again comprised a large amount of time and decision making. It seemed like the obvious place to be for oatmeal and granola and granola bars. However, again, too much selection. One can truly make sense out of the cliché "kid in a candy store" here.

Oatmeal, oatmeal, oatmeal. The most controversial of all Trail food and the one most misunderstood. The hiker boxes conveniently placed in post offices, hostels, motels, and other public places along the Trail that hikers frequent always contain oatmeal, usually hiker-packed, and no decisions were necessary. Either you needed oatmeal or you didn't. Here in the supermarket, however, the oatmeal section alone required much study and consideration. Gone are the days when one merely had to select between minute oats and the real stuff. Now there is every combination of flavored oatmeal that one can image. Everything from brown sugar to cinnamon to raisins to blueberry to every imaginable fruit that can be added to oatmeal and still leave it edible.

It wasn't until later that I learned about oatmeal resupply from the hiker boxes. For some reason, hikers got rid of oatmeal quicker than anything. One book on a thru-hike even went so far as to say that oatmeal wasn't "real food" anyway. And the hiker boxes stuff was free for the taking. No decisions as that was simplified to having just what was there. The main thing about oatmeal on the Trail was that actually it is better for the evening meal. More time to just kick back and enjoy, and it was always so much more filling in the evening.

But this was my first shopping trip, and I didn't know anything.

When I went into the store, I had thought in terms of about 3.5 pounds added to the pack, necessary commodities. Food that was needed to fuel the machine to continue to do 15-mile days. However, this is such a fine line, and one constantly debated along the entire length of the Trail. How much food is enough? The issue being how much food is needed following the line of reasoning that when one is carrying too little and forced to ration versus having a little too much and the emotional lift that provides knowing that the night camp will be somewhat of a feeding frenzy. The psychology of having too much buoys a hiker enough to more than offset the extra weight carried. One can debate the issues involved and maybe approach it scientifically as to the extra energy expended carrying more than enough food. Of course, *enough* can never be defined within the confines of a reasonable approach. One thru-hiker strongly advised that if you are carrying food into the next town, you are wasting energy with the extra weight. I used this as somewhat of a guideline, and it wasn't too long before I totally abandoned that train of thought as being much to inhibiting. For then one has almost planned to the mouthful just what one is going to eat through each and every day. Some days I just simply could not get enough to eat. I loved telling people that after about the first day away from a supply stop, I could have sat down, opened up the food bag (a large plastic trash-type bag was all I ever used for this), and eaten everything that was in there. Period. Out of food right there and with three or four days to the next supply place.

So a system of rationing had to be developed early on. With that as a mode of operation, then the all-too-welcome situation of having some extra food presents itself when one finds oneself making more miles in a day than normal. Getting into a bind the other way and the uncomfortable position of either upping the daily mileage or cutting down on eating rears its ugly head. One is always on a tight-schedule thru-hiking. That never goes away. Lie back and relax and think of just taking it easy for a while, and soon you have a food supply shortage.

So after that digression, I am still in the dilemma of making my way through Ingles. Which finally works itself out as well as it can at this early stage of the game. I stuff my backpack with all of the goodies, wondering what it is going to feel like after getting back on the Trail. Soon I will find out. For the time being, it doesn't feel too bad.

However, the Hiawassee ordeal, as was so often the case in the AT experience, started turning to the pleasant side. While packing in the front of the store, an attractive older lady stopped and asked if I have a ride back to the Trail. She was cordial and friendly; and even though I haven't yet taken on the lean and drawn look of the thru-hiker, she must sense from my look of determination, and the huge pack, that I, indeed, must be going a little farther than just a day hike. I was surprised but answered that no, I was just working my way back to the highway to stick my thumb out and hope for the best.

She said, "Wait right here, my husband will be here in fifteen minutes." And with that she was gone. I was somewhat skeptical having yet to learn about this symbiosis of sorts that seems to exist along the towns of the Trail. A fifteen-minute wait seemed much more pleasant than the prospect of thumbing and the chances of hitting another maniac and a hair-raising ride. So I spent my fifteen minutes in a rather-constructive way scratching marks on my expandable walking stick so that I would have not to guess just where the little click would take place. I was just about finished when a vehicle slowed to a crawl and a pleasant-looking man smiled at me and sprung out the door to help with my pack. We soon had it in the trunk and were heading back east on Highway 76. Back to my mission and to my new life.

We talked at length for the entire time. He turned out to be Corsican, a thru-hiker from just a few years back. A retired physical therapist who now just merely enjoyed being a "trail angel," giving rides back and forth during this busy time of the hiking year when the mass exodus hits the

Trail towns with northbounders with their long gazes and a lot of hopes and dreams and brimming with inexperience.

Corsican was full of advice, and one bit stayed with me throughout. Possibly it was the difference, the catalyst that kept me going. It was just too simple; but it struck home deeply and, like most good advice, adhered to the keep-it-simple (KISS) rule. "Don't quit."

"Whatever you do, don't quit."

Those words rang clear for the next months and when all else failed. When rationalization tried to tear me away from the madness, when common sense kept saying that you are doing things to yourself that your body and mind are rebelling from, those words were always there. "Don't quit."

It was too early in the trip for me to have presence of mind to get some sort of contact number or address. Later I thought of just writing to "Corsican, Hiawassee, Georgia," and see if it came back. What would I say? Just merely thank-you. It was the only thing that made sense. Of all the advice and criticism and questions and head shaking, only Corsican had a real deep influence on my actions over the months that followed. Thank you, Corsican, thank you.

No, Corsican is not a play on words for I asked him that. Of course I can. No, that's not what it was. Corsican was originally from Corsica; and the addition of the *n*, the possessive, just simply turned out to be the perfect trail name.

I thought about him often as I made my way up Blue Ridge, feeling for the first time the additional weight and realizing that ironically we would always be coming out of these resupply places with a full pack and going uphill. Empty downhill, full uphill. The nature of the beast. And maybe it just fit all too well with the philosophy of the Trail. Nobody said that it was going to be easy, and if it were, would anybody be out here trying it? We all knew the answer to that.

In the meantime, my mind wandered back to those first clumsy efforts at trying to bring this thing to fruition. I had no equipment, no experience to the extent of this venture, and most importantly, tended to be rather naive and idealistic. Let's go back a little.

# Chapter 7

## Neophyte

The prospect of walking 2,175 miles in one stretch seems rather ludicrous when first contemplated. However, what starts as ludicrous is merely the bud of an idea, and as the idea starts its own long mental journey to reality, the absurdity slowly transforms as the mind slowly begins to accept such a radical idea. Today it seems absurd, tomorrow it seems like a possibility, the day after a probability, and then the physical plans start to take place long before the mind could actually accept it. For with these actual physical preparations come the process of the possibility, and with that, the mind is tricked into thinking that all of this is okay. Tangible evidence of an abstract idea and a clear case of doing something even if it seems impossible or improbable to complete such a task.

Without the physical, there could be no possibility of mental acceptance; and therefore long before the would-be hiker feels comfortable with such an impossible endeavor, the plans start to come to fruition and then the other processes hopefully will follow suit. Equipment will be needed for the mission; and to that end, a process starts to take place with purchases and, with that, a commitment begins to form. Then as this procurement process continues, one hopes that one passes the point of no return; and then the mind will just accept the inevitable and no longer question the why, the how, or the most difficult, a valid and believable explanation to others. I shrugged my shoulders a lot in those early days of planning and procurement.

The conversations were much too predictable.

"You're going to do what?!" Maybe not really a question.

"Ah . . . hike the Appalachian Trail . . ."

"What's the App . . . what is it . . . trail . . . what?"

"It's a foot trail that starts in Georgia and goes northeast along the chain of mountains through the northeast part of the United States ending up in Maine."

"Sounds like that will take some time to do."

"Ya, about six months."

"Six months?!"

"Ya, it's over 2,000 miles."

"Good grief!"

Shrug the shoulders and apologetically offer, "Just something that I always wanted to do."

And so on.

I bought a tent! With much trepidation, I bought this tiny little thing stuffed in a bag and not very impressive. After much gnashing of teeth, I finally got it up without poking out any screening in the Florida room with the long tent-support poles, and it sat out there all put up and beckoning. Only it was not the beckoning with comforts such as the invitation of a bed with its softness and nightly ritualistic trance. No, this beckoning was more like a dare. I dare you to lie in here. I dare you to think that you could actually be comfortable in here. Think about it! You are going to be in here, thinking that this little piece of nylon-waterproofed flimsiness is going to keep out torrential downpours and wind and snow and all the other things that nature is going to throw at you. You aren't going out there for a few days. You can't pick and choose. You won't be allowed the luxuries of thinking, "Aaah, here we go, a couple of nice days of sunshine and niceness . . . now is the time." No, nothing like that, there are going to be long periods of un-nice. Long periods. Wet and nasty long periods.

I dare you to call me home. Even for a day.

I laid it in only to find out that my six-foot-one-inch frame just wouldn't do well parallel to the long walls. All of my research as to the best possible tent somehow wasn't quite what I expected. And even after laying out all of the gear and what was assumed would be the format for where stuff would go, it slowly came to realization that this just would not do. My sense of neatness would either have to change or something else would have to change, and I was too old to start thinking differently, wasn't I?

Lying diagonal was something that neither my body or mind could accept, an oxymoron, sort of like lying the other way in bed, with your feet where your head normally goes and vice versa. For one thing, the corner of the tent did not allow for any fabrication of a pillow or head support or whatever. Triangles just do not exist in the camping gear market. Most things are made square and rectangular for the most part.

But lay diagonally I did. Against all sense of tidy and proper, neat and organized, diagonal finally had to be accepted for nothing else would work. Much to the objections of neatness and order and making triangles of the rest of the space, I became a forty-five. Well, maybe a thirty. Whatever. It didn't seem right; but oh well, for the time being, these had to be the least of my worries.

The sleeping bag came next. It just seemed like the natural order of things; shelter and then sleeping in the shelter. So sleeping bag research started in earnest, and it became quite complicated. However, sleeping bags come in about every size and shape and weight, and so a culling process had to start taking place. Weight and size were the utmost priorities. Comfort and roominess were second or third on the list. And when the would-be hiker starts to add up things and the pack weight starts approaching forty pounds and one becomes tired before even having taken a step, one gravitates to the priority way of thinking weight, or absence of it, being paramount.

The first night at home with the sleeping bag was a nightmare. *Neophyte* could be the word of choice here in dealing with this, but just plain *stupid* would better cover the situation. Thinking again along the neat and tidy way I attempted to fold the bag and roll it and then very carefully place it in the tiny bag provided for transport. Stuffing just was not an option. It was like sticking wet noodles in a half-open plastic bag, hoping that they would all come out straight in there. The slippery nylon fabric would just kind of go its own way, and soon the bag was full with still about half of the sleeping bag trailing away like an errant child. The stereotypical ten pounds of you know what in a nine-pound bag.

I later realized that when the instructions said "stuff," it meant *stuff*. Just grab a corner and push and stuff, and magically the sleeping bag disappears inside the tiny bag, resulting in a very tidy and neat package. Actually stuffing serves a purpose too. Stuffing means that there will not be created folds that tend to damage fibers in the sleeping bag. The bag is meant to be stuffed. Neophyte. Part of the learning process. But to first learn, one has to accept, and stuffing just was not in this psyche. Later, when I could get up, get out of the bag, and have it stuffed in the storage bag in a matter of about a minute, I would smile and think that I was, indeed, becoming an *advanced backpacker*, a word that my wife questioned when I came home with the book.

Actually, *Advanced Backpacking* (1) was the first step way back in the later part of the summer before the year of the hike. I had browsed my way through Barnes & Noble and had pretty much decided that was the book of choice. I had the usual cappuccino and paged through the book, feeling somewhat insignificant and certainly not worthy of thinking about some of the stuff in there. I hadn't even done Hiking 101, and here I had taken the leap all the way to "advanced backpacking." Probably it was the reasons for Kris's speculation and doubting.

The chapter that got my attention right away was the instructions and information dealing with the art of dealing with weather. Hiking through high country, primarily above tree line and having to think about lightening, was something that stays with you. I tried to imagine what being above tree line was like. I could not anticipate what the actual experience would be and so blundered ahead in my reading and tried to think that when the time came, I would do the right things and wouldn't need to be rescued in the high country by a team that dropped out of the sky from a helicopter. Nothing could be resolved by reading and thinking and then not knowing and reading and thinking some more. Too similar to reading about how to ride a bicycle without actually having access to the bike. Okay, so now after throwing your right leg over the frame and straddling the seat and with the pedal in the highest position and with your right foot firmly placed on it, start to press down the pedal; and as you do that, push ahead with your left leg to start to accelerate. Then as you feel yourself leaning too far to the right, lean to the left and compensate; and while doing this, try not to turn the handlebars too much for changing direction is achieved not as much by the turning of the handlebars as by leaning and so on.

So dealing with lightening above tree line would just have to come with experience. Above tree line certainly would be a natural thing to do and the doing would take care of the knowing resulting in an intelligent approach and things would just work out. However, it was usually the first terror-ridden notions that came stealing into the night. The lay awake at night and try to imagine what it would be like periods. In those deep dark times of the early morning when everything takes on macabre overtones, my mind took me to far and distant and dangerous places, and all sorts of monsters were lurking everywhere and the idea of actually doing this thing seem much too much for comprehension and actual execution totally impossible. It seemed that for a while, the nights would bring an absolute certainty of abandonment of the whole project; and with daylight, new assurances would come and the planning and educating processes would continue.

In these wee hours, the first lurking thoughts sneaked in and reeked of uncertainty, of dangers beyond comprehension, of falling, falling, falling. Minutes turned into hours saturated with this yoke of burden and why, why, why had I made such huge commitments. No little nibbles of adventure had even been hinted at. No, I went for the big time. Big shot. Why couldn't I have just kept my mouth shut and not told people: relatives, friends, people at church, the guys at the outfitters. Why hadn't I just set realistic goals of, say, trying to make it through Georgia. Maybe through the Great Smoky Mountains National Park, maybe the stretch through Maryland. Or not even doing the Appalachian Trail and stay close to home and maybe do just the 60 miles of Florida National Scenic Trail through the Ocala National Forest. Or just little bites. No, I am doing the entire thing. Two-thousand-some miles. This sixty-two-year-old body is going to walk through fourteen states and climb mountains and do wonderful things, and I am wonderful and on and on. No, I had climbed way out on the limb, leaving myself just hanging there. I had left no alternatives for excuses to quit, no avenues of escape. No recourse for cold feet and sweating and crying and anguish late in the night when all were asleep in their secure little worlds of amenities that would be there forever, not worried about the rain or the cold or the wind—all comfort knowing that the cupboard was full and the refrigerator always beckoned with ice cream, cheeses and milk, and leftover roast beef and stroganoff, and various culinary delights.

And those nights when the rain fell with dreadful poignancy and looking out into the world looked very alien and cold and threatening, the idea of being comfortable out there in all that just seemed totally impossible. I had a long way to go to start developing a new set of standards for comfort and acceptable levels of dry and warm.

*Advanced Backpacking* (1) dealt in depth with the concepts and accepted ways of dealing with wet, the nemesis of the thru-hiker and backpacker. Wet. Rain. Soggy clothes and socks. Most everything one bought prioritized toward dealing with the utmost problem of the wet. One hiker, when asked about how he was dealing with the hike so far, replied, "It's merely a matter of moisture control." Or out of control. Or training the mind to think that unless everything was just plain saturated and dripping, everything was under control. Or training the body that it just didn't matter. That wetness was a state of mind. That the driest socks were the choice for the day and that putting on a wet T-shirt was in the best interest of keeping the other one dry for those times when it was really needed, when hypothermia was setting in and the difference between life and death was a half pound less of heat draining water, the emergency procedure of putting on your driest shirt. We all dealt with moisture in various ways. Some cussed. Some endured silently. Some hiked harder. It was quite comfortable hiking in the rain. High mileage days are often in the rain. Running cooler and needing less water, and there was no compulsion to take leisurely breaks at those wondrous spots that beckoned on sunshiny days. Push on. Push on in the rain. Stay warm. For when one stops, it doesn't take long for that wet chilliness to set in. For that start of the terrorizing uncontrolled shakes and, if the mind is working okay, to realize that death really isn't that far away.

But then hiking for the day eventually has to stop no matter what the weather. Then you're faced with dealing with the problem of everything being wet. My first really truly wet-on-wet setting up camp was on a day that I had hiked 19.4 miles in Vermont. I arrived at the Stratton Pond Shelter only to find it totally full, that is, except for one small space in the loft. I clambered up the vertical steps, nearly falling in the process as the steps were huge giant steps designed for someone that is about seven feet six. I nearly collapsed as I struggled for the final step up on the second floor. There wasn't room to turn around, and I had to at least attempt to make some effort to dry something off. I was dripping on everything, on everybody. This wasn't exactly a place where I was welcomed with open arms. All the other hikers had troubles of their own to keep warm and try to dry their own things out.

I left in a hurry. The day was rapidly ending, and there was only a little daylight left.

The North Shore Tenting Area is in conjunction with Stratton Pond Shelter, totally separate from the shelter and off the AT along a side trail. It was rather difficult to determine just where it was. The trail junctions with the AT going to the right and the camping area indicated as being straight ahead. I continued ahead and started to realize that this tenting area was going to be much farther than I really wanted to detour off the Trail. A shivering cold had started to set into my body, and I knew that I was bordering on being in trouble. A stereotypical case of hypothermia seemed to be developing, actually more like setting in, beyond control now.

I abandoned the designated camping area idea and headed back to the AT but was wrestling with another stealth camping night as this just was not a good area. The underbrush was thick as was the ground cover of various types of vegetation. There was no chance of making it to higher ground with coniferous trees, the ideal for undergrowth, and complying with Leave No Trace camping. I was cold and wet and now very tired; my options had been reduced to only one, stealth camp or place myself in a position of needing rescue.

I chose a site that met very minimal past standards and knew that I would have to hurry. I was already starting to cool down rapidly and was starting to shake uncontrollably. I managed to set the tent down and not flatten too many plants right adjacent to the Trail. One hiker came by, ironically my old nemesis, and his downtrodden demeanor didn't do much for my mood as we talked about the bleak prognosis for the weather in the upcoming week. A week of rain was being predicted. Not something I needed to hear right then.

The tent was up in no time. I threw the pack inside. Not a night to screw around with hanging the bear bag. Priorities would just have to rule here, and I needed to get as dry as possible and warm up quick or I was in trouble. Besides the priority idea seemed to hinge on whether the bear would find a food bag inside the tent with a fairly warm and healthy hiker or the food bag nicely hung outside with a comatose body somewhere near the tent. I was already in trouble, but not that far along. The prospects of a bear being a problem in the area seemed rather remote, and that precaution was thrown to the wind.

I mopped the excess water as best as possible with limited resources and inflated the air mattress. Then more or less corralled the gear into the driest corners and opened up the sleeping bag which was for the most part at least semidry. I undressed as much one item at a time as possible and changed into the other, and drier, clothes which were about the same status as the sleeping bag and then put the rain gear back on over it and climbed in the sleeping bag. With the exception of the drenched clothes that were just discarded, I had on every piece of clothing that was in the pack, including the sweater.

From my sleeping bag, I could reach outside and cook through the tent flap and managed to get the noodles cooked, always to perfection as there is no such thing as bad trail food especially when cold and wet conditions further enhance taste and gratification—one of the perks and joys of the Trail, amenities usually so taken for granted. Soon I was lost in the trance of hot trail food, and my chilled insides were slowly escaping what may have been a little too close a dance with hypothermia, the much-too-subtle danger that sneaks up so quickly.

In retrospect, the incident left me rather shaken. My vulnerabilities and the manifestation of such made me aware that even though we may feel like things are under control sometimes that can change without actual awareness that control has been lost. In our normal states of being surrounded by amenities and lavish creature comforts, real threats to health and well-being just do not exist. Excluding riding in automobiles, probably our most dangerous activity.

Long before any conscious plans had been laid for hiking the Trail, an innermost battle with the ways of society had raged within. Often, the thoughts occurred that were Henry Ford here today, would he or could he justify what was the original plan—to make motor-driven transportation available to virtually everybody? And could he face the fact that things had gone amuck. Transportation as he envisioned it, we would have to think, amounted to a supplement to using our bodies to get around and not as the sole mode of getting around as has become the case in our so-called modern society. Health and well-being of the human race has deteriorated as a result of all of this convenience, and ironically, we have become slave to—*handicapped by* would better describe it—this steel monster. That the intention of making life easier had propelled us metaphorically toward those steps so often mentioned in songs and musings of man of becoming physically useless because the natural demands normally placed on our bodies had disappeared. What would Henry Ford think about drive-thrus? Or more correctly stated, the gross abuse of such things. These were the seeds that subtly entered the fiber of my soul and would result in such rebellion as hiking the Trail and throwing all of that convenience away for a while. To become more appreciative of what we have. To become reliant upon myself again.

Within the core of this being lay strong urges to rebel. However, healthy outlets for such don't exist without some innovation. And within that core, the seeds were subconsciously sown—a rebellion and the manifestation of hiking the Trail slowly came into being and toward the baby steps of fruition. For that endeavor is so huge that justification has to be many-faceted, at least for this being. Just simply saying that it was something that was always a yearning to be done would not have been inspiration enough to actually do it. There had to be huge reasons. This little caper was more like a massive expedition, and reasoning behind it had to be ample and varied, enough so to take me through the hard times when the glory factor had long disappeared.

I suppose that I am a hiker, camper, outdoors person by nature and something that runs deep within my heart and soul. However, the prospect of giving up all creature comforts and throw amenities to the wind had to have strong motivational background. Rebellion is such a good tool when that energy is turned inward to manifest itself into constructive endeavors. And so rebellion was a large part of the base that was set down for hiking the Trail. A very large part, indeed.

So the preparation phase of doing the Appalachian Trail not only encompassed the physical aspects of training and gear acquisition and education to adhere to techniques that were proven from past hikers thrown into similar situations. Actually the largest part of this phase was the conditioning of the mind to accept this crazy idea with iron conviction and to instill enough desire to carry me through. It proved to be adequate in actuality; however, at no time did it seem like it had been enough. Each day, each hill, each rainy day, each new trail test brought back the same insecurity, the same fears; one just simply had to press on.

Time to dry out—
Lamberts Meadow Shelter
Virginia—May 24 mile 700 (about)

# Chapter 8

## Kris

*Spring 2003*
*Somewhere on the AT*

*Dearest Kris,*

*This, of course, was written well before I left. How could it be otherwise? But the thoughts were already there and the message had to be conveyed.*

*Maybe somewhere in the world there would be another woman that could be as understanding as you. But I would have to actually see that woman to believe it. A woman that could "allow" her husband to be off on some harebrained adventure not only belies such possibility, but in addition, to encourage such folly could not be possible in another wife that is out there anywhere. At some time in the forty-some years that we have known each other, your Swedish intelligence either came to the conclusion that he is either totally out of his mind or that the best way to deal with it was to just go along with it, for to argue was counterproductive.*

*And on those days when my feet and back and everything else hurt and I am wet from head to toe and haven't slept good in about two weeks, I can blame you for not talking me out of it as the good stereotypical wife should do and know that you already know that I would. But on those wondrous days when the sun is on my face and the wind is at my back (if that is possible hiking "north" on the Trail) and all is downhill and I look to the heavens and say, "Thank you, God," then I can be thankful that you are who you are with an open mind and had sent me off with your blessing.*

*In my mind's eye, there will always be those frank and intelligent blue eyes looking at me, cheering me on, wishing me well; and the reality will set in eventually that even though my body and mind are subjecting themselves to my self-inflicted torture, none of this could have been accomplished by myself. There would not have been somebody to do this for. If you were not there waiting, there would not be inspiration for doing this. You, the gracious lady that somehow always could reason things out to the why, and you alone are my reason for living and doing and being what I am. The understanding beneath that Swedish intelligence can only be understood with the highs and lows of our relationship. Had everything been "perfect," it would not have been. Someday I should write about that concept as too often in today's society we give up on the other person when disappointments and shortcomings inevitably happened, but you wouldn't hear of such foolishness. Having you made life so satisfying for beneath the trivial failures (which is something we all do) lay the ultimate conquests, and you somehow knew that way before I or anybody else ever did.*

*When I think of you, my mind also sees your Dad. Such a nice influence to have had. However, there had to be you and your basic self to have had that chemistry turn out as it did. He was much too reasonable for this world. Much too logical and kind and understanding. Other daughters may have rebelled against such radical thinking. You espoused it and made it you.*

*Kris, I love you dearly and could never imagine having lived life without you. Though there are things lacking within our relationship, the positives far outweigh the negatives. The subtle things that makes our life together is a rare thing.*

*So as I hike, I will be reliving those wondrous years that we have had together and will be so looking forward to telling you about my adventure. And mostly I will marvel at the fact that in your love, you could allow me to do this thing that has burned within me and endorse it and support me.*

*I shall be forever grateful to you and love you so very much,*

*George "Ole Smoky Lonesome"*

I had placed the letter in a strategic place so that she wouldn't miss it. Maybe out of guilt, maybe out of a sense of responsibility, maybe as inspiration to keep mailing those mail drop boxes, all twenty-one of them.

Or maybe as reminder that our life had never been "normal" and that my wife would again make her usual whimsical conclusions, that being that her husband in some ways was not a well man.

She had always amazed me, this Swede of mine. Her stoic approach to life, her eternal optimism, her unnerving, steadfast dedication. Her love ran so terribly deep that there was not a need for constant reassurance. I thought of those utterances from so long ago when we had said "I do." The Swede had sure meant it and had gone the spectrum of those "agreements," having seen me at my worst and my best, had seen me through sickness and health, through good times and bad, and, somehow, had never wavered.

Never once.

And sometimes when she is at my side with her hand in mine is all the proof needed to manifest that there is a God, that He had a plan, and that Kris had been set aside especially for me. A truly humbling experience.

And when our nomadic life became a yoke sometimes too heavy to bear, her deep inner strength would once again surface. I thought back to 1972, our ninth year together as husband and wife and yet another field assignment.

In the fall we made our usual southern trek—this time from Britt, Iowa, to Ozark, Arkansas. This time the move was somewhat complicated in that Kris was quite pregnant with Will. Ozark is not exactly the mecca for health care (even by Arkansas standards), and she soon found out that there was not one doctor in Ozark willing to take her case. Fort Smith, 40 miles away, was the closest and most promising.

With that information, we commenced into house hunting. After a few days, the health care situation looked pretty good when the comparison was made to the housing situation. By about the third day of viewing "cold-water flats," as they so lovingly became known, I made my way by myself, leaving my vagrant little family holed up in the local mom-and-pop, the kids being rather content in knowing that the longer this took, the longer it would be before they would have to return to yet a different school.

My mood was bolder, more reckless by this time, somewhat on the edges of chutzpah, but also with much lower expectations—the thoughts of an ideal home had pretty well fallen by the way. By this time, reality starts to rear its head; and with that, the glamour of USGS field life comes back into perspective. So in this bold and brazen mode and virtually at the state of panic, I unilaterally rented a house, the best pick of the rather deplorable litter. Just did it. Ballsy move on my part, but hey, our bosses back at the USGS offices in Rolla were metaphorically hovering. Guilt was setting in. They would be wondering why I wasn't making maps yet.

Having made the choice and agreement to rent, I was then faced with conveying the news. There wasn't too much joy to be garnered from the situation. We made our way over to "home" that we later lovingly referred to it as "a naice tait litle ole haus" (translation: nice tight little old house), slum-word jargon for leaving much to be desired. *Mum* was the word as we maneuvered our utility trailer into the front yard of the pink bungalow from which one had trouble wrangling even one ounce of charm. The unpacking process began.

Kris fights best by being totally silent. We shuffled back and forth carrying various pieces of what we then referred to as "our furniture." Silence. Back and forth. Shuffling. Lethargic. Using elbow points. Gestures. Back and forth. Floor getting covered with the jumble. Not too much organization yet, more of an emptying of the trailer process than anything else.

Somewhere back in the purchasing process, we had obtained our prize: an eight-foot-by-ten-foot fire-engine-red carpet all rolled up into a neat but unwieldy roll. Kris at one end, carrying this monster as well as she could in her condition; me at the other. Shuffling and plodding, tripping over everything as we made our way first through the front door then around things to the assigned room for the carpet.

Agitated and angry by this time, communication was virtually nonexistent. Stepping over and around things jumbled in heaps here and there. Carpet wanting to go where it wanted to go. Losing our balance seemed to come rather on cue, and we both went down with the carpet still somewhat in tow. Down into the jumble, carpet on top. Lying there hot and disheveled and sweating and angry.

The mind works so well with absurdity, eventually no longer able to ignore how one must appear to the little mouse (of which there proved to be many) observing all of this. The emotional dam broke, and the laughter began. Soothing, relaxing, releasing, tumultuous, belly-down laughter of the richest kind. Tears-streaming-and-rolled-down faces-laughter. Peacemaking laughter. The crisis was over.

But as life always has a way of timing things to her quirks, my survey field assistant chose this exact moment to report for duty on the job, having just come into town. He had been in Britt, Iowa, also and was ready for some more rodman work, this time in the South. He had come through the door about the time we had hit the floor.

He stood there a long time in a rather stupid but questioning state of suspended disbelief. He must still have that scene firmly and forever embedded in his memory. A scene symbolic of the life of a USGS mapmaker, a life of certain disappointment that seems to find rewards in the most unlikely places. A life of diversity and the unexpected and of finding pleasure in not what you have but more so in what you don't have.

Only Kris could have survived such a life so well and drawn so much from it. Only Kris could have faced another day still fully expecting the "better" part having had more than her share of the "worse" part. And now, thirty-one years later, only Kris could have let her husband follow his dreams yet one more time. Only Kris would have the patience to send out those twenty-one boxes and wait for the phone calls, ever optimistic. Thru-hikers need a lot of support. And only Kris could have done so well while I worked my way north, knowing that she was always there for the phone calls and the encouragement. And it was nice knowing that the packages would always be there in the post offices in the towns on and along the Appalachian Trail.

# Chapter 9

## Epiphany

For five months I hung around with people with names like Buffalo Bobby, Dreamwalker, Aussie, Gear Guy, Horizon, Rocky Top, Batch, Shine, Odyssey, Geriatric, Train, Sloop, and Jamaica. There were no Jims or Johns or Janes or Marys. The names were varied and descriptive, sometime mysterious, always interesting. For all I knew, these people could have been running from the law, taking on alias names, seeking sanctuary on the Appalachian Trail.

In the early days of the hike, it was rather awkward calling somebody Dreamwalker or Buffalo Bobby, but it was the ways of the Trail. After a while, nobody questioned it for this was an atmosphere of little façade, and an anything-goes sort of attitude prevailed. I grew comfortable with my trail name, though it evolved into other forms as other hikers attempted to add other names or inventions of their own making. Most people wanted to call me Smoky Joe, and I quickly would correct them. My name had been well thought out, and I wanted it to stay just as originally intended. Too much thought had gone into the selection process. I smiled, thinking back to an earlier conversation in a phone call to my dear cousin Doris.

"Hey, I have a trail name . . . finally. It's been so hard to come up with something that would not sound too self-indulging . . . or narcissistic for lack of a better term, but yet have some meaning and be something that would fit just me."

"So what is it?"

"Grinder." I was so proud of my choice and knew that she would just love it and be so enthusiastic.

Long pause at the other end. "Oh, you mean like bump and grinder."

"Good grief, I hadn't thought of that!"

Laughter. Pause. More laughter.

"It just seemed so perfect. Being older I probably wouldn't really be tearing up the Trail but would just sort of be grinding it out. Now, having told you, it doesn't look like Grinder is going to work too well."

"So is that all you thought of so far?"

"Well, I had thought of a couple of possibilities. One was to just not start with a trail name and just let the chips fall as they may. The actual correct, or I should say proper, protocol is to have another hiker or hikers name you. Usually something that happens along the Trail that would just sort of evolve into your trail name. Then I thought what if it just doesn't happen. Or worse yet, what if I end up with something like Fart Blossom or Booger, who knows."

More laughter.

"And I really do want a trail name. That is part of the mystique of doing this thing. I've never had a nickname and George just is not one of my favorite names and it just seemed so nice to get rid of my real name for a while.

"Then for a long time I really wanted to call myself Quixote for Don Quixote. My favorite author is John Steinbeck; and when he took his trip around the country in his camper truck and wrote about it, the book is titled *Travels with Charley,* he named it Rocinante, that being the name of Don Quixote's horse. Steinbeck was very impressed with Cervantes's book, and it just seemed like the right name. So since I didn't want to be named after a horse and since Don Quixote is one of my favorite fictional characters, it seemed right for me. Then I got to thinking that most thru-hikers are well-informed and well-read and they would have questions that I couldn't answer. I have never read the book all the way through, only some parts of it. I doubt that my understanding of the book is correct. It would place me in a vulnerable position."

My comments had been much too long, and it was time to move on to another subject.

"You'll come up with something. I just know you will."

Back to the drawing board.

My wife, Kris, and I have always loved the movie *Fried Green Tomatoes.* For some reason, the movie had been going through my head in recent times while making my trail preparations, and suddenly my name just appeared. Right then and there. An epiphany!

Ole Smoky Lonesome!

It's perfect. I'm old. I'll be going through the Great Smoky Mountains. I'll be very lonesome for Kris. It was perfect.

In the movie, Smoky Lonesome wanders in and out and is a rather-desolate soul that doesn't seem to belong anywhere. As he drifts in and out of the movie, Idgie always welcomes him back with open arms and always has a hot meal waiting at the Whistle Stop Cafe. Of course, he always accepts for it looks like he hasn't eaten in a very long time. Also, he enjoys the company of the gang there.

His character is perfect for someone hiking the Appalachian Trail. Lonely. Lost. Desolate. Emaciated. Homeless. In need of help from his fellow man. The name was absolutely perfect. Just the description of most thru-hikers! As the saying goes, the difference between an AT thru-hiker and a bum is the GoreTex.

My quest to find a trail name didn't last that long. And when I finally thought of it, I never had a doubt as to whether it was correct for me. And I could never dream just how perfect it really was. Much later—looking at the photos of myself—Smoky Lonesome, in the movie, looked better than the emaciated person looking back at me in the photos. The name fit me well, and as I progressed up the Trail and my body dwindled, it fit me even better. And other hikers were comfortable with it. It was perfect, and even now long after the hike, I still hang on to it. A nostalgia trip back down the Trail, I suppose, and maybe it is just a name that I'm comfortable with.

Trail names are intriguing to say the least. However, in some cases, people just did not want to be called anything except their given name. Such was the case with a man named Dick. He was from a small town in Missouri; seemed to keep pretty much to himself and was very quiet. He was well liked by all the hikers and it just seemed like he needed a trail name. Buffalo Bobby tried to call him Quiet Man. Dick didn't like it. Dick and I crossed paths quite often as we progressed north, and I developed a respect for the man; and after realizing that he just was not comfortable with anything other than Dick, I let it go. Dick it was, and it stayed that way.

Hike your own hike. If a trail name does not suit you, so be it. Just another fascinating aspect of doing the Trail. What worked for one probably wouldn't for somebody else. So as Ole Smoky Lonesome, I made my way north and grew into my name and grew more comfortable with it until it came to the point that I didn't want to give it up when I returned home.

In retrospect, the selection of a trail name is critical. Possibly the difference between a successful hike and otherwise. Names are important. Reflect upon successful novels and stories and the author's selection of character names, vital to the success of the story: Cruella di Vil, Oliver Twist, Huckleberry Finn, Clint Bunsen, Ebenezer Scrooge, Captain Ahab, Elmer Gantry, Rip Van Winkle, Atticus Finch, Adam Trask, Ichabod Crane. Characters come alive just having the correct name. And after all, while hiking the Trail, we are playing a part, being somebody else for a while, an escape from a sometimes-dreary existence. And the name selection should be the person we want to portray or should reflect ourselves in the truest sense if that is who you chose to be. There aren't that many situations in real life when we can be somebody else for such a long period of time.

Chose your trail name carefully. I pondered my choice of names as the training began. My conclusions about training after reading all of the books never were strongly formulated. However, there was a need to do something while waiting for the magic day.

# Chapter 10

## Get a Life!

The thought of it really is mind-bending. An assumed normal man walking around with forty pounds of sand in a backpack, a total of forty-seven pounds. Walking around. Certainly it must appear masochistic to the outsider looking in. Up and down, getting nowhere. Same general route every day. Same bag of sand. Hopefully, maybe, nobody knows about the bag of sand and just assume that the pack is empty or just stuffed to appear so. Nope, can't fool anybody. When one is carrying forty-seven pounds on one's back, there is a certain stride, a certain leaning to offset the weight—anybody would know. You have gotta be hearing "get a life" as people misinterpret the meaning in all of this. There just have to be better ways to spend one's time.

The real physical aspects of doing the Appalachian Trail as a thru-hike cannot be anticipated without actually doing parts of it as a section-hiker. However, section-hikers and thru-hikers seem to be leagues apart. One is usually one or the other. And maybe if one section-hiked too much, there was just the tendency to stay that way as a continuous expedition on a year-to-year basis, eventually doing the entire trail if one is persistent enough.

So when one hits the Trail for the first time with intentions of doing a thru-hike, there is usually no precedent, nothing to foresee what lies ahead. Living in Florida could not have provided the terrain that is needed to get some idea and for the body to prepare properly. My old external frame pack with the forty-pound bag of sand made about 400 miles along the streets and highways close to home. Drainage retention areas, fancy terms for huge rectangular holes in the ground adjoining development of subdivisions and other buildings, provided the only semblance of hills. By Florida law, these DRAs are required to be built to provide places for rainwater to drain into and held so that it can soak back into the ground. I chugged up the twelve-foot climbs and tried to imagine what doing that one hundred times in succession would feel like. It just was not possible mentally to put that into perspective.

The street hikes became somewhat of a joke. However, I was resolute in doing it daily and tapered off in the later part of the three-month training period. I began to refer to these "hikes" to my cousin Doris as "painting my face black." Meaning that I was assimilating some demented military type on a mission and with a vengeance and being rather clandestine and threatening walking around this peaceful neighborhood carrying a forty-seven-pound pack hiking to nowhere and back. Very few people actually knew what I was up to and had to come to their own conclusions. From the outside looking in, I had pretty much lost it wandering around, carrying all of this weight, apparently either meaninglessly, or as some form of self-inflicted torture, a study in masochism.

I became more painfully aware of this on one evening hike into the inky black night that turned into a relatively serious rainstorm. I was on a mission to recover my truck which was at Pep Boys for some repair work. That was about 4 miles away. When I walked into the waiting room, I received some rather-shocked looks at this reprobate drenched to the skivvies and dripping on everything; and then when the pack hit the floor with a thud, there may have even been fear in the eyes of some of the waiting customers, wondering if there was a bomb in there or something bordering on a weapon of mass destruction. Cleverly, of course, deeply hidden within the forty-pound bag of sand would just be part of the shrapnel flying when the thing blew up. Sitting seemed to dispel some of the worried looks; and when I withdrew similar waiting room items such as books, albeit soaked books, the atmosphere in the room went pretty much back to normal.

This training regimen continued for approximately three months, and the daily hikes were anywhere from 2 miles up to about 10 miles. The later "hike" of 10 miles was actually on a walking track at nearby Jervey Gantt Park in Ocala, which has been home for the past seven years. The walking-running-jogging track manages to wend its way around the park and attain a distance of 2 miles even though one can see almost any part of it from any other part, except the extreme northeastern partially wooded or savannah-like area. Portions of the Trail parallels itself within about twenty feet of where you had just walked a few minutes before, a series of hairpin turns stacked up against each other. Quite uniquely built for the small acreage that is available for such a facility. It was always crowded, usually with the stereotypical hard bodies and the menagerie of first day of the rest of my life types that are usually there in desperate hope for instant results after too many years of abject neglect. I was the only "backpacker" on the trail and usually received some rather-odd and questioning looks, and often people would stop to talk and ask me what I was up to. Of course, I was more than willing to tell my story. A role that I would play over and over during the training and later during the hike.

So the 10 miles amounted to five times around with that now-more-or-less-hated forty-pound bag of sand strapped to my back. I managed to make 4 miles an hour on this venture, so I was done in less than three hours, including taking a short break after the third time around. All during the "hike," I tried to transcend this experience to the real thing, thinking that it was possible to have 10 miles in before noon. That seemed like necessity just simply to be able to accomplish the thru-hike. I knew that there were other purposes for doing the hike—seeing the marvelous scenery, inter-relating with other hikers and local people, and just enjoying the rock formations, the trees, birds, and wildlife. However, my objective and priority was to be a thru-hiker—that came first and foremost. Nothing less than the entire AT was going to satisfy this longing and could justify the attempt. Stopping short of the end just was not an option.

So with the reading that I had done of previous thru-hikers, the studying that I had done, and the conclusions that I had reached all indicated that one just simply had to have a daily average of somewhere around 13 miles for the duration of the hike. So throwing in zero days from time to time, the actual daily hiking mileage had to be somewhere around fifteen or preferably closer to sixteen. It seemed impossible that day at the Jervey Gantt trail walking around and around for 10 miles. However, I knew that something within would probably kick in above and beyond my abilities, beyond my endurance, and beyond my capabilities. It just seemed to be the way of the Trail.

By that second time around, it was boiling down to quite a boring activity. Around and around we go. I could never realize at that time just how often I would have these same feelings while actually doing the real thing. One can only look at the same types of things so many times before a certain amount of boredom sets in. However, with the same methodology as I often emphasized in repetitive surveying procedures, one can instill interest by merely setting goals. It was either that or clock-watching, and I wasn't about to relegate myself to that after all the years that I had always set goals in one capacity or another to add zest and interest to activities that otherwise might not be that interesting. Setting goals adds interest, makes for accomplishments, and makes time go by quickly.

My mind was in fervor by the time I finished the fourth time around. I hadn't finished 8 miles yet, and I was hoping for daily mileages of double this on the Appalachian Trail. I knew it would be difficult. The days would have to be long with some breaks incorporated. Hiking common sense tells you to take a pack-off break about every 2 miles. My ever-favorite *Advanced Backpacking* (1) recommended it as did other sources of information on hiking long distances. That seemed like something that I would do on the Trail. However, until I developed good hoisting methods for the pack, it was almost more tiring to take the pack off and on than to just leave it on and lean against a tree or sit on a rock with the pack on. In reality, pack-off breaks just did not occur too often. And there were days on the Trail when I never did take the pack off until relieving myself of it at the end of the day, sometime having the pack on for approximately as long as ten continuous hours.

Another nearby trail facility that was used a lot was Baseline Trail. It was a marvelous asphalt trail about ten to twelve feet wide. A truly world-class trail that had been recently constructed and no expense had been spared. Here I met numerous different people engaged in a plethora of activities, ranging from the usual runners to bicyclists, skate boarders, roller-skaters, and speed-skaters. Walking this course that is 5 miles round-trip just never was boring. I walked along the edge of the blacktop to assimilate something similar to the Appalachian Trail; the blacktop surface was just not going to do that much good for conditioning and preparing for the real thing. Irregularity and the hardest route was always sought, an interesting concept for when the real thing was encountered; then the reverse was true, trying to find the easiest places to place my feet in threading my way north.

The training in retrospect was of questionable value. In all probability, it was advantageous as just simply starting totally unprepared on the AT would have been foolhardy not having done hiking with a backpack. It doesn't take too long to realize that different muscles were incorporated and technique had to be developed. Of course, not having hills there were limitations, and there just was nothing that could be done about that. One can only work with what is available.

Also, toward the end of the training period and for about a month before the actual hike starting date, about twenty deep knee bends with the pack on were added to the repertoire. These became a dreaded part of the workout. Deep knee bends just never were fun for me, or probably anybody; and adding forty-seven pounds made it almost unbearable, easily easier to hike uphill.

However, once I started on the real hike, I knew that the training was of value for I had already established some of the proper thinking that was necessary for the grindlike aura that a thru-hike takes on. Thru-hiking is so much different than the pleasant day hikes I was accustomed to. Day hikes usually mean a leisurely pace, one tends to stop and just relax and enjoy the scenery. Hurrying just was not necessary.

Thru-hiking the Appalachian Trail was one of the most grueling schedules that I was ever on. Not just in terms of the repetition of day after day, but also the daily routine just did not allow much room for goofing off. I developed a routine not unlike routines in jobs that I had done, in work with USGS or in private surveying. A certain time in the day should mean that a certain amount of miles had already been accomplished. If not, there was a tendency to hurry, and that was not what I wanted to be doing.

It was amazing how a long a mile could be! I had always prided myself in thinking that I could estimate how far I had walked. I swore that the mileage shown between destinations was just plain wrong on the signs placed at or near road crossings or at shelters. I would mumble and be absolutely certain that I had passed a particular landmark. Then, lo and behold, there it would appear; and usually long after I thought that I should have been to that point.

I did not start with a watch. That ended up being a mistake. A watch serves more purposes than can be imagined on the Trail. So many evenings, especially early on, were totally cloudy; and that presented a problem in the later parts of the day. If the sun was out, a relatively accurate assessment could be made of just how much farther to go and when to fill water bottles for the evening if a good source was crossed or near to the Trail. Also, a watch works much like a pedometer. There are very long stretches along the AT (possibly some places as long as 10 miles) where there are absolutely no landmarks. With a watch, one could pretty well use a rule of thumb of about 2 miles an hour and, in that manner, have some idea where one was. Also the watch served the purpose of simply allowing a way of knowing how you were doing for no two days were alike.

Many evenings prior to obtaining a watch I would shut down for the day much too early; thinking it was later than it was and not wanting to be caught between good places to camp for the night. Also on numerous days, water was carried much too far, not knowing just where I was and not knowing how much daylight was left.

So when I arrived in Daleville, Virginia, that was a very high priority. It took some searching for I wanted a digital model and it had to have a light. The model that I finally settled on turned out to be a rather-attractive kid's Timex. I couldn't wear it and didn't want to have it on my wrist, so it usually hung from my fanny pack strap and that worked out real well. Until Daleville, a distance of 700 miles, I just made do and found myself asking hikers for the time constantly. Having my own watch proved to be one of the better additions to my gear.

So in retrospect, the training and acclimation for carrying a lot of weight on my back would not have been traded for anything. When I hit the Trail, there were no particular problems except for the aches and pains that everybody experienced when first starting. My age required preparation. Many of the younger hikers allowed time for conditioning and just let the hike itself prepare them for what lay ahead. Nothing was wrong with that line of thinking. As they say, doing it was the best way to prepare for it. Having the advantage of starting at the south end which is much easier than what lay ahead in the northern half also helped in this acclimation phase, a luxury that southbounders could not afford.

So to train or not to train is similar to debating about religion, with no apparent right answer. It's best to follow your instincts and do what works for you.

# Chapter 11

## The Appalachian Trail

*April 27—Day 23—Mile 322—(Journal entry)—met Sweet Tooth and his wife on the trail (he's a trail maintainer who was checking this part for a friend)—they left cookies and sodas in his white Dodge pickup on the road*

The Appalachian Trail is amazing. Though primarily a woods trail, it manages to be as diverse as this country is varied and provides views of about anything conceivable, from a zoo to a major automobile racetrack to airports to cities and towns and rivers and mountains, lakes, and major works of man. This mammoth project was the brainchild of Benton MacKaye, but actually bringing that idea to fruition would never have happened without the efforts and work of his colleague, Myron Avery. Though at odds about many of the details including location and terminal points and just what the Trail should encompass, these two men were the driving force and the catalyst in the creation of the Appalachian Trail. The unsung heroes in this saga, however, are countless thousands of selfless volunteers who initially build it and now maintain it; but the Appalachian Trail somehow survives, and probably the original concept and overall idea is stronger than ever.

No book on the subject of thru-hiking the Trail should avoid at least trying to make some sense of a description that could be somewhat all-encompassing without being too confusing. It is so immense that the descriptions I read just added to the confusion. For the Trail is huge. At the visitor center at Amicalola Falls State Park, that also included the Approach Trail, the distance is shown as 2,108.5 miles. However, utilizing a ruler on a U.S. map and simply converting the straight line into mileage reveals a startling fact. The direct route from Springer Mountain, Georgia, to Mount Katahdin, Maine, is a mere 1,100 miles. It is difficult to believe that an additional 1,000 miles, or almost a doubling, can be added by simply following the topography or ridge summits and whatever other diversions are added for various reasons. For further emphasis, consider the fact that the mileage from my home in Ocala, Florida, to Mount Katahdin, Maine, on a direct route, a distance of about 1,400 miles, is considerably shorter than the Appalachian Trail.

One of the precepts or missions of the Trail is that it be meandering. One wonders if possibly that concept wasn't a little overdone. Yes, the ultimate distance when the Trail was first conceived was to be 2,000 miles, but one wonders for what purpose. I do know that as the hiker makes his way north or more specifically northeast, there are numerous places when one is going exactly in the opposite direction. The segment leaving New Jersey into New York is true manifestation of this as the northbound thru-hiker is going south and southeast for about 25 miles.

The general theme of the hike is to attain a ridge and follow that ridge until it either plays out or one is purposely taken off the mountain to gain access to a highway or road or to go into a town. It is supposed to be a wilderness experience, but still for thru-hikers, there are needs and that usually requires a town and the services that provides. However, the number of towns that the Trail actually goes through is (arguably for *through* can be subjective depending on what you consider proximity) a mere twenty-one: Wesser, North Carolina; Hot Springs, North Carolina; Erwin, Tennessee; Damascus, Virginia; Pearisburg, Virginia; Daleville, Virginia; Troutville, Virginia; Harpers Ferry, West Virginia; Boiling Springs, Pennsylvania; Duncannon, Pennsylvania; Port Clinton, Pennsylvania; Delaware Water Gap, Pennsylvania; Bear Mountain, New York; Kent, Connecticut; Falls Village, Connecticut; Dalton, Massachusetts; Cheshire, Massachusetts; Williamstown, Massachusetts; Hanover, New Hampshire; Glencliff, New Hampshire; and Caratunk, Maine.

It is difficult to describe the Appalachian Trail and have it make sense to the reader. It is best to avail oneself of a map, preferably a topographic map that shows the entire eastern seaboard. The U.S. Geological Survey has published a map that shows the entire chain of mountain ranges, and from that can be ascertained some sense of the overall picture and how different mountains are separated or connected. To say the Trail follows a ridge is much too simplistic as the Appalachian Mountains actually are a series of chains that have numerous names or fall victim to colloquial reference depending on the locale. The Great Smoky Mountains, the Blue Ridge Mountains, the Green Mountains, the White Mountains, the Mahoosuc Range, the Longfellow Mountains—all comprise some part of the Appalachian chain. The purpose here is not to confuse further but to acknowledge that as with most human perception, the story is more complicated than it has to be for the casual observer.

However, for the purpose of poignancy and to emphasize the enormity of the Appalachian Trail, some compilation of what is encompassed should attempt to be made.

The AT goes through fourteen different states, seventy-two different counties, eight national forests, two national parks; crosses and recrosses and parallels the Blue Ridge Parkway, twelve state parks, twenty-one villages and towns; skirts (somewhat in proximity) six major cities (Washington, Baltimore, Philadelphia, Newark, New York, and Boston) and numerous smaller cities such as Roanoke, Virginia, Bristol, Tennessee, Harrisburg, Pennsylvania; and supposedly goes within relative proximity of Camp David. It crosses twelve interstate highways at least once and the Pennsylvania Turnpike, twenty-eight U.S. highways at least once, approximately eighty state highways, hundreds of county roads, and an undetermined number of woods roads and trails. It crosses approximately a dozen major railroads and follows remnants of ones long abandoned. It goes through fields where cows and horses are pastured and where various crops are grown—including corn, wheat, and oats and along a wildlife preserve—and skirts or goes through areas that manifest the spoils of man where trees are dying, over mountain balds where the view is forever and through "green tunnels" where nothing is visible. And on a map requires a lot of paper for a proper rendering of its topography, enormity, and diversity.

The set of maps that portray the entire Trail at various scales (1:62,500; 1:100,000; etc.) that show important details is huge. Stacked up in trail ready form, the forty-one maps are six inches high. The set is sold and distributed by the Appalachian Trail Conference (now Conservancy) and costs $225.90. The beautiful thing about these maps is that they show profiles that the hiker can, at a glance, see how many ups and downs he/she has on any section, an absolute must. Some quick addition will quickly inform the hiker how much climbing there was to be done that day.

Approximately 377 peaks are surmounted in traversing the Trail's entire length. It goes through or adjacent to a number of Civil War battlefields, crosses two large dams and thirteen major rivers from ones as historic as the Potomac and Hudson to one as mysterious and varied as the Housatonic. It passes points where major watersheds are determined. It passes through watersheds that are major water sources for numerous towns.

A peruse of the AT on an U.S. atlas makes the potential hiker feel as if this venture were about to take him/her through a continuous urban area. However, it is uncanny how totally isolated one feels while surrounded with so much humanity; and some nights in the tent, one wonders if the airliners were ever going to stop. An oxymoron of mammoth proportions!

There are also some quite unique installations that the Trail skirts. One in direct conflict of what it represents is the Lime Rock racetrack, a major stop in the IMSA circuit of Le Mans—type racing for very professional drivers and teams. It is adjacent to the small Connecticut town with the same name. A group of us thru-hikers sat at an excellent viewpoint on Sharon Mountain about a mile from the track, watching with rapt interest as high-powered race cars went through the series of curves while practicing rounds at very high speeds. Also a number of other vehicles were doing purposeful power slides, obviously testing tires. Yes, much in contrast with our nonmechanized activity, but it proved to be somewhat of a refreshing reminder of those other aspects of our complex and diverse culture.

It would be sad if the entire trail had been built within a certain mind-set and did not vary as it does. Possibly the original intent was that it be strictly a wilderness experience. And one has to wonder just how much wilderness one needs. Wilderness can be boring when experienced at about 2 to 2 1/2 miles per hour and when day after day one sees virtually the same scenes. The variety of towns and highways and works of man not only are more representative of this country but also provide the change necessary to make hiking the Trail exciting and interesting. However, the line has to be drawn back to the original intent which is a good one; and with the checks and balances that are usually provided with such endeavors, this hiker finds no criticism necessary with the proximity of other than natural things. I welcomed the towns if for no other reason than for manifestation as to why I was out here in the first place.

It has to be noted that a thru-hiker eventually loses the big picture, a lot of the time not even totally aware geographically of what part of a state one was in. Dealing with the esoteric large-scale maps for the Trail that only have map margin notations for nearby towns of interest to hikers, you can go within 34 miles of New York City, as an example, and not even know it. A thru-hiker is for the most part intensely interested in things basically within walking, or reasonable hitchhiking distance of the Trail.

So a description of the Appalachian Trail serves no other function except to attempt a manifestation of the enormity. However, a writer usually will fail in that endeavor for that task cannot be achieved by mere words. That can only come in experiencing the Trail step-by-step, tasting the tang of the winds on the balds and savoring the tart cold of the streams as you splash its originality on your face, immerse in the damp frigidness of the morning dew as you evolve from your drenched tent, luxuriate in the warmth of those virgin rays of sunshine that filter through the canopy of trees, strain against the taxing of your cardiovascular being chugging your way toward yet another summit, and expound in the fragrant evergreens that perfume the still evening night futilely clinging to what is left of your body's strength and endurance as you patiently wend your way to the terminal point of your adventure. No, writing words in lieu of experience is only a study in futility.

# Chapter 12

## Technique

*April 23—Day 19—Mile 261—(Journal entry)—about 3,000' climb to Snowbird Mountain—paced myself—stayed aerobic—went good—got water about 1 1/2 miles out*

By the third week, I knew that I was in trouble. All that I had read about doing the Trail just was not quite working out as planned. This was also about the time that Buffalo Bobby and I sort of joined forces. Walking across Fontana Dam and entering the Great Smoky Mountains National Park seemed to be a good time to take on a partner; and he seemed to be my kind of friend, easygoing, laid-back, and somewhat humble. Therefore, we would not be a threat to one another. A thru-hiker had enough problems without having to deal with a too strong personality that was loaded down with insecurities. Most of us that may have had those traits could hold them in check, and that was a must on this endeavor. And being with somebody was a good thing. However, it also meant trying to maintain a pace conducive to such an arrangement, and that just was not working out. Either I was just a wimp or something serious was happening with my body or mind or some combination of the two.

Along about this time was when I developed "my own particular" style of doing the ups. It varied on the day, the length of the climbs, and other factors. Energy levels seemed to vary from day to day. The huge problem with ups is that a hiker was usually loaded down on the longest climbs, the ones to major peaks. Resupply was always at the very lowest elevations for that is where the rivers and major streams are and consequently where the towns and resupply are. Highways in mountainous country are for the most part built along river valleys and consequently so are the towns.

So ironically, the hiker would cruise into town or to the highway going to town fairly well depleted of food, and the pack was as empty as it ever would be. These were always such delightful times for hiking: downhill (usually for long distances), not much weight in the pack, and the anticipation of the pleasures of town awaited. However, later coming out of town, the pack was again filled to the capacity needed for that stretch; and usually one found him/herself struggling with the additional weight. And going back uphill, back to the mountains where, indeed, the Appalachian Trail is and should be. Also, in the back of the mind is that easy stretch going down into the valley and town. Now, again, one was struggling and yearning for another one of those downhill cruises.

So at first, when nobody was watching, I started doing it. Six steps and rest. Eight steps and rest. Six steps and rest. My body just would not, could not continue and continue and continue taking on the uphills without the rests. Whether it was mental or physical was rather moot. It worked! And ironically it was faster, and more fun. Removing the mental anguish of attacking a hill thinking that I had to do the entire up without stopping was just too much for my overwrought psyche. The likelihood of physical pain in a continuous uphill climb was inevitable and was just too much to deal with.

Six steps and rest. Six steps and rest. Six steps and rest.

At times I felt like an idiot. Good grief, here was Mr. Macho, with the powerful good-looking legs wimping his way up the hills like he was looking for the handicap section of the parking lot! Of course, the athletic prowess conclusions are based on a few choice encounters in life, mostly with a couple of old patronizing aunts. The rests, mind you, were not long, about three to four seconds; but it was definitely a stop. But it was enough and added a lag in the process that gave a chance for muscle renewal and rest. At first what the other hikers thought did make a difference and then it slowly started occurring to me that they weren't getting any farther than me in a day's time. Hike your own hike. The ever-useful, constantly repeated statement was becoming a hackneyed term. So hike my own hike I did. Six steps and rest. Six steps and rest.

Later analysis as to physiological or psychological reasoning to causes of lack of energy and strength were many and varied. All of us older hikers seemed to be having similar problems, some worse than others. Some apparently made attempts at hiding the fact; and others blatantly admitted that, hey, they were having a hard time. It wasn't easy. And usually added that if it were easy, we probably wouldn't be there. Probably just one of those things we said while hoping that it could be easy, for difficulty came in various other ways and physical pain just didn't fit well into the picture.

Lactic acid buildup was considered the culprit by many. On one particular long uphill of about a thousand vertical feet when I insisted on not stopping the entire distance, I finally took a sit-down and pack-off break and ate Snickers, thinking I would have downhill from that point on. Upon starting again, it soon became evident the stop was a huge mistake. The mountaintop was relatively level for a long time after cresting; however, my body would never know it. It seemed to still be going up as my legs felt like Jell-O, no strength, and constant stops were necessary merely to continue.

Patterns soon developed as ways of dealing with the problem evolved, doing whatever it took to continue. For some reason, again maybe the lactic acid theory, afternoon hiking was usually the most productive and most pleasant. From about 2:00 p.m. on, the legs did much better and were capable of longer distances going up without stopping. However, getting through the morning hours just seemed more painful knowing that each day required a long warm-up period, so the rewards of the afternoon surge appeared to have its drawbacks. Also, the leisurely early stops were reward for the day's efforts and were not to be denied. It was unsettling to hike too late and then have to hurry to get all of the domestics out of the way before retiring for the evening. A pleasant meal—enjoying at least an hour of daylight that slowly evolved into dusk and allowing plenty of time for journal entries, reading, and personal pampering such as foot massages—made the exertions of the day well worthwhile. I never grew tired of the ritual in the evenings.

I slowly became aware of the fact that the weight of the pack just didn't seem to make that much difference. That my legs were just wore out, and actually in a lot of ways, the pack added the counterbalance for this new way of walking. Hiking without it seemed almost clumsy and also took away the excuse for stumping along at this alien snail's pace. At first it was disturbing when going for water, always downhill to the source from where you were camped and only carrying the water bottles. When coming back out, it seemed as difficult climbing up to the campsite, dispelling any notions that slackpacking would be the way to go. Maybe it was just as well knowing that. Slackpacking was something that I never considered and just did not approve of; for safety reasons and simply because it seemed to defile this pristine act of thru-hiking, of taking yourself and your body cross-country having all of your needs upon your back. A clean and honorable endeavor if ever there was one. Free of the encumbrance of our society's enigma of the automobile and the handicapping effect that it was having on our populace. Also, safety reasoning being that possibly, a hiker would get caught in bad weather or was injured requiring setting up the tent and being safely sheltered with plenty of food and needs of the human body.

Of course, most of the younger hikers just cruised by. Some of them wouldn't say anything as they went by ensconced in their own little hiker world, and if another hiker was struggling, it was not their concern. However, there were many that would provide encouragement. Six steps and rest. It was getting me there. Eventually it became my trademark. First acknowledged as such by my rapidly becoming favorite thru-hiking couple, Foresight and Check Mate. They made comments about my unusual 'style' and provided support with the old mantra "hike your own hike." They seemed to pop up when least expected and most needed and were instrumental in my feeling comfortable with my technique.

Also back in the archives of reading material in preparation for the hike, I remembered reading about the rest step. Usually, I suppose, associated with real mountain climbing where much steeper surfaces were encountered and often while at very high elevations where there was depletion of oxygen; however, the reasoning and resulting rejuvenation were similar. The maneuver was called a *rest step* in mountaineering jargon and was acceptable. So even with the relatively moderate steep inclines of the Appalachian Trail, the ploy was serving my purposes; and I was still holding a credible place within the repertoire of outdoors activities no matter at what degree of difficulty, it was good enough for me.

Six steps and rest. It was working. It was actually working quite well. Usually at the tops of long climbs, I would just keep going for no rest was necessary and time was made up quickly for my body and physical makeup did well on level surfaces and literally flew downhill. Yes, the Florida training ground had not provided for real conditions of mountains, and the actual hike was manifesting that early period.

Six steps and rest. Six steps and rest.

# Chapter 13

## Pack Weight

*April 25—Day 21—Mile 290 (Hot Springs)—(Journal entry)—then to Smoky Mountain Diner—ordered Breakfast Skillet—wrote in journal while eating—breakfast was huge and awesome—ate it all—very full—didn't eat again until supper*

The great pack weight debate raged throughout the hike, though not as much in the later parts and certainly not as vigorously by the time a hiker reached Pennsylvania or beyond. A thru-hiker eventually came to terms with it and what he/she carried was his/her business and to further discuss it after a while was considered a waste of time. Some hikers became obsessed with it. Couldn't think of anything else. Such was the case for Mourning Dove.

I met Mourning Dove at Deer Park Mountain Shelter on April 24, the night before getting into Hot Springs, North Carolina. He was hiking with another older gentleman with the trail name of Falcon, and they seemed well suited to each other, a somewhat plodding sort of hike. Buffalo Bobby and I had a good day of 17.5 miles, having hiked together for most of the day—this, the result of a silent agreement to hike together at least for the time being. I preferred to hike alone for each day my energy levels varied, and having to maintain a pace above or below current capabilities seemed to just add burden that seemed unnecessary. However, Buffalo

Bobby had many endearing qualities, and it was hard to say no. He was a pleasant person, was one of those rare people that really listened when other people were talking. He was intelligent and always seemed to see only good in other people. Had a vote been taken by hikers that knew him as we progressed northward, the consensus would have been that Buffalo Bobby should be Mr. Congeniality 2003.

Mourning Dove was doing quite a lot of cooing about backpack weight and lack of preparedness as we fixed our evening meals and set up camp for what looked to be another rainy night. He was obsessed with weight, and the old debate started again. My contention had been early on that I had done everything possible to pare unnecessary items before starting, that what I had provided mandatory creature comforts, and that to dwell on it just made the pack feel heavier. Pack weight seemed rather moot within the confines of good judgment for everybody had to have a certain amount of gear, and with the supply of water and food constantly changing, that number could vary by as much as ten to fifteen pounds. So why worry about whether your tent weighed 3.2 pounds or 4.6 pounds. It all seemed rather silly.

Mourning Dove had already decided that gear changes were necessary to be able to continue. I thought that what had to be changed was attitude toward that encumbrance strapped on your back and go with it. He insisted on showing us his hammock-type tent that weighed some nothing of about two pounds. He was intent on leaving a number of things behind in Hot Springs and making changes in what he deemed necessary to continue. Of course, town meant more zero days for making these adjustments and to regain strength which also seemed rather premature. He had left Springer about two or three weeks ahead of me, and I wasn't exactly burning up the Trail. Hot Springs to me was a major milestone for it was the first town on the trail, one that reeked of Trail history and magic, but this was not the time to start shutting down and making excuses.

Our gear discussion continued and somehow my Leatherman became a topic within that realm. I handed it to him, and he held it in his hand, estimating the weight at being about four ounces. This wondrous and compact little multitool felt good in your pocket and served the functions of scissors, knife, tweezers, screwdriver (for eyeglasses), and various other things. I could not have dreamed being without it.

Mourning Dove handed it back to me. "Too heavy," he opinionated. By this time I was reasonably sure that Mr. Dove was just looking for an excuse to get off the Trail. Pack weight was about the best place to start deeming the entire setup insufficient. The next morning, I saw him in town hanging around the Bluff Mountain Outfitters. He was planning his next few days in town and, of course, all of the gear changes—the same record was still playing about weight and conditioning, redundancy prevailed.

I never saw Mourning Dove again. Never heard another hiker even mention his name once. I never did find his name in the *ATN* publications listing completed hikes and do not know if he finished. If he did finish, it must have been much later in the season.

# Chapter 14

## Naivety

*April 20—Day 15—Mile 219—(Journal entry)—a mess breaking down—hung everything and the tent was unpinned—the entire tent blew over the top of me—good God Almighty!*

Buffalo Bobby had to be wondering just what kind of a maverick he had become involved with! We had been together loosely, as that seems to be the ways of the Trail, since Fontana Dam and had struggled together in the wet and inconvenience of the Great Smoky Mountains National Park. We had not hiked together, preferring to allow for our own pace and not encumbering the other with being placed in a position of keeping up or slowing down for the convenience of the other.

We still observed each other at a distance and were at that stage of friendship where conclusions have yet to be drawn about the other person and character and trust were being weighed against the merits of worthiness and value in the relationship. Possibly that is placing too much emphasis on the mental processes involved; however, there was a certain amount of jockeying for position involved whether it was admitted or not.

The day that we had walked across the dam together and then sort of went our own ways for the duration of the day had allowed brief introduction of the form peculiar to the Trail. It was always somewhat awkward in those early days to not use one's real name, forsaken for some strange label of clandestine background. The other had to be wondering if you were, indeed, what your name implied rather than that you were hiding the fact that you were an ax murderer taking refuge from society with an alias name and, if that the truth be known, the cops would be there in a heartbeat.

However, he seemed to be able to accept that I was indeed Ole Smoky Lonesome, and there didn't seem to be anything wrong with calling him Buffalo Bobby. If his intention had been that Howdy Doody or Clarabell should be somewhere there with him then he had cast the proper aura for he seemed to be of such a vein. His easy smile and relaxed manner indicated that he would do well surrounded by beaming kids waiting for some sort of magical act of delight and kid pleasure.

By the third morning, we had grown somewhat relaxed with each other; and to other hikers, it would appear that we were "together" as at times it seemed that it was better to be with somebody instead of being alone on the Trail. Lord knows we were already all thrown together in this fraternal order of misfit society, and who knows what the other person was imagining that you were either hiding or running away from. And being alone could only cast more macabre overtones where such were not desired or needed. For one thing in these early days, one could only surmise as to one's intentions. At a mere 200 miles, we could not possibly know what the other person was capable of even if he or she was casting about wild and crazy claims about hiking all the way to Maine. At this point, Maine seemed like the moon. We only said that to bolster something inside that seemed to require it and lend some credibility as to what we were doing here.

So when it happened that rainy and dank and gloomy and windy and misty morning trying to garner some sort of physical comfort drinking coffee and making vain attempts at camaraderie, there were already some suspicions and mistrust. Goodness knows looking like an absolute idiot could do nothing constructive in this friendship of infancy. It didn't help that we were at such a place that could be named Silers Bald Shelter. We were just two days shy of being out of Great Smoky Mountains National Park and starting to feel kind of good about ourselves and what we could accomplish.

My tent was lying on its side at a ridiculous effort to rid it of some moisture as there was more of that there than tent fabric. However, this was early in the hike, and precedent was based mostly on ignorance; and if anything, the tent was gaining moisture rather than losing it. From time to time, the tent would bellow up in the wind and take on a life of its own.

Maybe one day I shall erect the tent on a windy and wet day and try this again. Aerodynamically what happened seemed impossible. And possibly there is an explanation in a scientific sense where one would consider such things as a vacuum being formed within the tent itself by some sort of Venturi process so that the outside air was heavier than the inside air—all of this seeming rather ludicrous considering that the tent in its construction is not really closed off, but that rather it is about 40 percent or better open to the outside covered only with mosquito netting. The rain fly was lying over in its own crumbled pile of soggy mass totally disconnected from the body proper.

I was sitting more or less facing the group that was about 150 feet away over by the fire more or less adjacent to the shelter. The tent was behind me, flapping about in the breeze. We, after all, were tenters; and they were, after all, shelter-dwellers. And even in this remote wilderness, a caste system seemed to subtly prevail. It seemed that most of the shelter-dwellers were short-term hikers, more like on a bent of doing the national park itself, possibly that suggested virtue to their endeavor, for they were better dressed and seemed to have food more of a gourmet style when compared to our noodles and granola. And as humans, there is always the tendency toward establishing us and them and the suspicions that are inherently existent with such thinking.

Peripherally, flying objects often belie the imagination; and certainly, reality could not have set in too quickly in this rather-surrealistic world of rather-high elevation and reeking moisture and fuzziness with the haze and fog.

The tent became airborne in a microsecond, did not touch me, and had totally ignored all of the physical rules that usually apply to objects staying where they are supposed to because of the other very important law of gravity. I suppose I exclaimed something like "Ju-hee-zus!" or something like that, but the journal does not state such and memory does not serve me very well on the immediate response. And possibly a furtive glance was cast toward Buffalo Bobby and his reaction. Preoccupation with the matter at hand left memory to later struggle with exact responses at the time. There was just too much to do for anything other than extreme concentration on averting total disaster as the final outcome.

The billowy balloon of tent was heading right toward the fire. And the highly disapproving contingent of shelter-dwellers were in a state of dismay now fully convinced that they were, indeed, of a superior class when compared with the tent-dwellers. As such, suddenly a lot of responsibility was thrown upon my frailty to protect our shoddy name and honor. Meanwhile the tent was flipping and bouncing in its frolicking flight of the Phoenix, almost joyfully mocking my ineptness as it made its way to a fiery demise and certainly not to rise again but remain merely a heap of humanly contrived synthetic ashes. There just was very little joy to be found in these anxious moments and this predicament that had so suddenly been foisted upon me.

Of course the ground was irregular and strewn with boulders, the trademark of the Appalachian Trail. I stumbled after the belligerent miscreant much in a state of aggravation and wishing that I were someplace else. I appeared to be chasing a naughty child gleefully running away much against the wishes of the very concerned parent trying to catch it and keep it out of harm's way. Possibly the irony of this object of so much affection suddenly turning on me could have occurred at the time, but I doubt it. Shelter being of the essence, this little four-pound bundle of comfort and protection, albeit rather frail, had been slowly winning a very warm place in my heart. So to think of this as a beloved child suddenly gone bad would not have been an analogy totally out of the question.

It should be noted that the tent was of the freestanding design intended to be moveable after being erected and that often for drying purposes I would lay it on its side in hopes of drying the floor which always seemed to hold more moisture than any other part. The tent, now in its balloon form, performed so well when wet made me wonder what it would do if it were totally dry and light as a feather. Maybe it would be somewhere above the heights of the surrounding trees. However, those thoughts were of little consolation as I scampered after it in hopes of avoiding what seemed to be its fiery fate.

The shelter-dwellers watched with intense interest for what seems liked forever; and finally just before the tent went into the fire, I managed to grasp enough of the nylon and hold on and, then meekly and with as much nonchalance as I could muster, made my way back to my place with the tent-dwellers, hoping that at least some semblance of self-esteem could still be salvaged from this reviling incident, though for some reason, nobody said a word. Possibly it was just the ways of hikers, or possibly it was better left well enough alone.

As I made my way back to my station, I avoided eye contact with Buffalo Bobby and hoped that he would still want something to do with me. In my weaken state of self-assurance, it was rapidly appearing that there was a need for all of the help that was available and certainly not in a position to be choosy about where it was coming from. The incident was never talked about. One could envision the guffawing and unbridled mirth at some later date. However, on that cold and blustery morning on the mountaintop enveloped in moisture and discomfort, our sense of humor was struggling just to stay alive.

Little did I realize that in my early state of neophyte, this small incident was merely a preview of coming events.

# Chapter 15

## Background

*April 20—Day 16—Mile 231—(Journal entry)—every step today was slop—trail never was dry anywhere—running water—gorgeous views, all day walking in the clouds*

So many factors are involved. Thru-hiking the Appalachian Trail is a concept that is foreign to most people. Something in the psyche had to contribute to the desire to do such a thing. Yes, a sense of adventure, but that could take one down so many avenues. Adventures for an average person don't usually last for six months! While writing this book, it occurred to me that my career probably was more of a factor in hiking the Trail than heredity, home environment, early influences in school, or those formative years.

My career as a mapmaker for the government cannot be overlooked. Therefore the reader who has bought this book to read about the Appalachian Trail will now be forced to take a stroll down memory lane. A hindsight look. The place from whence I came. Please forgive this intrusion; however, it is important. A nomad has to start somewhere.

My career with the U.S. Geological Survey started in a rather-innocent way; a job *application* for lack of a better term in a gas station where my friend worked. The government man came around looking for help. My friend came running to the back door of Cox Bakery, and before I knew it, I was hired. The mystery man disappeared; I was to report to work in a few days. I didn't know it at the time, but the USGS was to become my life, a severe left turn in life if there ever was one. Unplanned, it crept into my psyche and enveloped me like nothing else that ever happened. This simple and innocent start of what at the time was just a job ended up being a career. However, with a USGS fieldman (*man* was still okay, *person* was still in the works down at the ACLU), this career became a way of life that would be firmly imprinted within the very fibers of my soul.

A wanderlust was starting to form that never would go away. For that career took me to places I would have never went to in a so-called normal mode, and a desire to always be somewhere else was always gnawing at me, especially at those moving times of spring and fall. It would prove to be a necessary ingredient for hiking the Trail. However, all of that was just in its infancy, and those yearnings were only in the developmental stages. I would reflect on that later and wrote about those early innocent days with USGS; a diametrically opposed train of thought of fond memories and times of stark terror as a young man that was experimenting with life was to learn of this organization and its dedicated and motivated workforce. I reminisced as I walked the Trail. For 164 consecutive days of walking allows the hiker a lot of time for remembering and reflecting. My favorite story of all did not start with such feelings of warmth and humor, for mostly I was trying to survive.

My entire government career could have ended with a splat! In one instant of insanity, a promising future as a surveyor/mapmaker for the U.S. Geological Survey could have come to an abrupt halt. A career prematurely terminated in one gruesome gory, vicious splat.

Nineteen fifty-eight was my first year out of high school, and using the term *career* then in reference to this new job would certainly have been a misnomer. At best it seemed like a good job and certainly was better than my previous employment which had been as a cleanup boy at Cox Bakery. Swabbing the bakery deck, wrestling with huge steel mixing bowls, and being knee-deep in bakery dung didn't come close to resembling a career. So when the promising new job presented itself, there was nothing pulling at me, certainly no feeling of loyalty or a guaranty of an illustrious career. Flour and yeast hadn't permeated my soul to the extent that I wouldn't consider accepting other opportunities that came along. I wasn't ready to dedicate my life to pumpernickel bread, banana cream pies, and chocolate éclairs.

A surveying job! Surveyors usually never are in the same place two days in a row, and especially if the final product is a map. Once it's done, it's done, with no reason to go back. It had the overtures that one must feel when called to sea or when seeking some other glamorous vocation that reeked of adventure. The idea was exciting to say the least, and the pay was astounding. Somebody was actually willing to pay a neophyte, one unsure of the spelling of the word *surveying*, a $1.95 an hour. The promise and allure were irresistible.

He came out of nowhere having drifted into town in a grey station wagon that had For Official Use Only painted on the door. The first impression was that he was rather odd or possibly better described as eccentric. His physical appearance was deceiving; he carried short and stocky quite well and emanated total self-assurance. His walk was a study in efficiency, a total mastery of this taken-for-granted skill. His was not an aimless amble. He obviously was programmed to get body from point A to point B in a hurry. The pudgy physique was not a hindrance. Not in the least. This was a being with a purpose, and that fact was manifested immediately.

He used service stations as employment offices. I was to learn later that a favorite saying of his was, "Gas stations is the best place to find good workers. Go to a doggone employment office, and all you get is dem lazy guys that ain't looking for a job anyhow. Just want the money and don't want to do nothin' to get it. Gas station is the place to go. Darn right."

His name was Buck Meade, and he had a crooked smile. Not an easy smile, but it was there—he seemed harmless. He came from Western Nebraska and placed heavy emphasis on first syllables, those succinct words sort of oozing out in a gravely drawl. The job certainly had some strong points, the work seemed fascinating, and the pay was good. I was seventeen and embarking on my first real adventure. I was to be a rodman! It was a neat term and disguised the actual title, topographic field assistant, that didn't seem to serve any purpose except to possibly impress friends and relatives.

My uncle John would comment later, "You're a what! A National Geographic assistant. What the heck is that?"

"No, no, no, a topographic field assistant . . . a rodman on a surveying crew."

"You mean you're just a darn rodman. Shoot, why didn't you just say rodman. I know what that is!"

"Ya, we survey up and down roads. It's kinda fun."

My Uncle John's comprehension of the world and all that went on around him may at times had been rather astute: however, certain things, most things, fell out of that realm. He asked, "What the heck is all of this surveying for, anyway?"

"Somehow, all of this stuff goes toward making some kind of maps. Topographic maps, but I dunno what that is."

"Shoot, you don't even know what it's for!"

"Naw, but it sure pays good."

When working, Buck Meade was not a patient man; and he had two very distinct modes of operation, working and nonworking. When in the nonworking mode, he seemed quite relaxed with the world. He enjoyed huge steak dinners and usually knew about the better restaurants in town.

"Where can a man get a good steak dinner around here?" a voice that sounded very similar to gravel skidding across a washboard.

"Geez, I don't know."

"You don't like steak?"

"Not sure, usually just eat what Mom fixes. Don't eat out too much."

"Well, by golly, I like a good steak. How about that place out toward West Fargo? Big place on the south side of U.S. 10?"

"I dunno."

To Buck, steaks and fresh cigars were seemingly the essence of life. And with regard to the latter, I would become an integral part of that enjoyment—a daily ritual that soon was to become standard operating procedure. As part of my early training, he accompanied me to the store, to the tobacco department, and explicitly demonstrated the proper way to determine freshness.

"Ya see, ya take 'um between your thumb and forefinger like this. Just kinda roll 'um back and forth. Should be kinda soft. Smell 'um like this. See, this is a fresh one, see how that smells. Smells good, dudn't it?"

"Ya, I guess."

Maybe smoking cigars is a rather-innocent diversion and a simple seeking of pleasure; however, it would occur to me later that a full-grown man was implicating a seventeen-year-old kid in his personal pursuit of sin. My daily trips to the store prior to "going out to the field" were traumatic, filled with trepidation. Certainly, the outcome of the day hinged heavily on my choices of cigars. Each day I tortured myself with this awesome burden. Throughout history, rodmen on survey crews have had a diversity of duties; however, none weighed so heavily as my responsibility of the selection of the day's supply of fresh cigars.

Buck Mead's personality transformed totally once the equipment was out of the boxes and the instrument was on the tripod. The working mode! The other face—another Buck. The surveying piece of machinery. Efficient. Precise but with a contradiction, for his left-handed scrawling was atrocious, something that had to resemble what could be envisioned as the final desperate note that the bush pilot hastily wrote in his buffeting airplane just before crashing into the jungle. However, his work was accurate—the best.

His were the hands of a surgeon as he manipulated the Wild T-2 Theodolite. The T-2 surveying instrument is a complex transit that is comprised of numerous tangent screws, mirrors, verniers, leveling bubbles, and capstan screws—the tool that was the ultimate in precise horizontal control surveys. Buck was the maestro with his T-2. He had to be one of the world's best, his movements were precise; there was never one wasted motion. He loved his work; and that passion manifested itself as he manipulated the stainless steel controls, plunged the scope, and effortlessly floated around the tripod. He was in his element, he was good; he knew that he was good.

In retrospect, it might have been a bad cigar day. Who knows! I had managed to survive two weeks of employment with the USGS, and each day represented a new kind of terror. What would I screw up today? That's not a question, it was an inevitability.

"Hold that doggone range pole straight!"

The perennial North Dakota wind was blowing, further complicating what was already complicated enough. I was staring at the north side of a power pole, and it seemed obvious that it was impossible to see through it. On the other side of this obstruction was what was quickly becoming my adversary with his T-2.

The traffic on U.S. Highway 10 was menacing! The semitrailers, cars, trucks. The main artery for anybody going east or west in North Dakota. We were about 15 miles west of Fargo.

"Hold that doggone range pole straight!" much louder this time. This just was not going good.

We were "running" transit traverse north on a gravel road. Transit traverse is a basic control survey in the making of topographic maps. The surveys determine position on the earth's surface (exact latitude and longitude) on identified points such as crossroads and T-roads and are used as control to make the maps true to scale. The operation employs a five-person crew: an instrumentman, two chainmen that measure distances and set stations, and two rodmen. Stations are rather impressive terms for mere sixteen penny nails speared through ribbon with a paper card nearby to mark its designation, the cards bearing recorded distances and designations for identification. The nails serve as temporary survey markers. For protection, they are set slightly below the road surface. The rodmen hold red-and-white striped range poles on the nails that serve as "targets" for sighting by the instrumentman who sets the T-2 precisely over the nails at the station sites and "turns angles," thus giving the mathematic solutions for determining distance and direction from known starting points, resulting in the final analysis of latitude and longitude.

Later I learned that the chainmen were at fault. They were responsible for setting the stations so that there would be no obstructions. However, this was of little consolation—the two chainmen were about 3 miles north of us and safely out of range and harm's way. They had set the previous station on the south side of Highway 10. The point that I was holding my range pole on was north of the highway, a permanent concrete mark set just north of a power pole. The chainmen should have gone farther (to the north of the highway) when setting the previous station; then the power pole wouldn't have been in the way.

Proximity was my immediate concern. I, the front rodman, was nearby, much too close to Buck and his increasing wrath.

*Vrrooom, shhwisshh*—trucks, cars. Where in the heck was everybody going?

"Hold that range pole straight!"

It should be understood that what I was doing was not necessarily difficult. As instructed, I was carefully balancing the pole between my fingers, standing spread-legged behind the pole with respect to the instrument—totally still.

I searched deep into my soul, contemplating how to improve what I was doing.

"Hold that damn range pole straight!"

Maturity has often made me wonder if my Ukrainian heritage could be a factor in governing my actions. Certainly being Ukrainian could have some effect on knowing when one has taken all of the abuse that one is going to take, a nationality well-known for having fallen victim to numerous cases of persecution. My next act was impetuous and reckless and satisfying. I grasped the pole in my right hand and held it to the side and brazenly stood in belligerent defiance. Enough was enough!

He didn't look. He didn't take the time to look. The odds were against him crossing the highway without looking; however, he miraculously dodged the murderous traffic on the dead run. He covered approximately three hundred feet in scant seconds. Obviously he needed to be close to convey his message. Very close! I suppose that I wavered some in my resolve during this brief time and may have even considered running, but it would have been contradiction to my intentions, so I stood my ground and waited for the onslaught. It would have been a vain thing to do anyway as he would have run me down like a helpless animal in pursuit and would have only served the purpose of making him more angry. If rationality was any more a factor, there was no point in that.

When he arrived, there was no need to listen intently as the gist was easy enough to catch. There was a lot of redundancy. *Fired* was used numerous times though it sounded more like *farred* with that Nebraska drawl and seemed more like rather-empty threats. The message certainly was clear.

The drive back to town was somewhat terse. He assured me that generally speaking, I was "doin' a good job." He seemed to have an odd glow and wasn't doing well in concealing that crooked smile. I had to wonder, obviously, he liked a rodman with some spine—one that wasn't going to take all of his abuse. Deep down I knew. We had come to workable terms.

But, tomorrow was another day.

I thought about those days making my way north on the Appalachian Trail and knew that the character-building aspects were making this venture possible. I thought about Buck Meade who unfortunately left this world much too young, not that many years after he had retired. Those early days with Buck at times were much too stressful, but reality was, that without his influence, I would not be hiking the Appalachian Trail without a part of his gumption within me. Hindsight is a beautiful thing. Back then, all I wanted to do was quit working for USGS and return to a job where the demands were less. Now that same principle applied. Getting off the Trail would be the easy way out, but that sort of thinking was simply alien to me.

Just keep going, the rewards will far outweigh the hardship and sacrifice.

# Chapter 16

## The Walking Stick

*May 2—Day 28—Mile 380—(Journal entry)—long, long hike up Roan Mountain—thought I was at the top—then the storm started—top of Roan was high winds—raining and thunderstorms—manage to get rain jacket on*

The walking stick was a gift from my wife. One of her many contributions to the "cause," stemming from wanting to be a part of it, a part of her with me away from home, a part of her with me on the Trail. I wasn't sure that I was a walking-stick sort of guy; and on my maiden voyage in the Ocala National Forest overnighter to check out gear, desire, and technique, it seemed like something extra to carry that didn't really serve a purpose. At times it seemed in the way. However, later when embarked on the real thing and dealing with mountains and seeing that almost every hiker had either something similar or, with younger hikers, two poles used somewhat as one would employ in cross-country skiing, I started changing my mind.

That walking stick became an extension of me. And it seemed unfathomable to forget it leaning against a tree as I had read in other accounts of thru-hikes for it became an integral part of the entire process. It would have been akin to forgetting a leg as its importance grew. In early groping of writings about the Trail, I wrote about it, more as an animate object. It seemed too important not to be a part of this book. And as it turned out, it became a story in itself.

A walking stick. A hiking pole. Same thing. This one was always called a walking stick. It never had a name, though it probably should have. Had I chose Quixote as a trail name for myself, it could have easily been called Rocinante, and Don Quixote could have rode again in all his magnificent glory. It made the entire length of the Appalachian Trail. Every step. Sometimes carried but most of the time, making it step for step with its owner. The walking stick had a little rubber foot that came in contact with whatever substance that the trail was comprised of as they went along. Sometimes rock, sometimes grass, sometimes dirt, sometimes sand, sometimes mud. Day in. Day out.

A walking stick. A third leg. A crutch; sometimes physical, sometimes mental. At times a mini-pole-vault. Sometimes a retriever. Sometimes a prop. Sometimes an anchor for tying off the bear bag string. And most importantly, the top knob and bottom foot came off as needed to secure it to the ground. My camera screwed into the exposed top bolt, and so this wondrous tool also served as monopod.

And always in the capacity of a weapon, should the need arise.

A walking stick. At one time, a nifty rubber foot left a cute little cat print should the ground consistency be capable of being imprinted. In the early stages when all was idealism and promise and hope, the walking stick was quite handsome with its finely finished wooden knob and firmly mounted foam rubber around the upper part of the shaft that felt good to the touch and cushioned the hand of the master. The walking stick telescoped to suit the needs of the moment so that the length would be ideal for the terrain. Long for downhill and short to provide leverage going uphill. The telescoping process was facilitated with a smooth catch that would click precisely into the neat holes that were hidden under the foam rubber. It was always satisfying to hear the resounding clicks. A warm fuzzy feeling radiated from the walking stick as master and tool became inseparable on this long and arduous journey. A sort of symbiotic relationship though that may have been a little beyond the scope of this description.

An honest estimate would be that the walking stick kept me from falling about two hundred times during the hike, at times was solely the difference between staying up or falling. Consequently it suffered a lot of abuse, a lot was asked of it, far beyond the intention of its design.

Now the hike was over, 2,175 miles. All behind us. No more mountains. No more swamps to slosh through. No more rain. No more heat. No more mosquitoes. Over 2,000 miles covering fourteen states starting in Georgia and ending on Mount Katahdin in Maine. An expedition, a journey with a purpose. An epic walk of giant proportions. And that one walking stick stood in the corner as witness, the only object, animate or otherwise, that knew each step and each day and each mile.

The walking stick was propped in a corner, now no longer needed. Being inanimate and thusly taciturn did not keep it from telling its story. Once proud and straight, trim and attractive, the walking stick now was bent. Actually bent in several places, and attempts at straightening it only seemed to make it worse. And eventually, the walking stick was permitted to take on its own shape, its own personality, the little rubber cat-print end very long gone. The foam rubber was mostly pushed down and was heavily wrinkled. Duct tape is wrapped around the top of the misplaced foam rubber, a weak attempt at trying to keep it in place at the top of the shaft. The wooden knob was scratched and was somewhat abrasive to the touch. A large part of the upper aluminum shaft is now exposed and is sticky from the residue of duct tape.

The story that it tells is long and complex. The deep gouges scream of the rocks, the boulders, the abrasive granite. For too often, the walking stick didn't stop where it was intended to make contact with the ground but went beyond that plane, between the cracks, scraping on the boulders that were strewn haphazardly along the path.

Too often the surface was treacherous, the boulders irregular, the walking surface parameters only determined by the two-inch-by-six-inch white blazes that adorned the trees and rocks and whatever surface was available. It was difficult to determine where the actual trail was at times. Normal steps were few and far between for many sections of the Trail. It was a rock dance, sometimes hitting the tops and other times dancing between them. Often the rocks or tree roots were the only means of avoiding wading in the mud. However, this was a tricky and dangerous maneuver, and soon it was realized that the rocks and roots were too slippery when wet and that it was just better to cope with the mud for whatever damage it could do. Wet feet were a way of life for the GoreTex only worked for so long and then the inside of the boot was as wet as the outside. The walking stick experienced all of this too, though the elements were of little consequence or discomfort to it.

On the flight back from Boston to Orlando and home, the packing of such an odd object required some imagination. It no longer telescoped, having been bent too many times to slide anymore. It was more or less permanently stuck at about four and a half feet long. It could represent a weapon on the plane and would never pass security so had to be checked. Since it didn't telescope down, it didn't fit in the pack. It had to go by itself as a checked item. So I simply attached a card to it with name and address and hoped for the best.

At the baggage claim in Orlando, it wasn't there. The question of just forgetting about it was not a consideration. It was history. It represented the hike, the difficulty of it; it was manifestation of each step, of each fall.

In its remarkably broken-down state, it told its story and could not just be forgotten.

I filled out the form at the airline baggage department, not really expecting to ever see it again. I was to be surprised as the next morning a call came, wanting directions to our house. It seemed a little much that somebody would be willing to make a trip of about 90 miles simply to deliver something that appeared to be a piece of junk. That is exactly what happened. I answered the door rather sheepishly and offered my story about the importance of this object. Whether the man understood or not was a moot point for he listened patiently. We said good-bye after my profusion of thanks, and we were both happy.

It will eventually make its way into some sort of frame suitable for display. Seeing it will be enough for persons wanting to know about the Trail. It is evidence enough—a picture worth much more than a thousand words. And now the last Christmas has produced the "before" version as a gift. "Before" and "after." The new one has proven nothing and, in spite of its good looks, cannot hold a candle to the real thing. Untested, the new one shines but cannot compete not having really done it. All show, no go. It makes for wonderful conversation, and the comparison is so stark. True manifestation that something quite profound did take place.

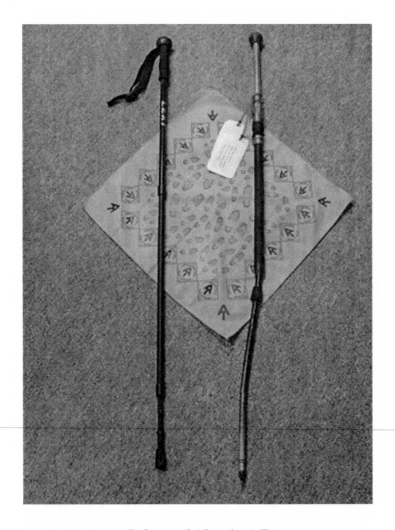

Before and After the A.T

# Chapter 17

## Kelly

Overmountain Shelter, TN
May 3

*May 3—Day 29—Mile 396—(Journal entry)—took detour to Overmountain Shelter and saw where* Winter People *(movie) was shot*

When she turns around on the barstool and makes eye contact with Tom, she has my intense interest. With her luxurious, radiant smile of feigned embarrassment as Maverick and Goose launch into their version of a popular love song, that intense interest is transformed into fascination. By the time Tom follows her into the ladies' restroom, I have become a fan of hers for life. Kelly McGillis is the epitome of femininity; gorgeous and intelligent.

*Top Gun* had brought her to the limelight, and she had to have been here during the filming of the movie *Winter People* in 1988 as we are led to believe. But movies are supposedly filmed in designated locations, and later one finds out that those scenes were shot in totally different locations. But as a dreamer, I had to think that she had, indeed, graced the confines of Overmountain Shelter, the converted two-story barn that now was capable of housing a bunch of thru-hikers in complete comfort. Good karma could be drawn by just being in this same place.

And just being in Tennessee lends credence to the mystique. The night before, I had slept in my last shelter on the Trail, Roan High Knob Shelter, with many adjectives to its credit; the highest shelter on the Trail being the most significant, hovering up there at 6,285 feet above sea level. I could have added a few more adjectives: *windiest, coldest, wettest,* but *last* was the best remembered. I had grown to love my tent; and the two shelters experienced early on in Georgia had fortified my original idea of what a shelter would be like—cluttered, noisy, confusion prevailing.

However, destiny was not kind on that second day of May, and weather was much too rapidly becoming a major problem. I had been tricked while making the ascent. At 5,500 feet, the hiker thinks, well that wasn't too bad and starts dropping off into Ash Gap being just a little confused and thinking that somehow the shelter and other things that are normally at tops of mountains were somewhere hidden and had been passed up.

Suddenly the real climbing starts. Steep, rocky, and unexpected. About a third of the way into this steep and rocky configuration, I had to stop and quickly don my rain jacket, not having time for the rain pants. The rain started to pelt me with a vicious intensity, but most alarming was the wind, estimated conservatively by me at being close to 50 miles an hour. However, this blustery unexpected torrent of reality did wonders for the glands, with adrenaline flowing freely. It wasn't too long before I reached the true summit and searched for the blue blazes to the shelter. Even this devout tent-dweller could not envision much comfort on this night in my little bag of nylon nothingness.

The blue blazing amounted to puddle jumping and rock skipping, and suddenly there it was. Quite substantial being an abandoned fire warden's cabin, it was totally enclosed with four walls for a change, was warm by the standards suddenly foisted upon me, dry, and most importantly, vacant. I quickly claimed my piece of shelter-estate, knowing the throng would soon be arriving.

And arrive they did. And arrive. And arrive. Soon my peaceful little corner was surrounded by wet and dripping hikers with wet and dripping gear and packs hanging from every conceivable peg, and my tidy and organized private little world had been converted to confusion and noise and clutter and stressful burgeoning humanity. I retreated farther into my shriveling space and contemplated whether it was worth it, but conditions outside had grown worse and darkness was setting in. I was trapped. I made preparations for the evening with expectations for rest not running too high.

I did manage to doze off from time to time. When awake, which for the most part was throughout the night, I found it necessary to make a game out of it. As the cumulative snoring rose to a crescendo of mammoth proportions and the reverberation was putting the old timbers of rugged construction to task, I envisioned having been eaten by a large and gruesome hairy and snarling animal. The beast was now digesting my remains with guttural sounds of appeasement and gruntings and deep rumblings of soul-soothing satisfaction.

Some semblance of morning finally and blessedly came with a vague lighting, possibly imaginary. That was close enough for me! As quietly as possible I gathered my gear enough to get it outside in about three tippy-toe trips of horizontal stumblings over the profusion of bodies while vertically dodging the hanging gear then packing as well as possible in the wet and the confusion. A wonderful elation overcame me as I took my first steps for the day, swearing to never *ever* stay in a shelter ever, ever again.

I was looking forward to my date with Kelly.

When Overmountain Shelter is first viewed, it is easily understood why this place was chosen for a movie for it is one of the most beautiful places on the Trail. And why a feature as grandly named as the Overmountain Victory National Historic Trail crosses through here. The valley to the south in early May was resplendent with luxurious spring foliage, that special virgin green of young leaves untainted by the sun and time. That view was never again quite replayed on the remainder of the entire hike. And amazingly, if all of the landscaping engineers in the world could have convened on this place and asked to properly place the barn in the most aesthetically correct place, it would have ended up right where it was. A work of genius.

I envisioned Kelly in her ultimate intelligence, strolling the trails around the setting, introspective and admiring and swaying to an inner cadence that only gifted and beautiful people are privy to. And as beautiful as the scene was without her presence, it must have glowed a rare iridescence when she was there.

The movie itself has drawn mostly criticism as sometimes movies do, and *Winter People* is a rather-inauspicious title. Lloyd Bridges was there too. As was Kurt Russell. I only cared about Kelly.

I sat in the barn and imagined that she was there with me, but only for a short while for I didn't allow myself to get too obsessed with this notion for my too-real world of thru-hiking had ways of occasionally crashing in around me. One should only live in a dreamworld for a little while. I did the true pack-off thing and made fresh coffee and basked in all of it and ate granola bars and knew that had I been there in 1988, I could have been one of the extras. It was one of my longest breaks on the Trail and certainly one of the best remembered.

Back home later in the year, I bought the movie in VHS form. My wife and I watched it, me with more rapt interest than her as I yearned to see something that I recognized and only think that in the early scenes that, indeed, is the spring that is east of the barn. But like other imaginations of this nature, one can never be totally sure. So ulterior motivation finally seemed rather moot, and soon I just lay back and enjoyed the movie. Not one of the best movies that I have ever seen. I didn't really care. I was mostly watching when Kelly was there on the screen, thinking that I had been there too. Dreamers have odd ways of looking at things.

# *Chapter 18*

## Damascus

"The Place"—Damascus, VA
May 8—mile 462

*May 7—Day 33—Mile 462—(Journal entry)—23 miles—40 miles in two days!—no water from Abingdon Shelter (not until about 2 miles out), so just kept going all the way to town—got here about 6:00-ish*

It was a day of evolution. The original plan for the day hadn't included a particularly long day or planned long mileage. On the Trail, circumstances usually dictate and control the days happenings more than plans, and the results were a rather-pleasant surprise. A day when things lead to things and soon miles melted away and possibilities loomed that hadn't been in the offing at the start. Those kinds of hiking days that thru-hikers wished were every day; effortless miles replacing the normal grinding out of tedious mile after mile.

However, another unwritten rule of the Trail, pleasantry usually was accompanied with contradiction. Today that was provided by being the day that the gnats decided to start biting. Gnats! Those ubiquitous little black forever there pests that helicopter around the eyes or front of the face, waiting to make a Kamikaze dive for which there is never a warning. All of a sudden, the inevitable blur, the plunge; and once again, you are walking along, trying to get the little black blob out of the corner of your eye. Even when the tiny body has been removed or thought to be removed, it's always in your mind that it still seems to be there as you plod along trying to remove the feeling; and what the heck, maybe it gives you something to do while you are walking. Nature has ways that are not understandable, and for the gnat, to what purpose is this act of futility for there is absolutely no chance of survival. However, this writ is performed again and again. An act from the annals of instinct that cannot be understood and only leaving some small space for tolerance.

The Oakley sunglasses really weren't designed, at least not for these sixty-two-year-old eyes, to be worn in the darker patches of wooded areas; but necessity being the mother, they eventually were donned most of the time that the gnats were out, which was most of the time, as the one last desperate means of defense. The gnats, once they started, were pretty much with us for the duration of the hike. Some days were worse than others; but for the most part for 2,000 miles, we were "Fly Face" from Dick Tracy walking along with little clouds in front of us. Never once was that name chosen for a trail name, possibly just hadn't been thought of, but it would have been perfect. I suppose some of us wondered, since we went from a southern climate to a northern climate, whether these were the same species of bug; but there does not seem to be information indicating that somewhere at some magic latitude we went to something different. So for the entire length of the Appalachian Trail, this one bug managed to be there, not cousins, not something else. Gnats. Day after day after day. We all hated them.

But today, they not only were hovering, they were also biting. Why today was anybody's guess. Wednesday, May 7. A little over a month into the hike with a light rain to start the day that went away before not too long with periods of sunshine and threatening rain later in the day. So the weather was about the same. Warm, yes, but not much different than the previous few days. An undetected message had been sent out appealing to all gnats that this, indeed, was the day. Bite! Bite! Bite! Stopping to rest for any length of time was nearly impossible.

However, I did stop for a short while at Abingdon Gap Shelter. Contemplating and planning out the remainder of the day. A tent was inside the shelter with the occupant deeply ensconced within, apparently taking refuge from the onslaught of now-biting gnats. I thought better than to talk and sat, quietly cussing the bugs attempting to enjoy a snack of mostly beef jerky having decided to make it a pack-off break. It was about two o'clock in the afternoon. However, this was a guess derived from sun angle for a watch was not a part of the camp gear. Damascus, Virginia, was another 10 miles; and I had already made thirteen and really had no plans to get to town this evening. Logistics, however, were not too cooperative. The water sources along this stretch were virtually nonexistent.

The ensuing 10 miles were quite flat and trending downhill as the Trail followed an old woods road for a very long ways and the mileage to town soon was cut in half and there was still no water in sight. My supply provided enough to drink, but it didn't look as if there would be cooking water for the evening. However, there appeared to be plenty of light left in the day, and soon my thoughts turned to the comforts of town—to town food and amenities. The decision to go for it was not difficult to make.

For the thru-hiker, Damascus, Virginia, is the second really big AT milestone, Hot Springs, North Carolina, being the first. Damascus probably is the most significant place of the early part of the hike. For one thing, this was entrance into the fourth state and really a time when a thru-hiker can start thinking maybe, just maybe, this is going to be the real thing. A thru-hike! However, this is all premature; but with this landmark, that really didn't make any difference. My efforts had already been classed a long-distance hike and with enough mileage under the belt to feel like a veteran and quite ready for whatever the Trail had to offer.

In the planning stages of the hike, I had thought about writing about the experience for I think of myself more as a writer first and a hiker, somewhat lower in my priority list of interests. The name Damascus seemed perfect to be part of the title, and *The Road to Damascus . . . and Beyond* was a title that I played with in my mind. It, of course, reeked of religious overtones which have nothing to do with the story; but maybe, the concept isn't that far-fetched. Many people that I talked to always mentioned those aspects in this type of a venture. Regardless, the name

Damascus was just too perfect title fodder to not be considered in some manner.

Damascus was cause for celebration even if it was just within oneself. For this was the Party Town of the Trail, however, really of not much interest in that aspect to this senior hiker. I was just looking forward to the amenities, the mail drop, possibly some extra things in the mail drop and possibly some gear changes. It was too early for Trail Days by about two weeks, and that was rather moot for there had been no intention of attending any of the festivities anyway. More than anyplace, I was curious about The Place; but more than that, I was looking forward to unlimited amounts of whatever food was there for the choosing and, of course, a shower—only the seventh one so far in this marathon. A shower! Commonplace, everyday thing, a shower was viewed by this time like basking in the lap of scrumptious luxury sinfully lathering and removing a two-week accumulation of trail gunk and dirty feet and smell. But town still mostly meant more food. Unlimited amounts of food.

It suddenly occurred to me! There deeply buried in the backpack were two Snickers bars carefully being protected as extra food, and now no longer needed for that purpose. Not rations for the day as those went in the more accessible fanny pack that actually rode in the front where the maps for the day and glasses and Band-Aids and necessary day items rode.

Snickers! Just the sound changed my trail personality. It truly was a Snickers attack! And if the candy company had been there that day, it is reasonable to conjecture that I would have received free candy bars for the rest of my life to just air this scene to aficionados of this culinary delight. A candy sales P R beyond the realm of any commercial maker's imaginations or dreams. Natural. Free-flowing. Convincing. Quick. Gluttonous. It would have been inspiration for candy bar connoisseurs beyond any conceived version of such and would have sold candy bars—lots of candy bars. I am sure of it.

With town just a few miles away and the decision that, indeed, that was the designated place for the night and an impending rain more or less upon me, it was a good time to get rid of some food. For as canons of certain aspects of life never vary, so it is with the Trail. Especially so with the Trail. One never leaves his wingman, and one never *ever* carries food into town. Just one of the precepts of thru-hiking. It would be a result of poor planning and not representative of being in the spirit of the hike.

The thought of not one but two Snickers bars suddenly accessible and truly available for consumption was akin to finding a metaphoric gold mine. In this state of near starvation and exhaustion, with a body eating up its own protein, the mind starts reverting to an animalistic state. Two Snickers bars all eaten at one time in this new world of scarcity and frugality defied all the rules of the Trail, but reasoning was beyond rationality. I euphorically anticipated the orgasmic experience as I tore the backpack off and dove into the food bag, a rather-empty food bag, and the source of my questing desire was soon pulsing in my hot hand and saliva was running rampant. Reasoning or hunger was not at issue here, rather just hedonistic and unbridled satisfaction. If it made any difference, I had earned it; but let's face it, it didn't make any difference.

I really did not think about it until later. I had momentarily transformed to more animal than human. The first candy bar was gone in mere seconds, and with trembling hands, I shredded the wrapper of the second. If any wisps of guilt may have been floating around in this onslaught of gluttony, they would not have been heeded anyway, not during these moments of unbridled culinary gratification.

In less than two minutes from the moment of inception, the dastardly deed was done, and I was holding two candy wrappers and licking my chops. Animal instincts merely answered to with no regard for anything else.

I put my pack back together and resumed walking and briefly reflected on that horrendous scene. As the alpha wolf would—before diving into the carcass—did I make growling sounds, deep guttural rumblings and did my eyes furtively scan my surroundings? As the cliché goes, I was scaring even myself. But who really cared, for I was ready for town and what it had to offer.

Damascus, Virginia, is a magical place. It is a small village with most of the stuff that you need to exist, but when the quality things of life are considered, it is the utopia where everybody that has been there wants to just stay. Life is good there. Slow and laid-back, people are friendly, the streets are safe to walk.

For the Appalachian Trail thru-hiker, it is the epitome. No other town along the Trail even comes close by comparison. Everything that you need is there. Excellent restaurants, hostels, bed-and-breakfast establishments, post office, showers, a place to tent, supplies, an outfitter, quaint little shops that provide those other things (the kind that you usually box up and send home), cultural things, beauty . . . ice cream.

Damascus is a major milestone for the thru-hiker. Just 4 miles prior to getting to town, another state has been attained, the fourth state, Virginia that has more AT miles than any other. If a hiker has reached Virginia, he/she has attained some serious credibility. But most importantly, the Trail goes right through town. It just could not get any better than this for the serious hiker. Through town the AT is also coincident with the

Virginia Creeper Trail and is a stone's throw from every conceivable hiker need. The ultimate Trail town.

And there is The Place.

The Place is a renovated house with sleeping accommodations and a shower that is a gift to the hiker-community provided by the Methodist Church. Most importantly, it has a wonderful yard and; room permitting, one just chooses a good place and pitches the tent and one has all of the amenities. The cost is a mere $3 a night, and that is considered a contribution; so if one were to be a total jerk, one could forego the fee and stay gratis. This hiker left more than was necessary to cover those that did fall in that category.

I arrived there on Wednesday, May 7; a little over a month into the hike and could be classified a serious thru-hiker with about 460 miles to my credit. I was very happy. It was time to just enjoy my accomplishments and take a day off. My first zero day! My first day of not hiking though I did cover some mileage walking around the town doing errands and just checking the town out. I felt courtly, feeling clean having taken one of those grinding-down-to-the-bone Saturday-night showers, and had clean clothes on. Basking in the lavishness of it all, I roamed the streets and talked to just about everybody.

I ran into eighty-one-year-old thru-hiker Batch who was looking fit and trim and enjoying a Coke on the main drag. In spite of his protests, I coerced him into taking his photo, one of my favorite trail photos. Batch had quickly become the icon on the Trail. Arguably the oldest hiker attempting a thru-hike, we all became attached to the man. He was an example of the human spirit. He was the epitome of chutzpah. He was defying the premise that old people weren't supposed to do physically demanding things. We all loved him, and seeing him again was elixir to the soul and body. Batch and his wife had thru-hiked the Trail about ten years before; he had gotten hooked then and was back for more.

A lady who lived nearby invited me over for a salad made with vegetables grown in her own little garden—an array of various greens that looked like something out of a how-to book for growing organic things. We visited while I was enjoying the excellent mixture of fresh lettuces and dressing, intelligent conversation about hiking, and most everything else. Her home was strategically placed hiker-wise, and she didn't miss too much. The Trail was a large part of her life, and this cordial and courteous lady with a fascination for the throng that went by her door each day made it a point to invite complete strangers into her life for a short time. It seemed to be the ways of the Trail.

Damascus provided me with something that I hadn't really anticipated, human activity subject to a lot of criticism. And since this was quite an anomaly Trail-wise, for the overall experience dealt primarily with positive and happy times, I shall not pass up this opportunity to remark on the things that were wrong. The people involved were in the minority; however, as with so much of what people do, it is that small number that influences the impression of the masses and the whole.

Having become very accustomed to the average thru-hiker—clean, helpful, ambitious, respectful, friendly, observant of rules, the epitome of what hikers should be—suddenly the scum of society were foisted upon us. Whether these were hiker-wannabes, hiker hangers-on, or just reprobates of trail society, there were a definite and disproportionately large number of undesirables hanging around The Place. Late into the two nights that I was there, it was party time. One thing about being sober is that it doesn't take long to recognize and identify where there is lack of such. Around about midnight, the loud voices and alcoholic-haze logic was ringing in the air. Opinions flew rampant about all conceivable subjects, and everybody was an expert on everything.

Not listening was not an option. Loud and profane beer talk, much too loud for about anywhere, let alone a place where there were about two dozen people that were trying to get some much-needed rest and sleep with nothing but flimsy nylon fabric to insulate them from the sounds.

The first night I finally sat up and wrote in the journal: *No use trying to sleep with all of the loudmouths sitting on the porch (probably drinking—against the rules). Now I know why I get out of town as soon as possible—the AT experience should be social; but I think, for the most part, it has lost its original intent (to be an enriching communing with nature and a test of making it on one's own with all one needs on his back). As I reevaluate my intentions for being here, I know that the best times and most rewarding restful times are when I'm alone in the middle of the woods away from shelters and people. As usual, people screw things up! No regard for others and quite inconsiderate. Watching the slackpacking and racing through the courses makes no sense at all. Back to lying and listening to the noise.*

In the very wee hours, I went to the bathroom to pee. Inside the shower door were the remaining three beers, what was left of a twenty-four pack. A slap in the face to the Methodist endeavor to help the community and to help the thru-hiker by providing this fine facility. I felt like screaming at the top of my lungs to wake up the participants if they were still there, hoping to see some bleary-eyed and hungover people.

Possibly of the most concern is that with enough abuse of this privilege, it will no longer be available. For the church does not want to provide a haven that would be totally against its canons. The Place was the absolute, a representation of what the Trail stood for. A symbiosis between town and trail, an oasis for the hiker and a welcome from the town to indicate that the relationship was alive and healthy. The beer (and most probably other mind-altering substances) and disregard of rules and common sense were the acts of a maverick few that would screw it up for the considerate majority. Why did so much of society hinge on the acts of that rebellious minority? The hackneyed term still applied here along the pristine aura of the Appalachian Trail. Rules are only made for that minority and are not needed by the good majority that would think not to be considerate. There would be no need for locks on doors or rules and restrictions if one could eliminate this shabby lot who seem to know only the low road in their hedonistic quest of doing anything and everything they could get away with.

Yes, I was angry and was happy to get out of town. Ironically so, for Damascus was the biblical origin of my voyage and provided deep reasoning for being on the Trail and for escaping some of the frustrations of the ills of society. However, deep down I knew that too much emphasis had been placed on my false idealism. That somehow because of the Appalachian Trail, people here could be different, almost fairy tale-like. In reality, whether in proximity of the AT or not, human beings still retain their true characteristics, oftentimes traits that we all eventually want to escape. The only respite lay in continuing to hike for only in that could we emphasize the positive, reaching deep to try to attain a level above the sometimes-deplorable state of the human condition.

And soon, my deep conviction regarding the goodness of people would manifest itself with the lifestyle and caring of one man.

Fence crossing—proximity of
Mt. Rogers, VA
May 12

# Chapter 19

## Trail Angel

*May 15—Day 41—Mile 582 (Bland, Virginia)—(Journal entry)—what a character!—he stopped with gutters tied to the side of the pickup—I wasn't hitchhiking—got in the bed, and he drove me to IGA where I ran into Buffalo Bobby*

The name even now elicits a smile. Often the thoughts of him reminds me of the *Reader's Digest* series on "My Most Unforgettable Character", for now away from the Trail, he is remembered best that way. Unforgettable, certainly, but absolutely certainly a character. A dynamo of animated energy and exclamation and motion. He barged his way into my hiker-life when possibly I needed him the most. Or maybe it should be stated, into our lives, for Buffalo Bobby was there too.

Fate seemed to govern the happenings of that morning and the events that would later unfold as the day progressed. It had been a pleasant hike coming down from Jenkins Shelter on as smooth a part of the Trail as had been encountered so far. Well, actually it had been a pleasant hike after getting a few destined moments out of the way, a way of the Trail that inevitably always provided some form of incidents falling into the category of arduous. Not too long after getting started, my stomach started churning, and it wasn't long before it became apparent that my body was not going to let it go. The business of dropping the pack, digging out the little shovel and toilet paper, digging the hole, all the while jumping around like a banshee, always provides much more excitement than necessary.

Then, as if to add insult to injury on what was otherwise a very pleasant morning, I fell in the creek. I had crossed and recrossed Little Wolf Creek one too many times; and stepping from a rock, taking the big step to another, my sole became a skate with a dull edge and down I went. As usual with these types of falls, of which there were many, I went down on my backside on the sleeping bag and tent tied to the bottom of the pack and no damage was done. A little wet, a little wiser, and slightly aggravated, I continued.

Soon the sounds of civilization invaded the peacefulness of the woods. Oddly, often the highways sounded closer from 5 miles than a mile. I listened to the trucks and cars doing their civilization staccato as I made my way toward the corridor leading to towns and resupply. This violation of noise actually came from two sources for I-77 crossed my objective, U.S. Highway 52, not too far from where the Trail crossed. Most of the sounds came from the interstate. It should be noted that highway sounds run contrary to the Trail experience. An anomaly. A representation of what we were trying to get away from and not something that we sought. However, highway sounds prevailed through much of the hike and, at times, were almost impossible to get away from. Farther to the north, I-81 parallels the Appalachian Trail for a long distance; and at times, the noise is almost oppressive. But one finds oneself seeking these sounds for it meant a break in the monotony and always meant amenities and overindulgence and pleasure, a break from the self-sacrifice that the Trail afforded. So it was with glee that I walked to the noises this morning, knowing that relief was there waiting.

This was a much-anticipated destination for it was the one place that I had been on the Trail before. I so hoped for recognition of the spot and remembrance of standing on this very site when this grand expedition was still a dream and plans were in their infancy. The year before in 2002, Kris and I were coming back from her fortieth high school class reunion in Wisconsin and had taken a detour off I-77 just so that I could actually stand on the Appalachian Trail. So we drove through the little town of Bastian with hikers milling around and made our way south toward Bland and the crossing. The highway map did its best being of small-scale and indicated that the Trail crossed at a huge switch-back curve in the highway. Kris stopped the car, and in a state of confusion, I walked up what appeared to be a driveway. In my naivety, I didn't know that every foot of the Trail was not stereotypical "real trail," and that sometimes, indeed, the Trail could be a driveway or a highway or whatever it took to connect it back to its original pristine state. So getting back into the car that day, I was somewhat disappointed that my image of this famous trail was somewhat tainted. A driveway just had failed to fill my expectation of quaintness; I had wanted to see a leafy and narrow dirt path meandering through an overhang of large trees that blocked out the sunlight. A year later, my images were more educated, and now I yearned for a crunchy driveway leading to town. Quaintness or ambiance had lost its allure in real time. Six hundred miles of the green tunnel on the Trail had narrowed my senses of adventure to rather weary and thin.

So this morning as a real Appalachian Trail hiker, my heart sang as, indeed, just before getting to the highway, I suddenly found myself on a gravel driveway and crunched my way downward, knowing that a year ago everything was just as it was supposed to be. I had, indeed, stood on the Appalachian Trail and not really ever convinced myself that it was just that.

The plan had been to go to Bastian for the town reeked of quaint the Trail, and I could remember that in one of the many books that I had read about the AT, there was a photo taken at one of the village shops with the hiker/author having an animated conversation with the shop owner. A scene that beckoned prospective hikers to come join the fun.

However, fate was working its mystique as events began to unfold to lead me the opposite direction. I had stopped to check out a trail magic box placed just before stepping on to the highway. It was mostly full of cans of beer which seemed a little odd for it was about midday and food and soda seemed more in order. Trail angels usually provide for all aspects of Trail need, and possibly, it had been placed the night before. While I was studying the box and looking for possibly a Snickers, it came to my attention that a pickup truck with the bed nearly full of hikers was waiting to see if I was interested. I asked which way they were going; and when the answer was the other way toward Bland, I started to say that, no, I was headed toward Bastian.

What was I thinking! A direct violation of a cardinal rule of the hiker seemed to be occurring, and I was the guilty party. In mere seconds my senses came out of this delirious state, making the adjustment to reality—one just does not look gift horses in the mouth while in the vulnerable position of thru-hiker. Soon I was happy to be riding in the laden bed of the pickup heading for, indeed, Bland. The other most important cardinal rule of the hiker is that one shall at all times be flexible and subject to instant change of plans no matter what that may be.

When the pickup truck got to the center of the small village, there was some uncertainty with the driver and his passenger as to just where we were to be taken. It was finally rather unilaterally decided to go west to I-77, to a truck-stop atmosphere complete with a well-stocked convenience store sporting a shiny new and beguiling Dairy Queen. Sounded good to all of us; however, this more or less took us back out of town. The other hikers were all young; thru-hikers rapidly becoming partygoers bent on making it back to Damascus and Trail Days. The proximity of the interstate was just what they wanted.

The Dairy Queen was another one of those kid in a candy store experiences. Wanting one of everything, I finally settled on the gourmet food of the thru-hiker: a hamburger, French fries, and a Pepsi. That topped off with a huge soft-serve ice cream cone, and I was loaded up with much-needed cholesterol and sugar. Calories, filling, satisfying—life was good.

By this time a contingent of young thru-hikers were out by the overpass thumbing, hoping to get south on I-77. It was surprising how quickly they were picked up. They were heading back to Damascus in search of what young people are looking for, fun and excitement, the best that Trail Days had to offer. Leaving this oldster with the task at hand, to concentrate and conserve energy to propel this body ever northward and to whatever glory that endeavor could provide.

After my gluttony, I decided with the short distance back to Bland that hitching along the stretch back to town was not really necessary and just merely started walking. Not too far back past the I-77 overpass, an older model pickup truck rolled by slowly. The driver's side window was open as the driver hollered something that I couldn't understand and drove on. However, he didn't drive very far, just to a good place to pull over. I ran with my encumbrance as well as I could and wrestled the pack up into the bed. This was a workingman truck, and the back was full of just about everything imaginable. I climbed in the bed and sandwiched myself between sacks of mortar and tools and equipment. He was talking the entire time and smiling and acted as if we had been friends our entire life. It was hard not to notice that along the passenger's side of the truck was about a twenty-foot-long piece of metal rain-gutter material tied to whatever rope could be attached to. Gaining access to the cab could only be attained from the driver's side.

The timing seemed to be perfect. I observed from my perch atop the confusion in the bed of the pickup that rain clouds were forming fast, serious rain clouds. He asked me where I wanted to go, and hearing IGA, we were on the way. We made some turns and soon were parked in the right lane of main street holding up traffic. I jumped out as quickly as possible and recovered my pack, did a pirouette, and was staring at Buffalo Bobby. We had just enough time to duck under the street-side canopy from the downpour that started about the time that we had made eye contact. Our mystery pickup driver was screaming above the profusion and noise of the main street traffic; something about being back shortly. Buffalo Bobby and I concurred that what he said was that he had some business to take care of and that he would return and take us back to the Trail.

"Buffalo Bobby, how ya doing, ole buddy!" It had been a few days, and it was good to see a familiar and friendly face.

His smile told me that he was doing just fine. He told me that the same pickup had also brought him here. "Did he seem okay to you?"

"Ya, seemed like a heck of a guy. What do ya think? Think he'll be back?"

We decided that in all probability, he would. I raced through IGA not totally sure of my immediate needs and, having not quite worked out my logistics for upcoming days, settled on the basics: the thru-hiker staples, oatmeal, packaged noodle meals, and granola bars, totaling fifteen dollars in about three minutes. It wasn't long before we were standing out in front of the store watching the increasing traffic on main street. And the rain.

Amazingly in about five minutes, the mobile rain gutter came rolling back down the street in the same direction. By now it was pouring, a classic cloudburst. We wrangled our now-heavier packs back into the pile in the bed. Then came a Three Stooges sort of drill as the three of us stumbled about and slid across the seat, getting in on the driver's side and dealing with the urgency of the downpour. The driver didn't seem to be rattled by much of anything, and soon we were all stuffed into the cab, dripping on everything but happy to be out of the rain.

"Name's Jack." He stuck out his hand, and we shook hands all the way around. He also told us his last name, but neither Buffalo Bobby nor I quite heard it. It was something unusual, not a run-of-the-mill name. Now there was confusion as to just what we were doing. The deluge outside didn't seem conducive to or a time to be heading back to the Trail. He started telling us about "my trailer," it being located somewhere in the country back to the north "a ways." I looked at Buffalo Bobby; and we shrugged our shoulders both about equally befuddled, finding ourselves in the much-reoccurring position of thru-hiker—just along for the ride, our health and well-being in the hands of a complete stranger. Dealing with the situation as serendipity would allow. Not enough time to ponder the consequences of such a vague venture.

He rambled the entire time. We listened intently, for anything that we could offer seemed rather frail by comparison to this guardian angel with transportation and shelter from the forces of nature. Vulnerability was a way of life on the Trail. A hiker was always courteous and considerate to somebody that offered some sense of security or housing or food or whatever.

He told us about the prevalence in the area of what sounded like "oxy-cotton" and of how easy it was to obtain and of how crazy it made people who were taking it like candy as their addiction grew. It wasn't until months later that I learned the correct spelling of the drug commonly used in the treatment of pain—*Oxycontin*—that it was a prescription drug, its possession strictly controlled and that it had become the latest designer drug for people with a flair for abusing their bodies in search of a quick high.

As he talked and we rode for mile after mile in the thunder and rain, my mind darted about in an effort to envision what was at the end of this excursion. We were definitely heading out to the country. To the backwoods. Let's face it, we were in Virginia, we were riding with a total stranger and a sort of subtle panic was creeping into my thoughts. We had by now learned his last name with a lot of trial and error: Agee. Jack Agee, and for the time being he was our guardian angel protecting us from the swirling surging rainstorm of growing proportions.

The macabre mood of the weather was catalyst for the fearsome thoughts erupting within my imagination. A mood of anxious gloom invaded the interior of the pickup truck. This one-door pickup truck with the twenty-foot gutter tied on the side. We were trapped! Buffalo Bobby, how could we have stepped into this in such ignorance? What were we thinking?! We were old hiker vets by this time!

In my beleaguered mind, the "trailer" evolved in stereotypical fashion at the end of a muddy profusion of ruts and ooze. And my wildly racing thoughts led me to wonder just to what extent this Appalachian Trail experience could reach. I ached for the comforts of home, for Kris, for security, for familiar scenes—possibly adventure wasn't my ticket after all.

"Just how far out is your trailer?" Buffalo Bobby apparently was becoming a little anxious also.

"We're just about there." Jack was still smiling. Still talking. We still were on blacktop roads. However, for the time being, anxiety was the prevailing mood within the confines of the pickup cab that was our only respite from the tempestuous weather.

Then there it was.

Oh good Lord of sweetness and mercy and forgiveness for past sins that still hang there for posterity, not to be forgotten by some and long forgotten by others. Surreal quickly turned to sublime and images of the past eons long moments of doom and despair dissipated as "the trailer" came into view. In its real form, it was an apparition hanging in the subtle mist of storm aftermath, a scene from a Kinkade painting barely hovering on the verges of reality, more of imagination than actual beams and wood and metal, the creation of a god rather than man. The lawn was manicured, weed-free and green, so very green and clean and orderly. Barely able to contain myself in my exclamations of praises and compliments, probably a little too joyful overzealousness, having so quickly been exonerated from my imagined sentence of just moments before.

The entire scene reeked of tender loving care and maintenance, of thoughtful pruning and mowing and clipping and responsibility. The trailer was located just off the blacktop road, and at a curve, we were looking directly into the yard proper when it first came into view. Trailer did not quite do it justice for it was actually a double-wide and probably more correctly could be called a *manufactured home* as the more sophisticated term of the Floridian. It had a wonderful porch attached to the back side that provided a place to sit and view the surrounding pristine countryside. It appeared to be Jack's pride and joy, and though the purpose for this abode was never quite established, it seemed to be there strictly for hikers at this time of the year when the major bulk of thru-hikers were coming through. Other hikers had recently found this very same to be home for a night, and it was stocked with the necessary amenities.

"Now, you guys don't worry about the wet clothes. Shoot, it will all clean up okay. The place ain't too clean right now, just had some people in there. There's coffee in there, but just use the water in the refrigerator, the water out of the spigot ain't too good, got a bunch of iron in it. So just make yourself at home there. Also, there are some sodas in the refrigerator and also some other stuff to eat there in the cupboards and you guys just make yourself at home. If you need to do some laundry, go ahead and do that. The washer and dryer work good, and there's soap in there. So just go ahead and make yourself at home. I gotta go take care of some stuff, and I'll be back in a little while and see if you fellers need anything. Maybe we'll take a little tour, and I'll show you boys around a little. Plenty of history round this place. You might want to see some of it. Got some stories to tell you guys you might want to hear."

And on and on and on. He never quit talking, was interested in everything that went on around the area, and appeared to be the heir-apparent for representing the local constituency in some sort of political position. He certainly had my vote.

Later Buffalo Bobby and I had become quite comfortable and very much at home. Our laundry was done, and we had eaten more than usual having just resupplied; and with the amenities and comforts of the trailer, we were truly enjoying our stay. We heard the vehicle pull up into the yard and really didn't bother to look who it could be. A knock on the door seemed rather odd, and when I answered it, there was Jack Agee himself. Knocking on his own door! The absolute gentleman respecting our privacy and was just another one of those acts of this amazing man to more endear us to him.

"You boys wanna go for a ride?"

There really wasn't too much room for a no even had that been our intention for he was just too entertaining. Soon we were heading in every direction for the roads wound too many ways to try keep track of where we were. It really didn't make any difference, and it was nice to be kind of lost after being so totally aware of my whereabouts with the Trail maps.

Then Jack started on his favorite stories. It didn't take too long to realize that we had clearly underestimated this man, regardless of his already-high esteem in our eyes. Some of these stories stayed with us. I made a succinctly worded list:

*   Lost car (Nash Rambler) at Pocono
*   Hillbilly making corn bread mixing with hand—kept mixing and inviting them for supper (as kids) and skinning the old groundhog with dirty feet
*   Getting paid for garden work with apple butter that was full of flies
*   Buried moonshine found when digging up an old cherry tree

And others that were just too numerous to remember. The lost car was probably the gem of the lot. Jack apparently had led an adventurous young adult life and had wandered to the huge Woodstock-type gathering at Pocono and had spent a number of days there. He had arrived there in a Nash Rambler. He had parked the car "somewhere." He never saw the car again. Ever.

The corn bread story was the most amusing with an obvious great deal of embellishment and elaboration. Apparently as a child, a residence that he frequented often was inhabited by a woman of somewhat sloppy hygienic practices. The account was probably a recurring scene during his childhood, but this particular time, the woman's hands were apparently filthy as she mixed the corn bread for the night's supper—no spoon—she was mixing the batter with her hands. An invitation to supper was a study in stall tactics having observed how supper was being made, especially when part of the supper was to be a groundhog that somebody had dumped on the porch. She had used her feet to aid in skinning the creature in preparation for cooking.

Jack had apparently led a life of hardship and hard work, and in his formative years a lot of his time was spent helping local people. Probably at the insistence of his father, though that is purely conjecture for he seemed much inclined to help people as just his second nature. And the gift of the apple butter story was told with a twinkle in his eye, for people that he was associated with would not have made an attempt to rip one another off. The people of the area were just as poor as Jack was in childhood and were thankful for help. However, being of this bent, payment in some form was usually the accepted manner for dealing with assistance. The apple butter probably wasn't made in the most sanitary of conditions and who knows where the flies came from or how they ended up in the batch. Maybe the most interesting part of this story was that if the flies were known to be in the apple butter or not, there would have been a reluctance to throw it away for being frugal was just a way of life, mostly out of necessity.

The buried moonshine probably manifested more than anything that we were in an area that could be stereotypical of hill people. The discovery of the moonshine came about rather innocently, but the burying part, it has to be assumed came about to avoid detection. It was the story that stayed with you the most, but the conclusion was the hardest to determine. Jack coyly remarked that the moonshine was well aged, and it's pretty safe to assume that the discoverers did not waste too much time in making that assessment.

And the stories went on until I could no longer keep mental track. Somewhere in the archives on my mind, a trip is planned back to see Jack Agee, to fill in details and for further elaboration and embellishment. The lore of the backwoods and backcountry is much too good. I mentioned to Jack that he needed to instigate the writing of a local history to which he responded that he had done some of that already and further attested to this remarkable man and to his goodness and accomplishments.

The next morning I struggled with leaving a note and some money. I was so intensely grateful for his kindness and caring that the need for conveying that was overwhelming. Though the monetary part just sort of hung there in my conscience and the proper manner to do this never was quite clear in my mind.

Jack provided the answer himself. About five thirty, there was another knock on the door, and again there he was ready to take us back to the Trail. He interrupted my note writing and my intention of leaving a $10 bill to help pay for electricity. The note had become wordy and blundering in my gratitude. He came in and sat down, and I stumbled into an explanation of my intentions. A scene ensued that would forever be etched in my memory.

He kindly stared at me for a few moments after my feeble attempt at explanation. His head drooped to the side. His eyes mirrored those of a wounded deer. My gaze fell in my shameful state as he uttered the words that would stay with me forever.

"Well, then it wouldn't be hospitality."

I had breached protocol to a man who truly lived the essence of concern for his fellow human beings. The "payment" was about to destroy all of the good that happened in the past hours, all of the good feelings, all of the camaraderie. Jack Agee had burned a place into the core of our hearts, and I was about to destroy it with my ignorance.

I quickly shoved the note and the money back into my pocket.

The ways of the Trail sometime are learned with some blundering, but if one remains receptive and open-minded, there is wisdom to be garnered. The Appalachian Trail was magic with its sheer ability to create good feelings and was the ultimate ambassador of goodwill, creating a sense of peace between us in this world of turmoil. I later reflected that there should be an Appalachian Trail within all of us where there is a need and that need can be fulfilled and we can come together as one. Jack Agee, in one fell swoop, had done more good than the combined efforts of many working for a lifetime, for such acts of kindness do not become static but blossom to affect many. The Trail had again worked its wonders.

# Chapter 20

## Reflection

*May 25—Day 50—Mile 714 (Daleville, Virginia)—(Journal entry)—to Econo Lodge by 10:15-ish—checked in and spread stuff out on veranda—took a very long shower/bath—walked to Shoney's and did the AYCE thing—full, full*

Assessments! As the awareness started to set in that hiking the Trail was going to leave permanent scars, that my body would forever be different, as would my mind, it became necessary to evaluate my venture from time to time, weigh the pros and cons. To, again, come up with additional justification to do what I was doing.

*Positives:*

* *Sleeping excellent*
* *Camaraderie*
* *Meeting challenges*
* *Learning limitations*
* *Sights, Smells, Sounds*
* *Educations*
* *Exalted position (peers, family, friends)*
* *Joys of camping*
* *Drinking pure water*
* *Tremendous sense of accomplishment*

    \*   *Being able to write about it*
    \*   *Benefit that others are deriving (Doris, Kris, kids, kids-in-law, friends, neighbors)*

*Negatives:*

    \*   *Weariness*
    \*   *Appetite*
    \*   *Discouragement*
    \*   *Physical appearance*

*It seems the lists tell it all! One just simply goes on. It wasn't supposed to be easy. There are subtle things here that are happening. The rewards will be (are) there.*

That was "An Assessment" from my journal dated May 26, 2003. A little over a month and a half into the journey and with 710 miles behind me. What provided inspiration for this at the time can only be conjectured in looking back for there was no real landmark here other than the Meeting. Us old guys had convened in the lobby of the Econo Lodge motel in Daleville, Virginia, that morning and cried on each other's shoulders and offered our deepest thoughts and reasoning as to why we were all struggling so hard. Old guys, after all, have a difficult time admitting stuff, that being that we were old and human bodies were just not designed for such abuse day after day. So we looked for deeper reasons and, of course, really didn't find any that could be considered an epiphany.

I suppose we left the meeting feeling better, or possibly we left the meeting feeling much as one does after an AA meeting. "Hi . . . my name is Ole Smoky Lonesome . . . and . . . I am a hike-aholic . . ."

We had spilled our guts to our fellow sufferers as a support group would do and, maybe in those admissions, would come the impetus to propel us on our merry way. The old trick of sharing, that these confessions would bring us to terms with what we were dealing with and that we would miraculously be transformed and up the mountains we would glide.

It should be noted that old guys really are no different than young guys when it comes to physical, mental, or even, yes, sexual prowess. We are invincible, always have been. It's the ways of the world of men. Too many of us that haven't bothered to read too much history still think that the ways of the world have always been dominated by men; and this places a lot of pressure, needless pressure, upon us to always be "performing." Had we taken the time to read about some of the ancient cultures or relatively recent cultures of South American and the Aztec Indians or even some of the cultures within the boundaries closer to home, our Native Americans, we could have eliminated some of this pressure by this needless machismo and conquering.

It was difficult to look when your body is aching and you're struggling your way up the mountain with each step and some lady hiker goes cruising by. However, one need only remember that she is drawing on instinctive strengths that she doesn't even understand. I have always thought that having a baby would kill the average guy, and after hiking the Appalachian Trail, I'm pretty much convinced of that. The women out there were usually cruising. Except downhill when knees came too much into play as a female's wider hips caused her legs to come down angular rather than perpendicular when absorbing the constant repeating shock. But let's face it, it just didn't do much for the ego to be telling the guys at derring-do macho break about how you cruised on by, say, somebody like Baby Steps going downhill. Just wasn't too impressive. So we just had to deal with it the best that we could.

My old boss and mentor, Novie Hudson of the U.S. Geological Survey, was famous for shaking his head with that wry smile and mischievous grin and mutter something about, "That male ego is a terrible thing." As a project engineer heading up topographic mapping projects throughout a lot of the United States, he had seen that "male ego" too often create situations that were dangerous and nonproductive, certainly not something that he could have ever wanted in guiding these cartographic ventures in quest of the good name of the U.S. government. He already had enough to handle with the frivolous weather that never cooperated and swamps and hills and brush and trees—all the nemesis of the map-maker. Yes, male ego proved too often to be the nemesis of sanely going about tasks that required too much, an arena for overaccomplishment and a feeding of self-image.

So this bunch of old guys also could not accept that their bodies might possibly not be designed or have adequate training for this type of abuse. Some of us thought that we would be floating along the yellow brick road by this time, communing with nature immersed in the smells and wonders, savoring each step like a fine wine, and eagerly anticipating the next step, the next mile, the next day. All an adventure and not the torture that seems to have taken over the Shangri-la. This adventure had turned into a masochistic torture chamber in the form of a narrow green tunnel in the trees, stumbling over rocks and wishing for the next "down" and that somehow the Lord would help you make it to the top of the next "up." No, this was not the way it was supposed to be.

So we turned to assessments. Return for our investment. Return for our sacrifices and damages done to body and mind. "Your path is arduous but will be amply rewarding."

By Daleville, Virginia, I was still waiting for some of the "amply rewarding" part and beginning to think that if that had happened, it was much to subtle. I needed "amply rewarding" to come in bigger chunks and much more often. I waited. Even at this writing, I'm not too sure just what the rewards have been and just possibly I had better interpret the deeper meanings of rewarding and possibly even look into deciphering *amply*.

Justifications! Assessments! A large part of such a venture.

The real assessments came when honesty was prioritized, looking at oneself realistically and without excuses. Those moments rarely came in the early or the late parts of the hike. However, around 300 to 400 miles and through what could be considered the middle part of the hike, the realization occurred that my body had changed. Much more than I had ever expected.

I was a plethora of blood vessels. That is rather a family trait. Some of my uncles seemed to be nothing but sinew and blood vessels. Some time after Hot Springs, North Carolina, after the novelty was starting to wear off and same ole same ole was starting to set in, I started making honest observations. Blood vessels were visible in my legs that hadn't been there before. I was rather alarmed to say the least.

And looking at myself in the mirror was painful. My shoulders seemed too scrawny, and my body appeared stringy. My stomach was absolutely flat to sunken. I prided myself even at 62 years of age in having a fairly attractive body and was in relatively good physical condition. The Trail was taking an awful toll, and during these assessment programs, there were times when conclusions were arrived at that it just was not worth it, that I had to live with this body and I planned on living a good life. My Ukrainian background seemed to indicate from family history that I could live to a ripe old age; my paternal grandmother had lived to 106 years old and was still quite active even into the hundreds.

I just really did not want to jeopardize risking my health. No, I did not believe in pansying around and avoid doing things for fear of hurting myself. However, much in the same vein, I didn't want to abuse myself to a point where I could suffer physically and mentally because of the hike. I did not want to lower my quality of life because of damage incurred during this venture. I place too much value on physical aspects of life.

In Waynesboro, Virginia, actual entries were made in the journal that I had prioritized and decided that it just wasn't worth it. I would get off the Trail and go home. However, after two days of rest there, I reprioritized and continued. This became much a ritual that lasted for most of the duration of the hike.

The assessments continued throughout the hike. Probably to some extent, there is still evaluation going on long after the fact. One has to wonder in retrospect just how he carried on. It would have been much easier to quit, to drop off the Trail. However, that is just simply a characteristic of the human mind to forget the anguish, to rose-color things. The mode of the mind during the hike is much different than when one is comfortably at home.

Now sitting and comfortably writing about this experience and musing and reliving, it is hard to assume that same mental bent. It would be difficult to get into the swing of doing another thru-hike. The physical aspects are about the same, but the possibility of completing a hike hinge much more on the mental than the physical.

I firmly believe that I could not do it again.

# *Chapter 21*

## Trail Magic

Food—food—food ! !
Trail magic
Hog Camp Gap, VA
Mile 800 (about)—June 1

*April 24—Day 20—Mile 278—(Journal entry)—Terry and Cindy from Belleview, Illinois, gave me an orange at Lemon Gap*

Trail magic. A concept that could serve us well in all aspects of life. A symbol of the symbiosis that exists between one person with another person regardless of stature, regardless of creed, regardless of differences. A need, a need answered.

In the case of the Trail, the symbiosis that exists between thru-hikers and the local people can only be described as its name implies. It's just magic. A caring shown through acts of kindness, whether that be food (in most cases for that is uppermost in the minds of thru-hikers who are always hungry), rides to town, free lodging, and trail "amenities" such as Coleman fuel or duct tape or thread or whatever integral item the hiker may need.

And therein may lay the secret to the immense success of this relationship between hikers and the people that encounter the Trail in other capacities. Extravagance does not exist for there is no room for extravagance. Need and extravagance after all are in direct contradiction. On the Trail, wants have been totally replaced with just needs, and the human compassion can always answer to needs. Wants tend to confuse the issue, and let's face it, our lives are much too strewn with wants. A grass roots' return to life as it probably should be led, but we in our American misconception truly believe that the more stuff we have the happier we will be.

The Trail quickly disproves the materialism-is-happy theory with a resounding manifestation, for after just a few days in a thru-hiking status, one discovers just how very little we need in life and conversely how very happy we can be with just those simple things—good food, good water, good companionship—albeit in a rather intermittent capacity as the Trail often dictates, for hikers go at different speeds and the logistics of the Trail often lead thru-hikers along just a little different schedules. However, that sense of togetherness and camaraderie never quite goes away. Hikers meet and remeet as the slow progression north evolves. Every week is old-home week all over again.

In my thru-hike, it only took until Hiawassee, Georgia, 75 trail miles, to encounter my first trail magic experience. Yes, prior to that there had been trail magic of sorts shown through the caring of fellow hikers; but those cases would not really qualify for the true meaning of the term, if there is an accurate and conclusive description of this phenomenon.

The story bears repeating. I had completed my shopping at Ingles Store and was packing these items into the backpack when an attractive older lady stopped to ask me if I had a ride back to the Trail. I told her that I didn't. She quite firmly told me to stay right there, her husband would be back in fifteen minutes. In exactly fifteen minutes, he arrived and proved to be much more than just a ride as he was a past thru-hiker, Corsican, and he not only gave me a ride back but provided the kind of encouragement that I was needing as he told me to not quit no matter what. Also, it was a good feeling just seeing this man's caring, for as we passed other hikers walking into town, he would holler to them out the window that he would be right back and give them a ride.

Most of the trail magic came in the form of food or soft drinks. Offerings too numerous to mention would just appear in various forms: cold sodas, cookies, Coleman fuel cans sitting on a stump with a note Help Yourself, candy bars, granola bars, sometimes even beer. My status of teetotaler, a recent attitude resolved when I turned sixty years of age, stayed with me throughout the hike; but at times the temptation was quite strong. Often the drinks would be lying in a stream where the ice-cold water was gurgling over the containers, an irresistible scene reeking of commercial appeal; but most of the time, the food and drinks were in coolers strategically placed along the Trail close to road crossings. Usually the coolers were placed far enough away from the road to not be easily seen by others—meant for thru-hikers only, a practice that was rarely violated. Also, it was interesting to note that rarely, if ever, was the trail magic code broken. A hiker would just never think of exploiting these freebies and take more than was needed, a few cookies, one soda, what have you. Need did not dictate greed for the hiker knew there were others behind and that this was a sharing thing, a kindergarten experience in true spirit.

Sometimes the trail magic was in conjunction with trail maintenance people doing their thing. I ran into a gentleman who was doing both. It was April 27 and the start of the third week on the Trail, here roughly following the North Carolina-Tennessee state line. Before ascending Sugarloaf Mountain, the AT crosses two improved roads that made a junction to the west before leading to the tiny place called Carmen. Another one of those sections of the Trail where the hiker was heading south under the auspices of being northbound.

He called himself Sweet Tooth and, on this day, was accompanied by his wife. Actually this section of the Trail was the responsibility of another maintainer, and he was just doing a friend a favor, a trait of trail maintainers of just never quite being able to give enough of themselves. He told me that at the second road, his white Dodge pickup was parked and to check in the bed. We shook hands and I thanked him and we wished each other a good life before continuing my trek. The truck was there, indeed, and it is hard to describe just how delicious some store-bought cookies and a canned pop can taste on a crisp, sunny late-April morning.

A true state of ambiance on the Appalachian Trail provided by Mother Nature herself. About six thru-hikers were there, and we took each other's photos before facing the climb ahead. We generously thanked him with notes in the trail journal notebook that he had left with the treats.

I thought about Sweet Tooth making my way up and felt very good about the world situation knowing that with more Sweet Tooth's, most of human complication would be of little consequence. Later the concept of the Trail being a linear diplomatic tool slowly formed and, with so much time for thought while hiking, had to wonder how this could be incorporated into everyday life. An idea certainly worth researching and developing. Of course, the line of thought that often dominated the thinking of our nomadic self-propelled way of life was that if we could merely get people out of cars and walk together, a natural state of peace could exist. We Americans only read about the quaint after-dinner walks in neighborhoods in France and Italy where people come together and grow to know each other and bond. We also know that in America, suburbia has made a major impact that has taken a huge toll on our quality of life. Road rage is simply a symptom of too much too fast, and what an elixir a little walking would be to alleviate this phenomenon.

The Dodge truck with a bed full of cookies and soda pop was the typical trail magic scenario, simple and direct and very effective. These cases were rampant throughout the thru-hike. However, on occasion, the trail magic would take on much more serious proportions. Planned and with numerous people involved. Virginia proved to be the granddaddy of trail magic, no-holds-barred, the ultimate.

June 1 started windy and gradually got colder as the morning progressed. It seemed hard to believe that one could be shivering in June in a state as far south as Virginia. The night before had been a study in trepidation near the top of Bald Knob where I had stopped a little early to allow some extra time to dry out. The gradually increasing wind provided more than enough drying power. However, the only place available to adhere to Leave No Trace camping was immediately adjacent to the Trail and directly under a suspect dead branch. The wind was making the branch do things that questioned the wisdom of selecting this place directly below it for a camping site. However, there just did not seem to be any choice; and so while eating my noodles, I kept one eye on the miscreant piece of dead wood and hoped for the best. It did not help that the wind got stronger through the night. It should be added that later in the hike and in the middle of the night when things take on macabre overtones, a nearby tree came crashing down. However, this night, the fiber within this particular dead branch had not given up yet. Morning found me back doing my thing without a big dent in my head.

When I reached the very top of the mountain, the wind was strong enough to make it difficult to walk with my billowy pack. I leaned severely into the wind, keeping my walking stick on the lee side to keep from blowing over and struggled along. Finding refuge on Cold Mountain (the irony did not escape me) behind a rock, I allowed for a morning pack-off break to enjoy a package of granola bars. While biting into the second bar, an unknown thru-hiker came by. He was all excited, saying that there was a huge trail magic party ahead at Hog Camp Gap.

I gobbled down my last granola bar and soon was at an assumed forty-five working my way downward and dealing with the pushy wind but happy to know that food lay ahead. Never in the wildest trail magic dreams could I have envisioned the magnitude of this trail magic party. Cost had been no object having been sponsored by five past hikers, at least one of them a thru-hiker from the year before. There was a huge fire ring and tents all over the huge grassy open area. I gravitated toward the large group huddled around the fire doing their best dealing with the wind. I recognized numerous faces and was so happy to again see Pippi and Buffalo Bobby. Old-home week! And that warm camaraderie unique to the Trail and especially so with the carnival atmosphere of the ensuing party of thru-hikers and our slow progression north. After a profusion of hellos, it was time to partake of the feast.

My journal included a rough list of what was offered: soft-boiled eggs, granola bars, oranges, apples, cinnamon rolls, potato hash brown nuggets, venison sausage, chocolates, blue berries—I had at least one of each.

Ironically the photo setup of the group responsible never happened. We had them all together and posed and smiling. My Olympus camera that had been lying on the ground after the first initial photos just would not respond. The automatic setting called for a flash, and the very cold battery just could not muster up the energy. However, the group is etched in my mind forever even if somehow in the confusion I had failed to get names recorded. Again, one of those cases of the buried journal and not taking the time to dig it out.

I left there feeling good, full of good additional and very much needed nourishment. Mostly, though with my mind full of good thoughts, the mental food, the real nourishment providing the drive and probably the most important aspect of staying the course on the Trail.

The trail magic stories abound with all thru-hikers, and many have their favorite that for me would be difficult to pick. In the course of the thru-hike, at least a hundred acts of kindness were bestowed upon me—ironically and sadly, more than had occurred in my sixty-two years here on earth in "civilian life." Just spontaneous acts of goodness triggered by nothing else other than an unselfish desire to be a part of this thing called the Appalachian Trail. I so desired to eventually live close by and participate in a like manner. I envisioned aspects of it and created in my mind the perfect trail magic scenario: offers of water and soda and food and friendship and encouragement. My mind toyed with the options and a feeling of warmth, and a closeness to mankind prevailed like none that I had ever experienced in my life.

# Chapter 22

## Musing

*April 19—Day 15—Mile 203—(Journal entry)—saw U.S.G.S. bench marks "70 RJN 1963—71 RJN 1963"—east of Spence Field Shelter—*

As I progressed northward along the Trail, there was so much time to think about so many things in my life, and more of the USGS happenings that had long been forgotten surged into my memory as if these now-cherished events occurred just yesterday. As it is with life influences making us who we are, these were the contributing factors in making me an outside person and one that would one day consider hiking the Appalachian Trail.

Working with the USGS for 24 years in the Field provided opportunities found in very few lines of employment. Most importantly, the work proved to be the catalyst that would one day find me doing a long-distance hike. For it seemed that wherever my mapping assignments were, there were trails—the seed was being planted and the love for paths in the woods and through the fields and meadows and through my heart was forever being ingrained into my being.

It is a strange marriage between hiking and mapping, a symbiosis for lack of a better term. It would be hard to imagine hiking the Appalachian Trail without profile maps and other cartographic information for planning and navigating in areas where numerous trails other than the AT exist. The profile information is derived from existing USGS topographic maps; the profiles merely representing the topography as a side view for a quick assessment of the ups and downs to be encountered on any section. I cannot imagine hiking the Appalachian Trail without knowing what lay ahead; especially with regard to long climbs.

In the line of duty as a mapmaker, my quest for topographic information found me in places such as the Boundary Waters Canoe Area and the Northwest Angle State Forest in Minnesota—the Bienville National Forest in Mississippi—Devils Tower National Monument in Wyoming—the Kettle Moraine State Forest in Wisconsin—the Ozark National Forest in northwestern Arkansas, and lesser known places such as the Russell Sage Wildlife Area in Louisiana and innumerable national, state, county and city parks and preserves all over the Midwestern and adjoining states.

Often I found myself using the expression "I can't believe that I am paid to do this." On a large portion of my mapping assignments and even in those stereotypical agricultural parts of the Midwest, it seemed that there were always at least a few recreational areas that included, of course, hiking and walking trails.

The mapping of trails provided a challenge for often these linear features could not be seen on aerial photographs, thus field identification was required. Numerous trails usually had to be walked or, in some cases, ridden with three wheelers (four-wheelers hadn't been invented yet), to be identified and located on the maps. Or, in numerous cases, the trails had to be surveyed with an alidade and plane table to accurately plot them on the maps; this usually was done in conjunction with other information gathering such as establishing elevations on map identified points or as part of the process of drawing contour lines.

The trails were varied and it seemed that each area had certain unique traits: snowmobile trails, equestrian trails, logging trails, winter roads and, of course, hiking trails. The winter roads in extreme northern parts of Minnesota are in remote areas of vast swamps, and are mostly there for the logging operations, being drivable only in the dead of winter when frozen. A lot of the snowmobile trails in these same areas of muskeg and floating bogs are in some places, corduroyed; usually with cut logs laid perpendicular to the direction of travel to provide a base. Also, in these same locales, there were usually a lot of abandoned railroads that had been relegated to recreational use or forgotten. The majority of these had been there for the logging operations and when the trees had been clear-cut, the railroad beds were left as the only evidence that something profound had occurred there.

Like the hiking of the AT, it seems that the business of making maps is also a rich environment for numerous stories and fond memories.

In 1980, while working out of Morton, Mississippi, I had developed a condition that was fondly referred to as just 'tennis knee'. My left knee had deteriorated to the point where it was painful to do much of anything. Overuse had taken its toll and some evidence of arthritis was starting to show its ugly head.

So, I administered a form of Ukrainian 'therapy'. I went for a hike. In the Bienville National Forest just to the east of Morton and accessible from old U. S. Highway 80 was an equestrian/hiking trail that looped around to the north and west and back south to the highway. It was in the latter part of the fall and the orb weavers (locally called banana spiders) were out in full force. It was difficult to find a section of the trail over a few hundred feet long where numerous cobwebs didn't span the width of the trail from tree to tree. It was impossible to navigate without busting through the webs. Eventually I became a walking cobweb.

The entire length of the trail is nearly 24 miles, very flat, very typically Mississippi terrain and very wooded with primarily deciduous trees. The Sunday weather was fabulous with temperatures ranging around 75 to 80 degrees. My first steps on the ailing knee were painful and the sanity of this venture was in question, but perseverance prevailed. The first two miles found the knee slowly loosening and by the third mile I was striding like nothing was wrong. By the five mile point, I was back to my old four-mile-an-hour pace.

I hiked the entire 24 miles in about six hours and was totally covered with cobwebs. Other than three very active cottonmouth snakes and maybe a deer or two, I had not seen any wildlife other than the banana spiders. On the way back to my rental trailer (my wife and children were living in Monroe, Louisiana during this period—this just happened to be one of those weekends when I chose not to go home) I stopped at a convenience store for a soda and some candy bars for energy replenishment. The clerk was shocked seeing my cobweb matted hair and entire being looking somewhat haggard and beaten. I made a speedy retreat back to the car and drove back to my trailer and collapsed in the easy chair, quickly falling asleep in a vain attempt of watching what the NFL had to offer for the afternoon. When I awoke about an hour later, I could hardly get out of the chair. However, the next morning, my knee was back to nearly 100 percent. My therapy had worked.

It was amazing how often this same methodology had to be employed in the hiking of the Trail.

Eventually, family complications led to some drastic changes in our lifestyles which were catalyst for my transfer from the field into the office in Rolla, Missouri. However, 24 years in the Field and virtually on my own had not prepared me well for working in an office with 350 other employees. And, the field always beckoned so strongly as did the nomad deeply engrained that had never really known a home town.

These inner cravings eventually found me seeking temporary assignments when transplanted field people were needed to fill gaps and balance workload. An application for an Antarctic assignment may have been done more out of rebellion than a tangible reason. So, when the acceptance came, it was quite a shock.

Probably my largest fear in going to Antarctica was the fact of 24-hour daylight. Being a perennial insomniac made me wonder about being able to sleep with daylight the entire time; with the sun going round and round, straight south at midnight and straight north at noon.

However, the portable military Jamesways at our base camp on Bowden Névé—located roughly halfway between McMurdo Station and the South Pole—were well light-insulated and as comfortable as my bedroom back home; well, maybe nearly so. The 6,000 foot elevation proved to be an elixir and the work was exhilarating. Our crew of four was flown by Huey helicopters compliments of the Navy's elite VXE-6 Squadron. We were in the hands of some of the best pilots in the world. Also, the thrill of landing on the snow fields in a Hercules C-130 is beyond adequate wording. Something akin to hiking the Appalachian Trail in that there was a freedom there that does not exist in our normal world. Huge airplanes usually need real runways to land and take off.

In the course of doing our horizontal control surveys, each one of our crew had the option of naming a number of the brass bench mark tablets that we set as recoverable points. I was allotted two, and chose, of course, KRISTIN for one, that, hopefully, is still imbedded in a rock at the top of Mt Sirius. My other choice left me in a quandary, for not particularly liking my first name, found me using the name UKE in recognition of my Ukrainian heritage. The work on The Ice allowed me a time to again be who I really was, a drifter and one who was always wondering what was over the next hilltop. It was a dream come true and the wanderlust was again being answered to.

Any field career with USGS finds one in places not quite as interesting with regard to trails and recreation areas. However, every place in this great country seems to have some redeeming quality or, if taken in proper perspective, places of interest that would not usually be considered such. Western Kansas assignments were usually a challenge in this regard. It is an area that has a tendency to grow on you with the extremely friendly people and the almost surreal openness. I clearly remember walking up to a house one day to get some water and turning around, became aware of the fact that the only thing visible for 360 degrees was the row of power poles into the ranch.

The lady that answered the door did not even hesitate as she invited me in and ran the water until it was properly cold and we talked as if we had known each other all of our lives. The warmth of the people in these areas of nothingness more than made up for the lack of physical features that we hiker-types normally crave. However, little surprises existed along the creeks that provided some break from the ubiquitous fields of irrigated wheat; interesting old trails and roads that were just barely visible, windmills and old watering tanks—proving that the ever present adventuresome spirit does not die without grandiose features, it just usually adapts as there is usually always something of interest everywhere that one wanders.

Hiking the Trail with the wonderful Appalachian Trail maps was like reliving those 24 years in the field. Each day was carefully planned around the detail and information so richly provided. Of particular satisfaction were the first two maps that provided coverage from Amicalola Falls State Park to Fontana Dam. These 1:63,360—scale maps are reductions of the original USGS 1:24,000-scale maps with esoteric Trail information added in larger type and symbols. It took a magnifying glass to read the original 1:24k information, but what a delight to see all the detail.

And, as an added bonus, in the Great Smoky Mountains National Park was a deja vue experience beyond description to this surveyor, having found three USGS bench marks! The man that had done the levels surveys in 1963, as stamped on the metal tablets, was a fellow employee, thought not one that I knew well. I was envious of his assignment in such an awesome place, certainly a "can't believe they pay me for this" location. However, the surveying mind always is working at the logistics and methods of executing levels in the steep terrain. Levels, as implied, are done with a level instrument, capable of only taking observations (shots) within a level line of sight. It had taken multiple hundreds of instrument setups to have traversed the steep Trail. The equipment is somewhat cumbersome, and, of course, merely working out the day-to-day details and where to stop and start had to truly have been a challenge.

The AT maps in Maryland and Pennsylvania are truly state-of-the-art! The enlarged insets provide detail that made my heart sing. The map of the day always was readily available in the fanny pack that I carried in the front. Of course, on those numerous rainy days, the maps remained ensconced in plastic and were usually only brought out in a shelter. My maps were going home with me and were going to stay in good shape.

Another aspect of use of the maps was to find water sources other than ones indicated with AT symbols and print. I stealth camped at Saltlog Gap northeast of Glasgow, Virginia. The map indicated a spring to the west of the gap. However, trying to locate it was quite challenging. Using the map it was fairly obvious that eventually there had to be a water source along the upper reaches of what eventually became Belle Cove Branch. And, finally about a half mile down my search was fruitful having found a number of excellent springs. The climb back was invigorating but tiring, especially on top of a 17.5 mile day on the Trail.

So, in retrospect, my mind wondered what came first—hiking or mapmaking? The mapmaking required walking, and, conversely, in my way of thinking, hiking the Trail required good maps to truly appreciate and logistically optimize the experience. Those early years in my career had indelibly established a need for walking and hiking. Having worked in the field as a surveyor/mapmaker for a total of 32 years (eight years in the private sector) garners a walking/hiking distance on this body at somewhere around 50,000 miles, that being a conservative estimate for not a day goes by in my life that I don't walk at least two miles. With USGS, a lot of days on certain phases of the work, walking a distance of 20 miles was not that unusual.

It turned out to be the ultimate in preparation for the hiking of the Appalachian Trail.

# Chapter 23

## Harpers Ferry

*Sunday, June 15—Day 72—Mile 1012 (Harpers Ferry)—(Journal entry)—then started walking to KOA to do laundry—made it to PO—a guy came by with two thru-hikers—hostel dude—actually hostile—a real opinionated guy*

A resounding scream in the early morning! I held back nothing, and the sound probably carried all the way into town even though that was about a mile away. My insides were boiling with the injustice of it all; and in spite of this idealistic so-called walk in the woods, a slow-fused anger had been building up, too much to try to stifle now when I was supposed to be feeling good about all of this. The weather, more than any other factor, continued to be the nemesis and was affecting too many aspects of the hike. Not exactly the accepted way to come into town, but I really did not care. Not exactly the celebration of getting to this important point. To this major milestone. It just wasn't supposed to be this way. For there ahead lay the psychological halfway point for the AT thru-hiker in front of me, just across the river and up the hill through those trees even though not visible from where I stood.

It was raining—again, or yet. Rain, rain, rain.

Harpers Ferry. A magical place for the Appalachian Trail thru-hikers. The place where the hiker could finally be accounted for, make a mark, albeit rather insignificant. For here was the home of the Appalachian Trail Conference (now Conservancy) headquarters. Harpers Ferry, West

Virginia, was approximately 1,008 miles from Springer Mountain and certainly close enough to halfway even though dividing 2,175 by two didn't add up. It was the place that one's psyche accepted as being close enough to halfway to be cause for celebration. Where one could strut about being a true thru-hiker, maybe even a place that getting off the Trail could be considered a remote option while still retaining some semblance of respect and sense of accomplishment. My mood should have been ecstatic.

I stood at the far end of the long concrete bridge over the Shenandoah River, about a mile above where it flowed into the Potomac River, ready to do my dance into town. I had planned on just holding the map in my hand, referring to the exact route to the various sites, sort of planning my route along the way. As with numerous places along the Trail, places of special interest had larger-scale insets on the map for more detail, and Harpers Ferry definitely fell into that category. Also, I had envisioned this major landmark as being symbolic of the ideal, that I would walk across the bridge with sunshine all around, a gentle breeze swaying the trees, and birds singing their songs announcing my grand arrival. I shoved the map back into the plastic in the fanny pack and started grumbling my way across the bridge, halfheartedly trying to lift my spirits. Shoot! I was in Harpers Ferry!

Minus the idealism, I just hoped that I could get to the hotel or motel or wherever I decided to stay not too wet. I had spent the previous night atop Blue Ridge prior to setting up to dry everything out yet again and had done a good job, and the night was fairly kind with simply some morning dew to deal with. I was arriving in good shape for a change and not having to deal with a motel room full of draped items with the all-too-common scene. The rain started just as I crossed the pedestrian underpass and started to ascend the concrete steps to the sidewalk that was part of the bridge along the northeast side. A slap in the face. Mother Nature was toying with any scrap of good humor that may have been left within my mind or body.

I was totally and completely mentally and physically spent. There was not enough energy within my being to hardly get across the bridge, let alone climb the hill to get into town. My legs were mush. I had fought with myself through the morning as to just where I should stay. Toying with staying at the KOA campground seemed to be financially the best choice. Also, from the guidebook, it appeared as if that was the location of the only Laundromat in town. However, the Hilltop House Hotel appeared to be closer to the places to eat, having a fine restaurant of its own, even if somewhat pricey. As I walked I continued my internal debate.

Harpers Ferry is an oddity as far as AT towns go. A tourist town reeking with American history, the most famous being the 1859 John Brown raid on the federal armory there and replete with sites and buildings and statues, a mecca for the history buff. It should have been the ideal Trail town; however, it wasn't. Somehow when all of this was laid out, it was forgotten that hikers are on foot. The facilities were there but so spread out that the hiker found it almost necessary to seek trail angel rides just to accomplish what needed to be done for basic town needs. The town is quite hilly, so the walks can be quite strenuous, especially carrying the laundry in a pack. The Laundromat at the KOA was about 3 miles from the center of town and the hotel. Or if one chose to stay at the Comfort Inn and somewhat closer to the Laundromat then there were no places convenient for eating. I wanted my map out so that I could plan this debacle while turning this over in my mind.

Pancakes! The inner turmoil and debate finally came to a close with pancakes. Priorities prevailed, and pancakes tipped the scale. Hilltop House Hotel and Restaurant beckoned with the promise of a Sunday-morning buffet, and certainly pancakes would abound there. I skipped through the old Storer College campus (now a National Park Service training facility), having taken the map out long enough to check the route to the hotel with the smell of pancakes, albeit imagined, having pulled me up the hill. A pleasant reunion with Aussie, Dreamwalker, and Gear Guy awaited me near the center of the campus. I took their picture in the idyllic setting of the lavish old campus. They were already full of pancakes, full of promise and hope and heading out, Maryland awaited. I was envious as they all seemed full of energy and—though somewhat drawn and thin appearing, as we all were—were destined for greater things. A condition that didn't seem to apply to me right at the moment.

After taking the picture, I made my way north on Jackson Street and walked past the Appalachian Trail Conference (now Conservancy) headquarters, about the last place that I wanted to be in my mental state. I continued to Ridge Street and turned east to the Hilltop House Hotel. The charm of the old hotel almost immediately raised my spirits; and the smell of breakfast, as I entered the lobby, dissolved what was left of the negativism. Food ever being the panacea for the ills of the Trail. It was time to pig out!

I bellied up, what little belly there was, to the buffet feed trough and started the gluttony. As usual, I went through the turmoil of what to load my plate with first and, of course, made numerous trips back and forth. There were leftovers from other meals, so the table not only was laden with the usual breakfast fare but also included cake and cookies and pie. Delightfully, I partook and partook. I finally just had to quit, feeling more like a pig with each return trip, albeit a very skinny emaciated pig.

I was then left with some time on my hands for I couldn't get into my room until about midafternoon. I sat on the verandah for a while and decided that this was as good a time as any to do laundry. Soon, with my pack on my back, I was walking west to the very distant KOA and the only laundry in town. I had only walked about a half mile when I heard a car horn and was invited to join the throng, other hikers that were heading to the driver's hostel. The driver was quick to note that my pack was too heavy and then insisted on foisting his opinions on me about every other hiking thing, including that his hostel was the only decent place to stay in the Harpers Ferry area. Having just completed a thousand miles in my hike in the condition that I was in, I really did not want to hear his opinions about anything. However, he was nice enough to drop me off at the entrance to KOA, and gladly I got out of the car.

My true condition started to really set in about this time. I finally finished the laundry and started the walk back to the hotel. Walking along a nice, smooth sidewalk may have manifested just how very exhausted I was. Possibly had I been climbing a mountain or stumbling along a rough stretch of trail, there would be justification in feeling the way I did. But there were no excuses here. Yes, my pack was on my back, but it was frightening to think that just navigating a smooth street should be such a challenge with what lay ahead.

About halfway back, I crossed Washington Street and entered a convenience store. The lady that waited on me was nice as she made a comment about my heavy pack and wondered where I was from. I touched on the story ever so slightly and told her that I had never been so tired in my life. Eating three strawberry shortcake ice cream bars helped some. Done so in the usual fashion of plopping down in front of the store and woofing them down, a manner that had become somewhat traditional by this time.

I called Kris and told her that I couldn't make it any farther. That it just was not worth it. That I was probably doing permanent damage to my body and would never recover, initiating a physical condition that would be my nemesis for the remainder of my life. I'm not sure just what that condition was, but I was fairly positive that it was permanent and incurable. A dejected has-been at the prime of life of only sixty-two years old. Living with the burden of failure being a mere "one thousand miler." Forever scorned by society as someone that just simply could not cut it.

I sat on that hotel verandah for four days! My life became an obsession with just what and where to eat next. However, the other places for dining were far enough away that I had no problem justifying the rather-pricey hotel restaurant. So I rocked in the conveniently placed nostalgic old-timey wooden rocking chair, assuming the role of a Southern gentleman-type living in a hotel, eating the fine food, reading the paper, nodding off from time to time and then rocking some more, and making conversation with whoever would talk and dreaming of that train ride home. Enough was enough. It was time to go home and do nothing more than some serious day-in and day-out pancake eating.

Ironically, there just across the Potomac River was Maryland and my sixth state. The combination B & O Railroad Bridge serving also as the Appalachian Trail was there just below me, about a third of a mile away and clearly visible. I looked at that bridge in my vegetative state for the next four days and thought how Maryland could almost be considered a Northern state in some ways. So Maryland beckoned, "Come across. See me. Add me to the list."

At least maybe six states would sound a little better. No, more correctly, Maryland screamed at me, "Come on, you candy-ass! Get out of that rocker and get going! Complete this thing that you started and now are trying to woos your way out of! What kind of man are you, sitting there in your rocking chair in defiance and doing everything contrary to everything that you ever believed in. Be a man!"

Maryland, Maryland, Maryland. Why do you have to be there so close? I want to go home and eat pancakes. Pancakes with maple syrup and strawberry jelly every morning for the rest of my natural life. Butter pecan ice cream every night. Until I balloon to up there around 250 pounds and really do not give a darn about anything, let alone this frivolous claim of a maligned hero living in this state of self-denial and sacrifice.

It was raining again on the morning of day 4 as I sat uneasily in my rocking chair. After the usual breakfast, I had taken refuge yet again, reenacting the verandah scene. I was trying to read a local newspaper when he came, Mr. Myer, a retired pipe fitter from New Jersey. He reeked of New Jersey. My mind was in turmoil, a jumble of indecision. I had actually called AmTrak that morning and managed to get through the recorded messages, managing somehow to push 1 when it told me to push 1 and then 2 to hear the prices and then 3 to hear the connections and then 4 to repeat a few things that I had missed, or something like that—the numbers having become rather moot in the process. It was difficult to tell; however, there possibly might have been a real person in that myriad of voices and that labyrinth of information and nicety, thanking you again and again for choosing AmTrak. I had garnered the necessary information and actually came away from the ordeal, knowing the price of a ticket back to Jacksonville, Florida: $196. A train would be awaiting me at the allotted time just down the hill right there in Harpers Ferry.

Oh, it sounded so very good.

Mr. Myer must have been in the process of searching for a life that morning. He slid his chair close to my rocker and said, "I should tell you about my brodder." Then with a dismissive wave of the hand much in the stereotypical frustrated Italian manner, he added, "Aah, you don' wanna hear about my brodder." Then for the next very long hour, he proceeded to tell me about his brother, complete with every minute detail of a move that he had helped this brother make to Florida, brilliantly emblazoned with opinions about the brother's lack of driving skills and how they "kissed" a pump island overhang with the rental truck. And on and on and on.

My mind was desperately darting about, going from pancakes in Florida to pecan ice cream to AmTrak to Appalachian Trail to New Jersey to some darn rental truck demolishing a gas pump island somewhere in between. All the time, the rain is coming down and Maryland is screaming at me, "Come on, candy-ass. Hiking is what you do. Come on, get going. Come on!"

"So I says to the brodder, if you would have just listened to me, we could be 10 miles down the road by now. But no, here we are with the police, answering all the questions; and now we are gonna have to pay for the damages to the truck and to the gas pump roof thing. And he looks at me with this dumb look on his face and then has the gall to say that if I wooda told him about the gas pump roof thing in the first place, it would never have happened in the first place; and then I says to him, well, in the first place . . ."

Maryland is screaming and screaming, "Come on, get going!" Pancakes and ice cream and Mr. Myer and trucks and the demolished gas pump roof thing and . . .

I fled.

Soon I was stumbling along, at least it was downhill, with my pack securely in place on my back and heading down Washington Street toward that now-infamous bridge and eventually Maryland. Walking along, I could see the AmTrak station there just to my left and below me. But strangely, Florida and pancakes and pecan ice cream just didn't seem that important at that moment. Who knows, but probably Mr. Myer had put me over the edge. It really didn't matter. I was going to be in my sixth state soon. Maryland had won. Mr. Myer would have to wait another day for a life of his own.

It should be noted that the AT and Washington Street are not coincident going through Harpers Ferry. However, being a true purist by this juncture, sometime during that four-day sabbatical, I had diligently walked back through the old college campus back to where I had gotten off the Trail and then hiked that section to the downtown area to the bridge over the Potomac. So maybe in my dementia, the knowledge was there deeply recessed that getting off the Trail was really still not in the offing. However, for the purposes of this dissertation, Maryland screaming at me and, indeed, Mr. Myer were the catalysts to keep me going. So, Mr. Myer, wherever you may be, thank you.

I could only pray for the good fortune of never having to run into his brother when getting back to Florida and having to be subjected to the other side of the story about the gas pump overhang thing.

# Chapter 24

## The Mother Lode

*June 21—Day 78—Mile 1054—(Journal entry)—got to Pen Mar Park about 3:45 p.m. (or so)—talked to groundskeeper about water which he pointed out—then noticed soda machine at concession stand—bought Pepsi and noticed Cakalaki*

Exhilaration! My heart fluttered as I thought of how close I was to Pennsylvania. Finally. Rain was threatening. Again. It had been a good day of hiking, and it was getting toward the later part of the afternoon. It was the seventy-eighth day on the Trail, Saturday, June 21; and miracle of miracles, after the long and doubtful days spent in Harpers Ferry, I was about to make it across Maryland and, with the entrance to Pennsylvania, would come a landmark of significance. And possibly provide the catalyst to regain the commitment that I felt earlier. Something about crossing the Mason-Dixon Line held a magic, an allure, a passing from the South to the North. I knew that better days, attitude-wise, were coming with that historic event.

Pen Mar County Park was just two-tenths of a mile from the line. The park is a gorgeous savanna of gracious large deciduous trees and open areas with large pavilions. It was Saturday and the place was jumping. There was a wedding reception at the huge pavilion that skirted the Trail, and the festivities seemed to be winding down as I walked through the area. A soda machine had caught my eye with the large bright-lighted Pepsi sign proving to be irresistible. I sauntered that way, feeling rather good about the day with 15 miles under my belt and the soon-to-be entrance into the second half of the hike with the official halfway point not too far away.

It had been one of those giddy mornings of good feelings, good people, and good trail magic. The pending rain couldn't dampen my spirits as I slogged down the Trail. Smithsburg was a mere 2 miles to the left, and approaching Wolfsville Road, the decision for some resupply was quickly made. It was only 9:30 a.m., and I basked in the luxury of excess time. I had walked a short distance down the road before a man named Rusty stopped to pick me up. His wife and young son were with him. Our conversation was of the usual thru-hiker/trail angel manner. Rusty was more than happy to take me to the Food Lion supermarket and shortly was dropping me off at the parking lot.

Within five minutes, I was sitting on the sidewalk in the front of the store, enjoying some Salisbury steak, steamed yellow corn, and apple cobbler while contemplating the slowly developing rain. My resupply tour of the store was quickly out of the way followed by a quick call to Kris to tell her of my whereabouts, and soon I was outside stuffing the groceries in the pack. An elderly lady was entering the store as I was involved in this process. She told me that she would be right out and give me a ride back to the Trail.

Giving me a ride back to the Trail seemed to fill her needs more than mine. She told me about working as a civilian in military clubs when she was young. She confessed that she had done "some awful things to people" and that helping hikers out was one of her ways of making things right within herself. It was the usual candor expressed in these symbiotic situations. She dropped me off at a small parking lot just beyond the Trail because the road was busy, too busy to stop in the traffic lane. We bid each other a hasty farewell. As I walked along the road and then up the Trail, her story stayed with me. This trail, this Appalachian Trail, proved so many times to be the panacea for problems and human turmoil for those fortunate enough to know her and know of the solace that lay within her bosom. What an honor to experience her firsthand with such a warm and intimate manner for such a long time.

So those good feelings prevailed throughout the day, and while dropping the pack as I approached the Pepsi machine, it was satisfying to find enough coins in the fanny pack to purchase a soda. Usually coins are just left in the little change tray when purchases are made to eliminate the unnecessary weight, but I usually wavered on such practice. The savory cold sweetness further brightened the day. Hardly a second thought in "civilian" life, a soul-satisfying carbonated drink was always a special treat in a thru-hiker state of depravation.

People were scurrying every which direction, apparently closing down picnicking for the day as the skies became darker and more foreboding with distant thunder coming closer and more ominous. It was always so satisfying at times such as these to be a thru-hiker surrounded by local people and feel kind of like the dusty stranger that had rode into town on his steed, not belonging to anybody, mysterious, with stories to tell. However, it seemed that nobody was too curious about this dusty stranger.

However there was a twinge of envy as I looked across the throng, thinking that for them, a dry and cozy world awaited by merely packing up the stuff, loading it into the nearby cars or trucks and comfortably driving to a nice dry home loaded with amenities. It was apparent that we were in for another wet night, and thinking of being hunkered down in my little nylon apparition provided little solace. Theirs was the world of true comfort, mine was merely doing the best that could be done to control moisture. It was getting dark very early with the storm clouds looming. The picnics were coming to an end.

As I gazed across the scene, a familiar face came into focus, a mere fifty feet or so from the soda machine. My mind was a little slow in accepting this for familiar faces usually just were not in the offing in a hiker's state of being out of town and a nomad. But a familiar face it was, fellow thru-hiker, Cakalaki. I had been seeing him from time to time as we made about the same daily distance in our northern progression. What the heck was he doing there? He appeared deeply immersed within the cocoon of a huge picnic mob appearing to be just part of the crowd?

He was grinning like a Cheshire cat and rubbing his hands together, bristling with anticipation of forthcoming gratification. It was then that I noticed the pile of fried chicken on a plate directly in front of him, possibly six pieces, golden, succulent, fried chicken. Cakalaki apparently had hit the mother lode of trail magic, something we thru-hikers dream of, but never quite believing such good fortune could ever stumble our way. Awareness of just what was going on finally soaked in as other familiar faces suddenly manifested themselves, thru-hikers knowing when serendipity was staring them in the face. Numerous starving thru-hikers, some recognized and other whose names I didn't know, were converging on this table of cornucopia with intentions of partaking of the generosity. The table was the usual display of picnic preparations, too much food had been brought and now something had to be done to get rid of it. Symbiosis in its true form: overladen picnickers, starving hikers with a few paltry items of trail food in their fragile inadequate backpacks. A display of human goodness of mammoth proportions was about to take place, evidence of the human spirit and kindness and giving and sharing.

Fried chicken! Cute little sandwiches made with dinner rolls filled with ham and cheeses and thinly sliced deli meats. Cake slathered with frosting.

Pickles! Dishes defying description: those age-old efforts of one picnicker trying to outdo the other picnicker as picnic tables have witnessed through the millennium. Hot dogs! Jell-O! Food piled on top of food surrounded by food. Delicate aromas of flavorful delights permeated the air.

For some moments, a state of surrealism overcame me. It seemed I was merely an observer of something that was not available to me. Was I dreaming? That aura quickly burst for the sounds and smells were much too real. Very quickly, Ole Smoky Lonesome finally came out of his trance and became a part of the scene, realizing that this was, indeed, not a mirage. The food was disappearing quickly, and it was time to make a move! However, when one goes from a state of depravation to such excess, it was hard deciding where to start. The hot dogs screamed the loudest and were the closest so that seemed the easiest place to start. Some of the dishes defied description, of that variety found on the back pages of cookbooks having found their way to this arena of experimentation. Between mouthfuls, I did manage to latch on to a piece of rapidly disappearing fried chicken.

Oh, life was so sweet at times.

The rain set in quickly, and soon we were scurrying to a nearby covered pavilion carrying as much of the feast as we could. A rare and wonderful feeling of camaraderie prevailed within the pavilion as we partook of our good fortune and exchanged recent incidents along the Trail. Deep within us, we knew that as the darkness set in, provisions for the night would have to be made in short order. However, for the time being, the inconvenience of the night and where we were going to sleep just did not make a difference. The night was far enough away to allow time to satisfy our senses, to gain strength, a time for some luxury even if that contrasted to our perennial state of need.

The rules are stated clearly for Pen Mar Park. That being that overnight camping was not allowed or that the pavilions were not for that intent. It was doubtful that any of us would pursue that route anyway. Common knowledge was that a hiker using the facilities for other than intended use could be fined. The younger hikers may have been willing to take that chance, but this hiker packed it up and headed for the Mason-Dixon Line. At least I wouldn't have to cook tonight and just concentrate on staying as dry as possible.

# Chapter 25

## Ice Cream

*June 24—Day 81—Mile 1103 (near halfway point—Pine Grove Furnace State Park, Pennsylvania—(Journal entry)—to camp store by 8:00 a.m. (doesn't open till nine), wrote in register—talked with Wanderer—got ice cream about 9:10 a.m. (took an hour to eat)*

*August 19—Day 137—Mile 1856 (Journal entry)—I am living on Snickers!*

Food. The essence of the hike! Necessary as the fuel to get you going and keep you going. Important, but also a source of varying views and controversy. An area that, if allowed to, can be the nemesis to the thru-hiker.

Keep it simple, or the old mantra: KISS. Food should be thought of on a thru-hike as simply nutrition. To attempt to mix the complexities of a thru-hike with too many other elements presents a conflict of interest; gourmet cooking is fine in other places but not necessary and thru-hiking is about necessities. The priority here is thru-hiking, and if food becomes too much of a burden, it can only complicate the main issues. If thru-hiking is the purpose for being here then priorities have to be established and listed somewhat like this: (1) the hike and the mileage factor have to be addressed each day and activities that divert from that one thing can only be counterproductive, (2) water sources—do not underestimate its importance for dehydration looms much too close—should be known

163

ahead of time and some planning needs to be spent each day, and (3) shelter—tenting for me about 90 percent of the time, and finally, food fits in there somewhere but not so that its importance would be out of perspective.

Food, of course, is uppermost in the hiker's mind. It just does not go away. However, it should not become the obsession, the excuse, the reason, the panacea. It will command a great deal of your time as it does in normal life. However, it just simply cannot be allowed to usurp the primary goals with frivolous urges or allowed to be the red herring. Hunger is such a pervasive factor while thru-hiking, to succumb to it, one has to always remember not to allow a rampant sort of lust to prevail. To stay in control. Hiking is first and should remain paramount.

The physical hunger for food on the Trail cannot be explained. And now at this writing, after being off the trail for a year, it is even more difficult to remember and has resulted ultimately in a changing of eating habits. As oxymoronic as it may sound, the sensation of hunger can truly be enjoyed on the Trail. The hunger that we feel in our day-to-day world is not really hunger. It is merely diversion from other activities and is more habit than a true need for food. A look into the eons of the history of man back when we were hunters and gatherers imply that this business of "three square meals a day" is something devised for modern man and is not truly physical needs as much as physical wants, whims of fancy as we wander through the cornucopia of assorted delights that are available to us anytime.

Hunger on the Trail somewhat pleasantly takes us back those eons and is a hunger that cannot ever resemble any hunger that you have ever experienced before. Everything tasted good to me. Everything! I threw nothing away. I dove into food boxes of unwanted items at the various places along the Trail, and it just did not make any difference. It all looked good and tasted good. One particular homemade variety of trail mix—or to the hiker, *gorp* (acronym: *granola, oatmeal, raisins, peanuts*)—taken from a food box seemed to be primarily dried bananas. The first bite seemed like heaven, and it wasn't long before it was gone as it just simply pulled at me until it was entirely consumed.

I lived on noodles. The carbohydrates are a necessity, and pasta is easy to prepare and is nourishing and, most importantly, filling. Prepackaged noodle meals come in a variety of flavors if one so desires, but that was never a factor. I mixed them all up and really got to the point where I didn't know what I was eating. It always tasted good. Amazingly good. It was mind-boggling at times to think that what I had eaten just twenty-four hours earlier could again taste so good and be so satisfying. This proved to be true day after day.

Probably manifestation of being able to eat anything presented itself most clearly at my first Appalachian Mountain Club hut in the White Mountains, Lonesome Lake Hut. The AMC policy is to try to provide "day food" (most of the time) of some sort for thru-hikers at the huts. I arrived there just before noon. Displaying good manners, I took off my boots and entered the pristine cleanliness and, in a state of awe, surveyed the surroundings. The pineapple pizza in a tray on the table beckoned strongly, with a sign that said seventy-five cents a piece. Five pieces later had done nothing to abate my ravenousness. The day cook was very understanding and said that there would be no charge and seemed adamant, so I put my money back in my fanny pack. He probably could see the all-too-visible physical hunger and most certainly could see my emaciated body. However, it seemed only right to leave some for other thru-hikers that would be coming through. So having already had more than my share, I finally dragged myself away from the pizza.

I was about to leave when another source of nutrition presented itself, a large bowl of not quite describable "stuff." It took a little time to determine that it was oatmeal. Cold. Lumpy. Dry at the edges. At best, a coagulated gruel! Probably prepared in the early-morning hours when the prima-donnas were just getting up and ready for the fare of the day, partaking of it in its original satisfying form, hot and refreshing and creamy. It had long lost those qualities. It represented food that probably nobody else would want. And quite frankly, even at home, I am the alternative to the garbage disposal. I dug in and finally just had to drag myself away, more from embarrassment than courtesy.

It was delicious! I thought later, however, that I had taken my "waste not, want not" philosophy a little too far. A perspective gained later at home was that the "stuff" could not have been choked down surrounded by amenities and wants. A rare contrast that our society never gets exposed to for real hunger cannot be truly appreciated. The Trail manages to transform almost any food to gourmet class just simply out of need.

Another time, I found a large plastic food storage bag full of a generic variety of trail mix. The bag was lying on the Trail, having apparently somehow fallen out of a pack. The mix was of the homemade variety. It only lasted until the next morning when it was the breakfast supplement to the normal pittance. The thought did occur that the owner should be found. However, that possibility seemed rather remote as it was doubtful a hiker would backtrack for something that was lost and the chances of catching the hiker to whom it belonged also was probably not going to happen. For me it seemed odd to lose food for I guarded mine covetously and probably could have accounted for every ounce that was in my pack at any one time throughout the hike. Every food item that was sent out in the food drop boxes, every food item that was purchased along the Trail, and any that could be added from donor boxes placed strategically in post offices and other public buildings along the Trail—all was eventually consumed. If there was an excess, that was just considered supplement to whatever had been allotted depending on how the logistics worked out for any particular section. Nothing was thrown away.

The diet should be as varied as possible for the demands of the Trail. This is a precept that I live by anyway, trail or not. It is just common sense that we humans, with our complex bodies, need limitless variety in our food, all food groups, and as many different natural colors as possible. So in towns, I tried to cover those areas that would otherwise be difficult to carry or supply, such as fresh fruits and vegetables and, of course, meats. Usually my only actual meat or meat product on the Trail was beef jerky. There were times when I craved beef jerky and would just have to stop and satisfy that need. Yet another canon of the Trail, listen to your body.

Breakfast was usually granola bars or pop tarts; some dried fruit such as plums, apricots, apples, cherries; and coffee. Always coffee as the pick-me-up, the only form of pain reliever in my pack and, also, the one very true form of morning pleasure that was so looked forward to and never missed except for those rare mornings when boiling water was just simply impractical or inconvenient or there was a shortage of water. Most of these foods were prepackaged and all my food drop boxes contained at least six bags of each and most were purchased at Wal-Mart prior to the start of the hike. All tasty and easy to carry. Foods that require special handling just do not belong in a backpack. Also for breakfast, a spoonful or two of peanut butter and, sometimes when there was enough between resupply, a Snickers bar.

Lunch usually amounted to little snacks of granola, dried fruit, and Snickers through the day except for those days when extreme hunger could not be ignored; and that usually meant stops with a mix of whatever was available, usually always beef jerky and, at times when supply warranted it, a can of sardines. The body has ways of letting you know that there is a need.

Supper was always either ramen or packaged noodle meals. These only took minutes to prepare; and depending on the amount of water added, sometimes I treated whatever the choice was for the night as soup, other times a hot dish. And usually this was accompanied with beef jerky, and a lot of times, oatmeal was considered desert. And throw in a Snickers and whatever there was enough of, that was it. And occasionally a can of sardines or something similar.

Not too much was changed from the eating habits from "civilian life." One of those being the ever-present daily multivitamin supplement. It is not the intent of this writing to espouse on the virtues or detriments of taking vitamins or whether they are needed or not. My personal feelings are that if, indeed, my body throws off unneeded vitamins then at least my body had access to such and could decide if my chemistry was lacking in that area. It seems to work for me, and my general health has always been quite good. It should be noted for those "older hikers" (above fifty or so), and pertaining more specifically to men is to be careful to not get too much iron. Multiple vitamins also come in a variety designed for the geriatric set that comes with little to no iron, the kind that I have been on for about six years now. However, for some unknown reason since the hike, I have had to go back to the iron supplement for when giving blood, my iron count has been down into the elevens.

Of course, the beauty of all of this more or less self-imposed abstinence from food while actually hiking easily justifies the food binges when hitting towns and at strategically placed restaurants. A well-placed cafe just did not usually get passed by a thru-hiker—within a mile or so from the Trail was certainly considered proximity. One usually has to be careful for some of these are rather pricey. Information about nearby restaurants was always available from other hikers. For the most part, the ones encountered were quite affordable.

Restaurants, and more specifically buffets, allowed one the opportunity to fill the gaps that trail food just simply could not fill. I went through the buffet lines, usually taking one of everything even if not a whole lot of one particular item. Again paying attention to colors, my plates were a kaleidoscope with representation throughout the spectrum. However, the favorites were always visited and revisited in a vain effort to subdue the craving.

Junk food! Yes, pancakes do have eggs and flour made from wheat but otherwise are on the junk food side of diets. I craved pancakes. Everyday visions of pancakes danced in my head. Golden. Succulent. Moist yet crisp. Buffalo Bobby, in a moment of culinary delightful zaniness, performed an embellished description of the hotcakes that he had for breakfast at a place that I had chosen to not stop at for whatever reason. His description stayed with me for more or less the duration of the hike and spurred me on to more mileage as the incentive of pancakes in town provided impetus, much-beyond physical and endurance capabilities.

Probably the most satisfying aspect of the food binges were that as you partook, you could smugly look around at those that had driven up in the family SUV that had lumbered to the food trough, obviously more for want than need. You, however, have more than burned up your share of calories and are there for the base purpose of nourishing your body. With this knowledge, you are armed with feelings of superiority, knowing that you didn't have to worry about such things as overeating; an oxymoronic condition that does not exist on the Trail. You cannot overeat, and that is a line of reasoning that is worthy of much discussion and provides insight into a side of life never before experienced.

In your role of an inferior person, one without transportation other than your legs and with all of life's possessions sitting in the pack leaning on the wall outside, suddenly you find yourself on the caste ladder quite a few rungs lower than anybody else. However, the caste system of the Trail at meal times reverses roles, for food holds a position in society not usually so revealing; and suddenly you become an ultrasuperior being. A person with the barest of possessions in a materialistic world, a substandard rung on the social ladder, and you can only be envied if the truth be known. Just simply too sweet. Just simply too satisfying. An experience that can only be brought about by a long period of self-denial and sacrifice.

Then there is ice cream.

Just the words *ice cream* conjure visions of the oasis. Of indulgence. Of overindulgence. With ice cream, thru-hiking opened an entire new arena and a new life for me. Seven times during the hike, I feasted on an entire half gallon of ice cream at a sitting. And that took on art form as time went on. Eating an entire half gallon of ice cream requires a certain amount of preparation and technique. Not for the neophyte to just jump in, thinking that there weren't skills involved in this act. There should probably be instructions on the carton, Do Not Try This at Home, with an illustration of one consuming the whole thing.

Justification just always existed. Standard operating procedure. A hiker probably walked farther yesterday than the average person walked last month, or two months. Quite to the contrary, the calories burned in the previous week would probably leave you open for a half gallon a night for about a month. What a joy knowing that this indulgence came free of guilt, free of encumbrances. Just a spoon was all that was needed.

I thought of the Pine Grove Furnace State Park tradition many times and wondered if I could even eat a half gallon of ice cream at a sitting. A certain sense of mischievous trepidation set in, and I wanted to "perform" well when the time came for I knew that there would be others there embarking on the same course.

As with anything that I have ever done in my life, I had to "train" for it. Waynesboro, Virginia, seemed like the right place. I had a very comfortable motel room, and it had been raining constantly prior to getting there, and the sacrifices by this juncture had been too much. I hated looking at myself in the mirror and avoided that about as much as looking close at those large maps of the Appalachian Trail posted in stores and public buildings. I looked like a concentration camp refugee, an emaciated reprobate, drawn and tired and broken. It was time to overindulge.

After checking out the Laundromat next door, I walked into the discount-food supermarket. A few other items made it into the little basket; a thru-hiker avoids shopping carts like the plague, the main goal being that half gallon of ice cream. I selected butter pecan out of the rather-sparse selection of flavors, thinking that would retain its virtue throughout this culinary marathon.

"How are you going to keep that cold?"

The voice was somewhat familiar, but as is the habit of the Trail, one just usually does not look around for somebody that you know. However, the face was familiar. She had stood in line with me at the post office, and as is usual, I talked to everybody on or near the Trail. Partially for information but mainly to be able to share my great adventure with others. She thought I was buying trail food!

"I'm not. I going back to my motel room and eating this entire thing."

We laughed, and she provided more comment and said that she wished that she could be so frivolous in her eating. I told her all she had to do was hit the Trail and she could eat all that she wanted, knowing that for women, this did not quite hold to be as true as for men. Life is so ironically unfair so much of the time.

I scurried back to my room in a delightful romp, anticipating this gluttonous excursion into this newly assumed world of hedonism. When else could one justify with such reckless abandon?

The actual eating was somewhat anticlimatic. The entire half gallon went down with ease. I even opened up the carton and licked the creamy residue clean that usually makes its way into the trash can. The thought of more did enter my mind.

I dispelled that notion and, instead, called my cousin George, a man that had served as my surrogate father in my fatherless childhood, a man that I deeply respected and loved. He had been mentor and disciplinarian, motivator and nemesis, and he had taught me about responsibility. He loved the story. He said that I should keep him up-to-date on the progress of the hike. He told me about the weather in Grand Rapids, Minnesota; and I related my adventures so far and his wife, Vi, also added comments. I hung up, glowing as if life could never have been better. And it had never been better.

The next day, my tongue felt odd. It didn't take long to realize that it had probably suffered a mild form of frostbite. Yes, I suppose a tongue is also vulnerable to frostbite!

An entire chapter should be dedicated to Snickers. However, redundancy already is too evident in this chapter on food, so we shall only touch on this most sacred of trail food. Usually it was the first item to hit the bottom of the supermarket shopping basket. The term *food* is applied somewhat facetiously, however, maybe somewhat in the same manner as Bill Cosby justifies having chocolate cake for breakfast when he found himself in charge of his children one morning can be applied here. Disregarding allergies, peanuts are nutritious. And there is milk in the chocolate. And dextrose is a vital ingredient for the brutal displays of energy that are taking place. No, it doesn't take too much imagination to defend the virtues of the Snickers bar. It is doubtful that too many packs along the Trail were absent of such.

Probably the largest disappointment in the posthike is that there is simply no way to reenact the pleasures of the true Trail Snickers break. The ambiance that can only exist under certain conditions has to precede the event to garner meaning, to experience *that* taste, to bask within *that* feeling. There is no way to recreate that scene artificially. That can only happen after a body has expended thousands of calories, has struggled up numerous mountains in succession, only after hunger has went to the next two to three levels, only when the mind knows that one bar is the only one available. The Snickers break off the Trail is to pardon the expression like kissing your sister, a lesson in futility.

Maybe eating to excess is a form of abuse, but let's face it, the entire concept of a thru-hike is abuse in the purest of forms. The body and mind are subjected to conditions never before encountered. The body is forced to respond to demands never made upon it. Like the lady having a diet soda with her burger and fries, there are oxymoronic circumstances evident, and to try to lend sanity to an insane situation only further complicates something already too much so.

So food on the Trail is merely a means to an end. A time when one is virtually free to do as one feels. That may not hold true to a lot of the women that were encountered on the Trail. Metabolism sometimes can be cruel. Men cruised while losing weight without trying and eating anything and everything that they could get their hands on while some of the women actually gained weight as their bodies transformed to muscle.

It should be added that natural foods do exist along the Trail, sometimes in abundance as is the case with blueberries that I ate from near Lehigh Gap, Pennsylvania, all the way to Maine. The blueberries are small but very tasty. I rarely passed the opportunity to grab a handful. Ramps, those wonderful high-altitude onions, were available for a short time in North Carolina and Tennessee and were wonderful. A lot of the hikers cooked them into their noodle or rice dishes. I ate mine like green onions, and what a complement these were to noodles or whatever hot was being cooked. Raspberries abounded in New Hampshire and Maine and, like with the blueberries, made a nice break in hiking and also provided incentive, thinking that they were just going to get better farther up the Trail. I managed to eat something natural for almost the entire length of the Trail, ranging from the scrumptious mulberries in Pennsylvania that were quite plentiful along the Trail north of Boiling Springs, wild apples in Vermont to pin cherries in New Hampshire.

I stayed away from the mushrooms with a lot of consternation. I just could not make positive identifications, and the consequences just were not worth it. Wild mushrooms under normal conditions are sometimes a gamble. Along the Trail should a hiker choose carelessly, the repercussions would just be too complex. Maybe even fatal. One is out on the limb with too many factors in a thru-hike to take chances unnecessarily.

Food was never allowed to become a factor or interfere with the original plan of keeping it simple. However, the more I tried to separate myself from complication, the more food, indeed, did become a factor. It is difficult to maintain food properly, in other words, to have enough without having too much. Food is the obsession with thru-hikers. For the most part for me, food was the inspiration, the dangling carrot to keep going, the reward for completing a section or a day. And early on, it was determined that too much food was always better than not enough for the promise of rewards were the very thing that kept me going.

But most importantly, concerning food, my thoughts went back to the epitome, my absolute favorite thoughts of food, that wonderful cook—my Mom.

Lehigh Gap, PA
Bridge over Lehigh River
July 4—mile 1245 (about)

# Chapter 26

## Mom

*June 26—Day 83—Mile 1129—(Journal entry)—loved the farmland hiking! took many photos—crossed the Pennsylvania Turnpike and I-81 (crossed nineteen roads today)*

"Now, don't go walking down by the Red River."

My visits to Fargo would eventually precipitate this comment from Mom after telling her that I was going out. My nightly walks usually took me this same route; and she usually would go through the same list of reasons not to walk down by the river, including a graphic description of all of the culprits, weirdoes, and reprobates that hung out there. And blacks, for Mom never did trust Afro-Americans. In Fargo, North Dakota, there hardly were any blacks until about 1975. There was one black man living in Fargo when I was a kid, and he was friendly and harmless, nonetheless a curiosity. Mom just never did understand that. But she had few faults, so maybe that one was okay.

Where Mom had formulated such ideas that this wonderful place along the river was merely an attraction for social outcasts can only be assumed as an association of "rivers" as simply being bad places. Mom never could swim and was deathly afraid of water. It was amazing that my brother and I would have ever grown up without the same fears. However, we both took to water like a fish, and Mom's paranoia just could not influence us otherwise.

Of course, most nights, the Red River is exactly where I headed. Not in hopes of finding some of these misfits of society but because it was a peaceful nature walk resplendent with those things that attract one to such places. For along this large stream that flowed north to Canada and formed the borderline between North Dakota and Minnesota comprised about the only semblance of wilderness in this wide valley of rich agriculture. The sparrows and robins and meadowlarks sang and squirrels catapulted back and forth, rabbits scurried about in the thick weeds and grass that grew lush here, and the good earth reeked of the smells that reminded one of soil and life and goodness.

I had hiked many miles on my great adventure before it occurred to me that the hiking of the Appalachian Trail could not have taken place until after my Mom was no longer with us. Albeit she probably watched the whole thing for to this day, I strongly believe that she is now in an angelic form flitting about on gilded wings, receiving the rewards that she so deserved. She had made do with so little while here on earth that if, indeed, we are to believe what we hear about the hereafter, she is regaling in her now-angelic being as a queen. Truly the meek should garner the rewards of the hereafter. However, in Mom's case, she was anything but meek, actually quite to the contrary.

This story cannot be complete without telling about Mom for she was a rare person, one that could only be described as a character and full of goodness albeit full of a contradictory orneriness. If the earth were full of Moms, there would be an excess of everything for she rarely threw anything away. Wasting anything ran contrary to the fiber of her being. My early influences from this woman left a mark for wasting things just never has sat well on my conscience. The influences of the little woman have now made it to the third generation for my kids, now full-grown adults also seem to be rather conservative.

There are some minuscule similarities in comparing hiking the AT to walking along the Red River. Most importantly, those walks were subtly creating a desire to do this on a grander scale. And the love of nature fueled by exposure here formed the base of wanting to see a lot of it. Just another one of the formative activities leading to such an undertaking.

With her propensity for worry, had Mom known about my hiking the AT, she may not have been with us even as long as she was. For the trepidation she experienced over my thirty-minute strolls along the riverbanks of this minor stream could hardly compare with a five-month expedition, with exposures not only to bad people but all manner of creatures, weather, and the rigors of exhaustion and overdoing. She could not have comprehended it, the reasons for it, and it would have been a lesson in futility to have tried.

Through the years, I managed to write or call her at least once a week, especially through my adult life. Part of that regimen was just respect and love for her, but probably most of it was that she demanded it. To go too long between these missives was to be flirting with a good tongue-lashing, and usually being a thousand miles away did not reduce the sting. So sneaking around to have accomplished the hiking of the AT would just not have been possible. She would have known anyway being the Mom that she was and being strongly intuitive as mothers have been since the beginning of time.

She would not have approved, an understatement of massive proportions. She could not have even envisioned her baby boy sleeping on the ground with only 4.3 pounds of nylon being the barrier between her progeny and all of the dangers of the wild lurking outside. Though Mom was not afraid of too many things (other than water and swimming) and could never be mistaken for some frail being that was paranoid or scared of things, she at times did not appear to be afraid of anything. However, where her son was concerned, her motherly instincts and imagination followed a much-different path.

Mom had done some walking of her own in her day but usually for short distances at a time. In her entire life, she never owned a car. It is possible that she never drove a car but probably drove the old Ford back on the farm before we moved to Fargo. However, she always managed to get to work or shopping, and most of the time that was accomplished with her two strong legs that took her where she needed to go. She rarely walked for recreation but did occasionally take a stroll for that purpose. Even after she turned eighty, she would still take her metal pull cart and haul her groceries home. One day while standing in her front yard and looking down South Fourteenth Street I was saddened to see something that I had never seen before. She had stopped to rest. It was the first time that I had ever witnessed such a thing, and it caused a stir of sadness.

Considering that Fargo is a fairly large city (by Midwestern standards), it could be reasonably estimated that she walked quite a few thousand miles herself. She never complained about walking, apparently enjoying it more than considering it a chore. One of the idiosyncrasies and one that was so endearing was her description of the joy that she derived from "walking on squeaky snow." Something that only true Northerners could know anything about. Very hard-packed snow, not to be confused with ice, under very cold conditions definitely does have a squeak to it when walked on. So on those nights when the temperatures dipped to the minus-thirty-below mark, Mom would be out there enjoying what maybe lesser persons would not have noticed and certainly could not have considered a source of joy. There is a lot to be said for finding such happiness in such a simple divergence. Not only butterflies are free to enjoy in nature. A precept that Mom maintained throughout life.

Mom left Dad in 1949. I'll never know just what happened, but my father did have a mean streak and made some pretty evil threats at times. Mom had put up with it for a number of years, for their early days were quite happy. One day she had enough. We made our flight in the dead of a bitterly cold night and headed for Canada. To Baba's house which was only about 5 miles away in Southern Manitoba, where we took refuge until arrangements could be made to take the train to Fargo and our new home. The ride on the Dingy, a very short train that was all passengers and no cargo, was imprinted on my young and impressionable mind.

In Fargo as was the usual custom when Canadian relatives moved to this mecca for lost and exiled members of the Badiuk family, we stayed with aunts. It is hard to explain why the uncles never got any credit when it came to these arrangements, one being that the uncles never seemed to live too long. So Aunt Wasylka's became home. This 1537 Ninth Avenue South address would be called home for about two years. I was nine years old, and it seemed like paradise. Indoor plumbing seemed like a luxury that only the super rich could afford. Life was good.

However, the sisters were all of the same iron will and determination, and when Aunt Wasylka threatened to move "out by the river" in West Fargo to live, Mom and her parted ways and we moved in with Aunt Cookie. Her name was actually Helen; however, that had long been forgotten with her zeal for baking as she always had a jar full of the things and always offered one upon coming through her always-open door. So to Second Avenue we moved, and that was home for me until moving from there when leaving town for the start of my career with the U.S. Geological Survey in 1959.

Mom probably never made over $5,000 in a year. It amazed me that somehow from her miserly wages, she somehow could set money aside and made her way to Fargo National Bank with every paycheck; and a percentage of almost nothing was set aside, her "nest egg." She was slowly buying a house the way that it was supposed to be done. Then one day, she had the downpayment and took the plunge that would make her a home owner. The bank did not hesitate with the mortgage, and she never missed a payment.

A number of years later, knowing that retirement was ensuing and that with Social Security being what it was, I took it upon myself to pay the house off. So with my wife, Kris, we walked into the Fargo National Bank and paid it off and brought the paperwork home to show her. She was confused, but mostly hurt. She just could not have totally realized that when she retired, there just would not be enough money for the mortgage payments. She was angry and called me a son-of-a-bitch, ironically a name that was well suited for the particular situation.

Mom retired and lived a miserly life on her $345-a-month Social Security check. This in spite of having worked for forty years tending to the needs and desires of the well-to-do that could afford maid service and a nanny for their progeny. Those that made a lot of money but didn't want to share too much of it as Mom's earnings did not quite measure up to their lauding of her and comments about her irreplaceable services. The compensation that my Mom received for her services was just enough to keep her in their employ, manifesting the ways of life of the "haves" and "have-nots" that is too sacrosanct to question. However, she never complained and just absolutely refused assistance. She lived her simple life, and the black earth of the Red River valley provided her a garden replete with vegetables that were the mainstay of her diet. There are many photos in the albums of Mom standing in her garden.

However, with the stress of making it on too little and with the stubbornness of her heredity, she finally succumbed to high blood pressure and failing kidneys and the ensuing strokes that came with it. Her frail little body finally gave out in 1998. The wee hours of February 1, 1998, to be exact. She somehow willed her way into the next month, and with that, the government had to send her one more of those three-hundred-and-forty-five-dollar Social Security checks. We'll never know, but I have to surmise that she did what she could do to help pay for the funeral expenses.

With Mom's passing, an era ended that can never be replaced. However, her spirit is here forever. I took it with me on the Appalachian Trail. She was there when I was too hungry. She was there when I was sad and lonely. She was there when I just knew that making it to the top of the next mountaintop was impossible; and she assured me that, indeed, it was possible. For in spite of her disapproval of what I was doing, she was not going to allow me to fail. For her, failure was never an option.

# Chapter 27

## Time to Think

*July 1—Day 88—Mile 1207—(Journal entry)—flimsy bear branch (bent under weight) just one toss though*

The frame of mind that eventually absorbs a long-distance hiker borders on reminiscence and introspection and a sense of peace. The sameness of so much of the Trail provides an abundance of time to think. Some of that time is taken up with planning the day; playing and replaying the logistics—where to stop, where to camp, available food supply and the next stop, number of miles—and the constant monitoring of the weather. At times, logistics becomes rather an obsession. With too much time to weigh the alternatives, every conceivable option is considered to a point where conclusions are hard to resolve. A mental round-robin eventually ensues in a rote manner that almost match the footsteps.

Then one day, your mind is just tired of doing logistics. Then you start composing great speeches. It is absolutely positive at some point in this excursion that you are going to thru-hike the Trail. And with that accomplishment, you would become a sort of anomaly, at least in your town or social group. So you will be in constant demand to talk to groups of people, whether it is esoteric hikers or church groups, or others that have a casual interest, or more accurately, a curiosity about why somebody would go to so much trouble to walk such a great distance.

So you rehearse.

"Hi, I'm Old Smoky Lonesome, and I thru-hiked the Appalachian Trail. [Pause for emphasis.] One day at the book store while wandering through the travel section some backpacking books caught my eye. And soon I was heading home with my choice selections and dove into the reading to find the subject much too fascinating. A wanderlust soon set in. Soon you are gazing into space . . . wondering . . . Soon you are at the outfitters. Then suddenly for some reason unknown to you at the time, you have purchased a backpacking tent. Then other books. More gear. And this gear is not of the sort that really could be used for anything except backpacking. Soon you are telling people what you are going to do. And before you know it, you have made commitments that will be hard to back out of . . ."

And so on. Great, wonderful speeches followed with tumultuous applause. Oh, this heady hero stuff is so good for the soul; but most importantly, it makes the adrenaline flow so nicely, and soon you have made 5 miles without hardly a thought about discomfort or hunger. So much better than logistics that usually leaves the hiker somewhat pensive.

However, soon your mind gets tired of composing great speeches. Then you turn to inventions. Great inventions by somebody that has been there, has done that. One that recognizes a need firsthand so has ideas for making the hiker's world maybe just a little easier. My list sort of replayed with a honing sort of process, constant little changes to improve the invention.

The first of significance was the bear branch launcher. Getting that cord over the tree branch presents problems that are not evident to the neophyte. The book says the food bag has to be ten feet away from the trunk and ten feet above the ground to insure that bear claws couldn't reach it. However, that appropriate branch is usually located in such a way that you are surrounded by low brush and obstacles, and it is difficult to get a good clear throw. It just didn't matter if the line was thrown underhand or overhand or some mutant combination of the two, stuff was just in the way.

Now, if a person could devise a sort of catapult that would take the weighted end over the branch and gravity would bring it over and down. The launcher would have to be light and portable, the same as all camping gear. Now, if it could be incorporated into other uses, it could be multiple-use, for that is the way long-distance hikers have to think. It is the height of irony that you have carefully selected gear and have culled things out of the backpack, and now you are going to add a bear branch launcher?! Logical thinking always boiled it down to a spring-powered gun sort of device. Probably similar to a toy dart gun that had a trigger and the "dart" has some sort of end that the weighted end of the bear line could be attached to. Point and aim, and effortlessly, the line would be up and over the branch ready for tying the food bag.

My mind toyed with this device over and over, but that image never totally materialized. So many miles were covered while trying to perfect such a device, knowing that there was a need and maybe possibly even a demand as other hikers would love to have one. Then various cute little names, the ever-important marketing tool, would come to mind: Bear-Bagger, Hi-Shot, Camp-A-Pault, and so on. Corny, yes, the type of mental food that evolves from too much time on one's hands and too much time to think.

The Therm-a-Rest for me provided more food for thought and diversion while hiking. Inside the tent, I was too tall to sleep parallel to the long wall. There just was not enough length. So the Therm-a-Rest was set diagonal, placing the head end as close as possible to the corner of the tent. However, this made for a triangle that was always difficult to fill with something to keep my head on top of the end of the mattress. It seemed logical that the answer would be a fold-out triangular corner to the end of the Therm-a-Rest that would snug up against the corner of the tent and avoid all of this shifting and filling in. A triangle seemed logical going through the virtues of this design while hiking and making mental improvements.

Then there was the problematic ground cloth. It was never determined whether it did any good, conversely actually seeming to hold water between the tent and the ground that eventually would seep inside the tent. My mind toyed with various ways of folding up the corners so that water would go under the ground cloth. However, nothing ever worked.

Eventually the ground cloth was abandoned. However, not as much that it didn't work for it always provided a sort of mental coziness. It was so satisfying to lay the ground cloth flat on those rare dry nights and so neatly arrange the tent cleanly on top. It was yet another one of those magical and cheap additions to the camping equipment, a purchase at Wal-Mart for a mere four dollars. It was light and just seemed like a necessary item and could be used for other purposes.

However, when the serious business of the White Mountains, the Mahoosucs, and Maine set in and additional clothes were again needed as a safeguard, the ground cloth just simply did not fit into the plan. Some things had to be eliminated. The ground cloth found its way via the postal service back to Florida. And as is the mantra for long-distance hiking, one wonders just what one does need for the ground cloth was never really missed. And it seemed that the tent stayed drier inside on those long, wet nights. So innovations for how to better set the ground cloth to avoid water getting on top of it proved to be rather moot. It is doubtful that this hiker will ever use one again.

Some of the "inventions" bordered on the bizarre. One that kept creeping back into the psyche was something akin to a golf cart for those days when the pack just seemed like such a burden strapped to your back. On those days when that toothache in the left shoulder would not go away and no adjusting of the pack could alleviate it. It was conceivable that a golf cart device would work. However, there are times when it would be better out of the way and then where do you keep it? Anything that weighs anything that is not useful most of the time has to simply be eliminated. Of course, in places like the White Mountains and Mahoosucs, there is just no way to roll anything up, over or down the huge boulders. However, on those relatively level stretches, the thought of getting the pack off your back and just simply pull it behind you seemed so inviting. A mental contrivance at best to allow some relief from having that pack strapped there day after day.

Other bizarre gadgets came to mind as different situations arose. Boulders of the North were catalyst for thoughts of innovation. While going downhill when one was reaching for purchase on slick rocks, it often occurred that you were close to repelling, but minus a rope. How nice it would be to have some sort of hook on a rope with a built-in release. There were numerous times, especially in the Whites and Mahoosucs, when it was downright scary to descend by merely sliding down the cascade of boulders, wondering if you were going to stop where there was a foothold. A tether of some sort would be helpful. Again, with so many of these frivolous devices, there were drawbacks. You would probably have to climb back up to unhook it from a rock or tree, ending up in a sort of Chinese fire drill.

Of course there is always time to wonder how Mr. Shaffer did it. And the thought always replayed, "How did you do it without Ziplocks, Earl?" For it seemed that eventually, everything was encased in plastic. Also, his rucksack must have weighed about seventy-five pounds! There weren't too many choices for backpacking equipment in those days when he is inventing the need by doing it. He became the necessity for the mother of invention. GoreTex and nylon fabrics and backpacking stoves were eventually waiting in the wings as a result of his efforts. Earl was with me in spirit throughout. In awe for the most part for the largest conquest is the one over doubt; and for him, there had been no precedent, no how-to books. Earl Shaffer was the ultimate role model, and he did it in the manner that it was supposed to be done; pure, simple, and pristine.

So the hiking went on, and the speeches and inventions and logistics were worked and reworked. That part was fun. After inventions, I went through a time period simply referred to as redesigning my backyard time. A wonderful microcosm of the Appalachian Trail was created right there in my own world on Thirty-fourth Street. Complete with white blazes and double blazes at turns. However, since the yard is small, it was hard to devise a way of having a blue blazer to the bathroom or refrigerator without making the place look like an extravagant display of one that had bought some paint on sale. And now in actuality, it is comprised of a few white blazes that take you through the gate and into the backyard and then around the back of the pool and then to the east side before going north around the other side of the pool.

However, it provides that much-needed déjà vu. I take my little thirty-second "hike" and muse and wonder and feel good inside, especially knowing that a comfortable bed and a full refrigerator loaded with a freezer of ice cream are very close at hand.

# Chapter 28

## Showers

*April 8—Day 4—Mile 49 (Journal entry)—bought $43.90 worth of stuff (including $3.50 for shower, $3.95 for carabiner, and $15 for rope)—the shower was awesome!*

At home, the shower just sits there. Not really noticed, taken for granted, nothing special. Jump in and get wet and suds down, shampoo the hair and out you go. Who doesn't have a shower in their home? Through a marvel of relatively recent modern technology, it has become such a mainstay it is like the old faithful dog, always there when you need it. Usually at least once a day, a pleasant little visit with not too much thought about the process. Maybe twice a day. A refuge at times from the tension of life in our too-busy lives, in the morning the wondrous pick-me-up. However, even though relied on for a lot, still taken for granted.

Until you hit the Trail!

Try to remember one shower that you took at home?! Go ahead, tell me about your favorite shower: time, date, particulars. Did you wash your hair and moisturize it? Did you luxuriate, or was it a quickie? One would be hard-pressed to come up with specific details. No, these home showers are nondescript. Unless, of course, somebody joined you and the shower became somewhat incidental to other things.

In 163 days of thru-hiking, I can remember every trail shower. There were only thirty-seven in that entire five months. Boils down to about one in every four and a half days. Try that sometime in civilian life and still say that you have friends and a spouse, people of significance in your life, that like being with you. It takes me back to childhood in some ways where a bath was considered a luxury, something we probably only did about once a week.

It took awhile to develop the skill to take a trail shower. Some, of course, were taken in normal places such as motel rooms and not too much different from the home. However, the Appalachian Trail means that not too much is normal when compared with everyday life and usually not convenient. The one at Neels Gap just four days out on the Trail will always be remembered even if brief and utilitarian, an introduction to the process. Trail showers usually required some innovation. At home, the towel and soap and other bathroom amenities are about in the same place all the time. Not true on the Trail. And to compound the problem, there is a need to do this quickly for usually other grungy hikers are waiting to use the same shower. Some of the showers are on coin-operated timers, and that is always a challenge. Stick in the money, wet down, lather, lather. Stick in some more money, rinse, rinse. Quickly. None of the ole-fifteen-minutes-under-the-hot-water luxury of home. Succinct showers. Bare bones stuff.

Until you get to the motel. Then it is just the opposite for there is some serious trail grunge to remove. It took about the third motel to realize that the stand-up shower just was not the answer. Eventually standard procedure became to fill up the bathtub, hoping that you have one and not just the shower-stall type. With a bathtub full, the process of removing layers of dirt was possible. It usually took about an hour—soaking, scrubbing, a changing of the water, or just finishing up with a good shower as the final rinsing process.

Some of the showers were unique. Maybe not even totally sanitary and safe, but usually that was not a concern on the Trail. The one in Glencliff, New Hampshire, at the Hikers Welcome Hostel was ingenious. There was no drain! Just the ground. The ground eventually became saturated, and the soaking-in process took just a little while. So a lot of water, mixed with a ground fodder, made up mostly of wood chips, at least kept your feet out of the mud. Of course, the drain fodder ended up stuck to the bottom of your feet; and while toweling off and dressing, some of it ended up inside your underwear.

It was hard to reenact trail showers after getting home. The luxury despite the conditions of the shower always held a certain mystique and aura, and that just could not be duplicated at home. It is amazing how quickly we humans become accustomed to luxuries. So much of what we have is expected after a while. The Trail brings one back to a reality that we have long since forgotten.

The Trail model that took the prize for most innovative was outdoors. It is located at the Denton Shelter, very close to Linden in Northern Virginia. The shelter is state-of-the-art, complete with a deck and a nearby cooking pavilion. The shower is located down a nearby blue blaze trail, a pleasant stroll to the spring, and is housed on three sides, giving somewhat of a sense of privacy. The spring provides the cold, very cold, water to a unique valve that supplies the reservoir for the shower water supply. Unless one has a capacity to adapt to the temperature, the shower here is quite brief. However, that briskness not only removes trail grunge for the exhilaration of the frigid spring water also revives the soul. There was an added zest while eating the evening noodles after this invigorating cleansing.

The Ritz-Carlton could not have topped it.

Basic trail amenity
New Jersey

# Chapter 29

## Humble Pie

Boardwalk—Proximity of Pochuck Creek—day 99
July 12—mile 1350 (about)

*July 12—Day 99—Mile 1364—(Journal entry)—I'm not going to make entries*
*for all things that happened today—I know why—nobody else needs to know*

Poop thing management was a delicate issue most of the time. Trying to compare the comforts, the convenience, or the amenities of home to such business on the Trail is impossible. Another classic case of something that we take for granted, never a thought otherwise.

When nature said it was time, there just wasn't time for contemplation, and pre-preparation became standard operating procedure. There are a lot of things to do, and if one is caught unprepared, there were consequences to deal with. For normal morning routine, the hole was dug the night before.

The morning of Saturday, July 12, had started well, considering the cloud of mosquitoes that were following me out of the Pochuck Shelter area where I had tented the night before. It was another gorgeous day. The morning greeted me with rays of sunshine through the trees, something that hikers just never tire of and shortly raised my spirits. Always stiff and not rock-wise in the early stages of the day, I took my first awkward steps up; thru-hikers always know when there was a good climb ahead.

It took awhile for the realization to set in, but my stomach was in a state of turmoil; and I just hoped that it would go away, as a lot of times were the case, for this early-morning business had become more or less normal routine. The crossing of County Route 565 came quickly and just served as a milestone and not a stop, and soon there was County Route 517. It was just the middle part of the morning, and with 5 miles already in, it was break time. I stopped to admire the start of what appeared to be a very long stretch of boardwalk, not realizing at the time that it was very new and was part of a recently rerouted portion of the Trail.

A little-earlier-than-normal procedure, it was time to take a Snickers break. I sat at the beginning of the wooden structure and faced into the warm morning sun, peering into the lush cattails and tall grass that surrounded the boardwalk. The candy bar was devoured quickly, and good feelings were evoked with the knowledge of walking flat and smooth boards. I was anxious to experience the boardwalk and soon continued on my way.

However other factors were at work within me as this stretch of trail was messing with my sense of direction. As one prepared to leave New Jersey and enter New York (actually entering New York for a short distance only to reenter New Jersey), the northeastbound thru-hiker is heading straight southeast for about twenty-five miles. The idea that I was backtracking just to have to eventually make the turn back to the north really didn't agree with my sense of purpose this morning, so I was in a state of dyslexia, feeling somewhat uncoordinated and rather disoriented. That didn't help my rather-nauseated state or my churning stomach.

I had "shut down" early the night before because of a logistics problem. I was making every effort to play by the rules when in New Jersey and keep my stealth camping to bare necessity. I had arrived at Pochuck Shelter about 2:30 p.m. To have made it to the next designated camping spot beyond that was impossible without chancing walking in darkness, something that for me was never considered an option. Wawayanda Shelter was another 13 miles, including the climbing of Pochuck Mountain and Wawayanda Mountain, both quite formidable. And extra time was needed this night just to dry out, bear line having been strung out once again for that purpose.

The mosquitoes were absolutely awful. The stories of New Jersey were proving to be true. For some reason, this state had the worst mosquitoes on the Trail. In all probability, most of these had followed me up the mountain from the Wallkill National Wildlife Refuge where they were totally unbearable. Ironically, there were strategically placed benches for hikers, ones that were designed to sit on with a backpack, being open at the back. However, after about thirty seconds of sitting and mostly swatting, the hiker was more than ready for movement as some form of refuge from the bloodthirsty little varmints.

The Wallkill National Wildlife Refuge quickly became and forever afterward was known by thru-hikers as the WallKill National Mosquito Refuge.

The boardwalk was fabulous. It curved in such ways to be ever aesthetically pleasing. A lot of thought and sound engineering ideas had went into the planning and construction, and it was especially intriguing that nails weren't used in the construction, it was all fastened with screws. A lot of extra work, a fact not lost on this hiker. I stopped to take numerous photos, trying to get angles that would make the photos interesting with the boardwalk enormity accented with the lush foliage as a backdrop. My stomach kept churning but didn't seem to be a particular problem. Yet.

I stopped at a suspension bridge and admired the construction. Shortly after that, I met a trail maintainer; and as was my custom throughout the hike, I stopped to talk to him and thank him for his efforts and to tell him that the work of the maintainers was much appreciated. We briefly talked about weather and about the intricacies of the extended boardwalk.

After about three quarters of a mile, I reached the end of the boardwalk, reluctant to leave this man-made marvel. I had crossed Pochuck Creek, wandered through a forest of large overhanging trees and finally to Canal Road. For some reason, I failed to see the clearly marked sign showing that the Trail simply crossed the road and continued more or less south. However, this was the point where the rerouted section simply reconnected to the original route and the map showed this road as part of the Trail. There appeared to be a white blaze to the right on a power pole, so I turned right on Canal Road. There were more blazes farther west as this had been the route before the rerouting after completion of the boardwalk.

By this time, the Snickers were in an angry frothing revolt and begging for attention. However, that attention was turned to the gorgeous homes along the road as I admired the views and made my way west, wondering why there had only been one or two blazes in the half mile before reaching Maple Grange Road. That was when I really looked at the map. And that was when I realized that there was no way that the Trail would have followed Canal Road since the rerouting had been completed. I had walked a half mile out of the way. The idea of walking back just was not appealing. There was plenty of trail without adding to it for no good reason.

By this time, I was feeling a lot of pressure. I would have to find a suitable place—soon. And there was nothing along the half mile back along Canal Road. However, no other obvious choices availed themselves, so back east I went. And sometime later, looking at the map closer, I realized that the boardwalk was a very new part of the Trail and that the road portions had been abandoned. Just one of those days when the very obvious just was not and that had been the reason for my confusion.

By this time, my body had gone into a cycle of about three—to four-minute intervals. There just was not much time to linger as the cycle became quicker and more intense. When I felt no one was looking, I applied massage to the afflicted area for the little relief that provided and was moving in a rather-bun grid-locked manner, backpack, fanny pack strapped in the front and all. The idea of stopping at one of the houses did occur but just didn't seem like an option. It was doubtful that any of the residents of these rather-lavish homes would be too receptive to a grizzly hiker who by this time was sweating profusely and for such a purpose. Also with promise of relief would come the accelerated urge, and the maniacal gyrations of this stranger would be alarming at best. It would not be a pretty sight. Most people have sort of a fetish approach to such things anyway. No, stopping at one of the homes just was not a good idea.

I was most of the way back down Canal Road when the urges became painful. The pressure by this time was of volcanic proportions as I felt what could only be a state of ooze beyond the control of muscular contraction. A body can only do so much. It hurt. Physically hurt. Not imagination. Real and intense physical pain.

So to sum up the situation, here was this hulk of emaciated sweating person, heavily laden with a forty-five-pound monstrosity strapped on his back, knowing that deep down within that pack was a little black plastic shovel now urgently needed; but that covering the backpack was the rain cover because it was always on for utility purposes and that the untying of the cord that held all of this together was always a time consuming ordeal. The shovel had to be extracted to attempt to dig a suitable hole, a suitable location was not yet available; and also, somewhere in the same place with the shovel was the toilet paper.

I was running by this time as well as one can do so with my encumbrance weighing me down. The pressure by this time was so intense that I had assumed a breathing pattern not totally unlike an expectant mother that was doing the dog-panting thing to alleviate some of the pain and discomfort. Though the comparison here would be total humiliation and insult to the entire Lamaze concept.

Yes, I was pretty much in a tight spot.

And clear panic was setting in. I then saw what appeared to be a trailhead with a small grassy parking area. One car was parked there. In futility for no other choices availed themselves, I asked myself. Why did the car have to be there? Was there anybody in it?

I now was at a stage of jumping up and down and bending over, then back up, then over again, gesticulating, appearing to be possessed of an evil spirit and frantically starting to unbutton my pants, dropping the fanny pack and at the same time attempting to pop the buckles to start unloading the pack. The anticipation was just too much for my body for all of this was indication that relief was on the way. That drove my body to urges beyond anything that I had ever experienced ever in my life, all this time dealing with the mental anguish of the digging of the hole and all of the preparation for this upcoming act, and maybe wondering why digging the darn hole seemed so very important at this time.

Then the will just simply collapsed, and my resolve dissipated. This mental and physical resistance to the unspeakable just simply went away in the face of extreme adversity. And with that came total—though momentary—mental release. A profusion of thoughts much beyond physical properties or endurance or resolve—or consideration for right and wrong. It just did not make any difference anymore. As one can only imagine the feelings that one must feel just before letting go of those futile fingerholds at the edge of a very tall building when there is just simply no strength left to hang on.

It was the most gratifying, the most releasing act—this spring that had been cocked oh so much too tight had suddenly and thankfully broken loose; and there was nothing there now except a loose, limp, languid, wet rag sort of feeling—a relaxation like none that could ever be imagined. Everything went down. Everything. And went down. And went down. It felt so very good. The very best and total and long-delayed orgasm could never have compared, ever, to this complete release.

The unspeakable!

I stood for a moment just enjoying not having this terrible burden to deal with, the yoke had finally been taken away. Of course, the realization took mere seconds for manifestation, and a much-larger burden foisted itself upon me and just loomed there. Huge and ugly and so contradictory to my senses of accomplishment, good grief, here I had hiked over 1,300 miles of the Appalachian Trail, and now I had succumbed to this.

For about seven seconds, suicide seemed like the only answer. No other solution seemed to offer any kind of appeal.

Then the thoughts of the authorities finding the body.

After suicide was pretty much eliminated, my mind slowly came back to the present and the enormity of the situation. The mental anguish would have to be dealt with later. There was a lot of work to do and some decisions as to just how to go about this. I had by this time pretty much determined that there was nobody in the car and that there didn't seem to be anybody around. At least now, I could take my time as much as possible while hoping the car owner did come back unexpectedly.

I managed to get rid of the fanny pack and the backpack and hoist it to the ground without too much bending or unnecessary movement. The hole would have to come later, but I did manage to get the little shovel out and the toilet paper, thanking all the heavens that I had been very frugal with its use, always anticipating an emergency. This must be the emergency.

As gingerly as possible to not move things around too much, I moved to the back part of the small grassy area and unbuckled my pants and managed to wiggle out of them. Then came the moment of truth. Even at the time of this writing, I will always be grateful for those ExOfficio brief-type underwear. May they RIP, for anything of lesser quality could not have contained the mess as well as they did. The digging of the hole went okay for that is never easy with the little shovel. Massive amounts of toilet paper later, I considered myself decent enough to don my hiking pants which were absolutely clean, sans underwear, and hoist the backpack and make my humble way up the Trail. Much in a deflated state of ego, groveling in dealing with my lowered status as well as possible. Ironically, not too long before in a gear-weight-reduction effort, I had sent home a pair of ExOfficio underwear. Now I was down to two pairs. Which proved to be the correct number anyway. It's amazing how very little we do need when necessity so warrants it.

I slowly and humbly continued my hike. Not quite as noble in manner but nonetheless progressing, ever northward, even if this part of the Trail was still heading south for the time being.

Possibly driven by adrenaline, this turned out to be one of the most remarkable days on the Trail. My most productive day in spite of all the delays. It also resulted in another frantic stop; however, this time, deep in the woods where matters could be taken care of in as correct a fashion as possible under again-adverse circumstances.

In spite of my deflated and grungy state, I just was not going to bypass the Heaven Hill Farm when reaching New Jersey Route 94. No hiker that comes within 0.1 mile of anyplace that has food would even think of not making the short walk to appease the ever-present hunger. Also, it gave me a real place to clean up. Really clean up and thoroughly wash my hands, something under the circumstances that I would never have done in a stream that I passed on the way being as all water in proximity of the Trail was a potential drinking-water source. One of the cardinal rules.

I made my way to the bathroom, which took asking to find and went through yet more massive amounts of toilet paper. Then a sink-washing of my hands with soap and hot water and a good toweling down. I was ready for ice cream which, here, came in the form of a double-scoop butter-pecan cone and, while at it, a nectarine and two large cookies. Though after the cone, the fruit and cookies would wait until later. However, my stomach was soon in turmoil again, but that is all rather moot as far as this story is concerned.

Then the real climb came for the morning, nearly a thousand vertical feet up Wawayanda Mountain. The boulders were huge and just would not stop for the longest time, and I wielded my way sometimes on hands and knees to navigate the jumble of rocks called a trail. However, whether driven by guilt or just venting frustration with physical activity, I managed to get to Wawaynda Shelter at the state park with the same name by 12:30 p.m. Thirteen miles and with all of the delays and side trips for food supplementing. Severe guilt was working wonders as it spurred me up the Trail!

I decided that possibly, just possibly, Greenwood Lake was not out of the question. However with ten more trail miles to go and then two more miles down the highway into town, it would be late getting there. So motel reservations seemed intelligent.

The lady at the park office was more than helpful after my futile attempt to make a credit card call at the pay phone produced no results. She allowed me to use the inside phone. Greenwood Lake was a local call, and soon I had reservations for the evening. However, I was now committed to a 23-mile day. However, my adrenaline flow was intense this day as I dealt with my state of guilt, and the miles just dissolved. However, the rocks entering New York were of a totally different nature and did not quit. More like rock outcroppings through this section; however, at least, the small boulders that require such careful placement of the feet was not necessary. Just a series of ups and downs, the kind named so aptly PUDS or MUDS (pointless or meaningless ups and downs).

The views from Bellvale Mountain, the ridge overlooking Greenwood Lake, proved to be about as scenic as anything along the Trail. I could see the village nestled at the north end of the lake, and even though there was some serious walking to get there, it was reassuring knowing that there it was in sight. It was somewhat disconcerting to think that the highway was just below me about one thousand feet horizontally when I was still about a half mile from the highway. The highway made a huge hook and paralleled the Trail on its way back into town. Also, I was somewhat apprehensive about getting a ride on New York Highway 17A for after all, the past reports on this state weren't all that favorable as to the acceptance of hitchhikers. However, it was reassuring to know that the walk into town along the highway was all downhill.

I did make a rather-feeble effort after turning right on the highway, not knowing if I really smelled okay to be actually picked up. My nose so permeated with myself that it couldn't tell the difference anyway. So my heart was not really into hitchhiking on this section. Besides, there was a more-than-ample shoulder, and the downhill walk on smooth pavement was quite refreshing after stumbling along on rocks for the previous 23 miles. It wasn't long before I had come to the point of no return as far as hitching went and was just content to walk along and enjoy the view.

The 2 miles into town were soon over. However, I took the wrong turn at the main intersection going southwest when I should have gone southeast. And the locals didn't seem to know a thing about the Greenwood Motel. After pretty well walking into the other downtown and past parts of town usually associated with where motels are, it was obvious that it had been the wrong turn. Just what was needed, some more walking. But after backtracking and going the other way, finally there it was. Albeit not the most gorgeous establishment, it was like heaven to me.

Later in the bathtub soaking the grime off, the mental grime was also letting go. With reflection on the day's happenings, things again started to come back into perspective, my "accident" took on more of comical overtones instead of abject failure as before. Human beings are, after all, first very human; and functions of the body cannot be denied. However, it was hard not to muse; and as I lay in the bathtub and layers of trail grunge came off, soon I was laughing—mostly just laughing. The day in itself had yet again provided a chapter to my book for there was no way that this could ever be kept a secret.

Quite a day. I walked about 26 miles—the most daily miles on the entire hike—visited a state park and calmly made motel reservations over the phone (the one and only time that I did this on the Trail), ate ice cream at Heaven Hill Farm, got to mile 1,364 on the hike, had my first bath or shower in six days, crossed the state line into New York, and for the first time since I was a small child, I had shit in my pants.

I laughed and soaked and luxuriated and laughed some more, knowing that this day, probably more than any other day on the Trail, I had learned and gained more and grown more; and all that it cost me was a little self-esteem and one perfectly good pair of ExOfficio underwear.

# Chapter 30

## Mandatory

CLOUDY MOST
OF DAY - IN CLOUDS
SOME SUN

(APRIL) 20

15.5 MILES

BLEW LIKE CRAZY THROUGH THE NIGHT
& RAINED - RAIN FLY BLEW LOOSE -
WET INSIDE TENT - MANAGED TO
REACH OUT & ANCHOR IT BACK DOWN

A MESS BREAKING DOWN - HUNG EVERYTHING
& THE TENT WAS UN-PINNED - THE
ENTIRE TENT BLEW OVER THE TOP OF ME
GOOD GOD ALL MIGHTY!!

SO WAS ALMOST THE LAST ONE OUT
OF CAMP
TOUGH HIKING TO CLINGMAN'S DOME!!
BLOWING MIST (IN A CLOUD)
FINALLY GOT THERE ABOUT 11:00 - ISH
TOOK A PACK OFF BREAK
LEGS REALLY ACHED IN P.M.
FINALLY SUCKED IT UP & BY NEWFOUND
GAP WAS GOOD. TOOK ANOTHER PACK OFF
BREAK (LOTS OF PEOPLE IN PARKING LOT -
A MAN TOOK MY PICTURE & WE TALKED
FOR AWHILE.
MADE THE 2.9 MILES TO ICE WATER
SPRING SHELTER IN ABOUT AN HOUR
1000' CLIMB TOO." (BY ABOUT 4:30)

LOTS OF PEOPLE!". TENTED AGAIN
(RIGHT BY SHELTER

FIRST TIME FULL FOR SUPPER

A HIKER GAVE BUFFALO BOBBY & ME SOME
SAUSAGE - IT WAS WONDERFUL!".
(ALSO GIVEN BY SAME GUY) COOKIE & CRACKERS
HAD OATMEAL, NOODLES, SAUSAGE, TRAIL
MIX, BANANA CHIPS, APRICOTS FOR SUPPER

16/219.

# 13
(BROWN'S GROC)
MONDAY
MAY 5

RAINING (HARD
@ TIMES) A.M.
VERY WINDY
@ TIMES
CLOUDY IN
P.M. - RAINING
AGAIN IN EVE.

11 MILES
PLUS 3.5
WALKING TO
BROWN GROC
& BACK

UP AFTER IT GOT LIGHT. DID THE POOP THING.
GOT EVERYTHING INSIDE THE TENT
& LISTENED TO IT RAIN - ATE GRAN BAR
& SNICKERS - RE-ATTACHED RAIN COVER
(A LOT BETTER NOW - HOLDS WATER (NOT
IN MESH) & WATER FILTER - IT MORE
OR LESS QUIT RAINING - BROKE DOWN &
PACKED WET TENT
LEFT ABOUT 8:30 ISH - WAS CLOSER TO
DENNIS COVE ROAD THAN I THOUGHT
PRESSED ON - TALKED TO FISHERMAN @
D.C. ROAD - TOLD ME ABOUT TORNADO
WARNING UNTIL 10:00 & ABOUT RAIN
THROUGH THE WEEK
LAUREL FORK GORGE WAS AWESOME IN
THE RAIN - SEEMED I WOULD ZIG ZAG
FOREVER THROUGH THERE - WATER FALLS
VERY IMPRESSIVE - GOT WATER
POND MOUNTAIN WAS TOUGH - GOT WATER
@ TOP & TALKED TO NUMEROUS HIKERS
GOT TO 321 ABOUT 2:30 - SAT @ PICNIC
TABLE (WATAUGA LAKE) TALKED TO COUPLE
FROM MONTANA & LATER "1/3" - INVENTORIED
FOOD - DECIDED TO GO INTO BROWN'S
GROC. - WALKED ALL THE WAY BOTH WAYS
BACK TO TRAIL - GOT WATER JUST A
SHORT WAYS - SHORT WAYS BEYOND NICE
EVERGREENS - CAMPED THERE
DRIED OUT THINGS - FIXED PASTA WITH RAMEN
BAGEL & FRIED PIE                    31  (422)
MONTANA FAMILY PASSED & WE TALKED

SUN AUG 24  TOTALLY CLEAR  **10 MILES**
(MAINE) !! SUNNY/VERY WINDY
GUSTS TO 50 MPH  LOGISTICS
(COLD) 30(ISH) TO  FOR MAHOOSUC
MAYBE 55(ISH)  PREVENTED
GOING ON

UP @ LIGHT. POOP THING (PRIVY). BREAKFAST:
COFFEE, VIT, POP TARTS, GRAN BAR - PACKED
& HIKING BY 6:45 (SO MUCH EASIER ON A
TENT PLATFORM).
THE TERRAIN IS ROUGH - SOME TRICKY
ROCKS - LOTS OF ROOTS - SHORT₽ P.U.D.S.
& SOME GOOD CLIMBS (ABOUT 1400' [TOTAL]
TO MT SUCCESS - VERY WINDY &COLD @ TOP!!
HOWEVER HIKING WENT GOOD (GOOD
ENERGY & STRENGTH)
SCREWED UP: THOUGHT I HAD GOTTEN
OFF TO ANOTHER TRAIL (BEYOND MT. SUCCESS
PEAK) - HIKED BACK FOR NOTHING - ABOUT
A MILE ROUND TRIP - THERE WAS ONE BLAZE
- FINALLY SAW IT - IN THAT 1/2 MILE.
GOT TO MAINE LINE @ 10:15 - TOOK A SNICKERS
BREAK & TOOK PHOTO OF ME KISSING THE SIGN.

GOT TO FULL GOOSE SHELTER @ 2:00. AFTER
MUCH DEBATING DECIDED TO STAY TONIGHT
& TACKLE MAHOOSUC NOTCH BRIGHT & EARLY
(STILL 1.5 MILES AWAY)
VERY NICE PLATFORM AGAIN - GOT SET UP
QUICKLY - WALKED DOWN FOR WATER - WROTE
IN SHELTER REGISTER - DID JOURNAL & ATE
COOKIES & M&M'S - ALSO B.J. & FRUIT & NUT
FINALLY COOKED NOODLES ABOUT 4:30
FINISHED OFF M&M'S FOR DESSERT
SPENT EVENING: PLANNING TOMORROW,
READING, X-WORD

ANOTHER GOOD DAY        (MAINE) 142
                        (1903)

*July 14—Day 101—Mile 1380—(Journal entry)—then it happened—took a very hard front-downhill fall (came down hard on my nose and right palm)—bloody nose—just kept going to road, and Hare and Agile were there*

It would be hard to take on something as ambitious as hiking the Trail and not keep a record or a diary or a journal. Journal is the euphemism for masculinity. *Diary* sounds school-girlish with entries about first kisses and prom dances. *Journal* is acceptable.

Journals! Diaries! Records! Whatever! Everybody called them something else. Almost everybody on the Trail had some method for documentation. A few didn't keep any kind of records, but not too many. It seemed absurd to embark on such a mission without some record of what happened, who you met, what you saw, and as an aid for remembering as we all would want to, something to jog the memory. Some carried minicomputer notebooks, making nightly entries that were downloaded when coming through towns that had libraries with computers and access to the Internet.

I originally started with a four-inch-by-six-inch spiral paper notebook with eighty sheets, actually three of them, dividing the trip into fairly equal thirds, as dictated by the locations of suitable towns with post offices that were in proximity of the Trail. The second journal was sent with my mail drop box to Pearisburg, Virginia, and the third to Salisbury, Connecticut. That worked fairly well, except that at certain times the entries got wordy, and other times just the opposite. So with Pearisburg at a distance less than one-third of the total, the first book ended up with empty pages for I wasn't about to carry an extra item for no good reason; and the second ran short, necessitating a book 2(A); and the third miraculously filled up exactly to the day of getting to Katahdin Stream Campground before taking a week off at Millinocket, Maine before completing the hike.

Entries for the week spent in Millinocket and the final day of climbing Mount Katahdin with my son to officially end the hike were kept in yet a fifth book that was more the size and shape that I normally carry when traveling. Being off the Trail, it was no longer necessary for a tiny little booklet that would fit into the backpack. In normal living at home, I have kept a journal for years. Now on the computer. Something that I always encourage people to do but find very few that actually do, my own adult kids being in that group. Journals are so vital in the living of life as time goes on for they become historical documents, nothing less than invaluable as time progresses and the memory doesn't quite remember events as accurately as when young.

The word *journal* in itself is misleading, seeming to be nothing more than just a record. However, it can serve many purposes. As a whipping board. As a stress reliever. As a record of all that transpired. As a record of expenses. And just for the sheer enjoyment of recording the events of any one day of your short life on this planet, a way of looking back with déjà vu and reliving those cherished moments. How one cannot keep a diary mystifies me. The events in life are much too valuable to not have some record of what was done, what happened, who you met, how you felt, what the weather was like, and so on. To not keep a journal implies that one's activities are not important enough to record, a concept that runs against my grain.

Many nights, the journal entry was like an elixir. A slow savoring of the day carefully worded and written; that on the nights when there was time to be exquisite and elaborate and wordy. Later when looking through the journals, a pastime now often indulged in, I was surprised at how neat they are. Other nights in the waning light, the journal entry was scribbled as quickly as possible; and then for the final sentences when the flashlight was hung from the ceiling of the tent, the printing became quite sloppy. Just from the neatness, without reading it, I could tell if I arrived at camp early or late, and usually could tell later without reading whether it was a good or bad day.

The journals were carefully packed so that they couldn't possibly get wet as they were written with ballpoint, and not only would the writing get smudged, it would be impossible to write in until the paper dried out. And on the Trail, that could be days. So too often when it would have been nice to have the journal handy for some quick entries, it was too often safely buried in the recesses of the backpack, especially on those days when the skies threatened and deluges seemed to be the order of the day. Later, looking for addresses and trail names of hikers met during the day and other information that was believed to be recorded in the journal proved not to be there. Improvising led to information getting lost, those little scraps of paper, whether receipts or other convenient fodder tucked into the fanny pack, would later have just disappeared. Information intended for the journal waiting for the nighttime and dry conditions sometime just got lost in the shuffle.

In retrospect a ready emergency journal could have been provided for; however, trail thinking is that the less there is to keep track of and carry is usually the best way. For most things, that theory did work quite well. The journals were sent home when the next one in succession was picked up with the food drop. The plan seemed to work out. The entries at times became rather predictable and somewhat mundane. However, as the trip progressed, there seemed to be more of a need for reflection and analysis of how things were going. This resulted in going from about a half page early on to about a page and a half for some days; and on those particularly difficult days, or when one just felt like it, the entries grew to about three pages.

So journal number 2 from Pearisburg on didn't make it without some additional space. It filled up with about two weeks to go to Salisbury; and so another booklet, smaller yet (three-inch-by-five-inch), was purchased on the Trail and somehow ended up with the label of 2(A).

There was always a certain amount of apprehension while the journals made their way back home via the postal service; but alas, all made it okay, and it was a relief to know that the cherished records would be there to be reviewed, to be referred to when the writing began and for wondrous nostalgic trips back down the Trail. The feelings of wonder and mystique never stop when comfortably sitting at home reliving those moments. Sometimes the nostalgia trips were better than the original experience, being able to pick and choose and enhance and elaborate. The memory is a wonderful thing. Selective memory, of course, and the gilded haze of memory were much sweeter if I faced the fact that in reality, some of those memories were much harsher when actually experienced.

A typical day (or, in reality, not so typical):

> *Saturday, May 31—16 miles—end of month—just shy of 800 miles—rain more or less all day—started about the time I got packed up (6:45 a.m.)—very windy in eve!—finally quit (raining) midafternoon but started again off and on * Bad fall today (see below).*
>
> *(Poop thing first) The day started real good with a good breakdown (the tent was just slightly damp). It was raining lightly as I finished packing up.*
>
> *The 800' climb to Bluff Mountain went good. It was really raining when I got to Punch Bowl Shelter so made the side-hike and visited awhile (told my 1492/1776 story).*
>
> *Got to the parking lot on Road 39 by eleven (see above) and snacked again. The trail was poorly marked at dam and ended up in caretaker's driveway. He offered me a drink of water (and directions to trail). *Somewhere between Road 594 and Brown Mountain Creek took a nasty fall in the red clay slop—what a mess, did manage to clean up good in the creek just beyond footbridge. Crossed Highway 60 about three thirty. To camping place (pretty much at top of mountain—2,000' climb went good) by four forty-five. Camp space right adjacent to trail—set up went good. Hung up clothes to dry in the heavy wind. Worried about branches blowing down. Supper: rice meal, ramen, peanut butter, beef jerky, dried fruit, two oatmeal, tea—very good meal. Had a second poop thing. Bear branch so-so (two tosses).*

> *At Punch Bowl Shelter (in heavy rain): Pippi, Baby Steps, and*
> *about three others—one was a day hiker from Lynchburg, a surveyor*
> *and drawer/compiler. Met a couple from New Jersey who had thru-hiked*
> *about five years before.*
>
> *Pippi said that Buffalo Bobby had just left shortly before and that*
> *he was down, had a cold and was tired of rain (also that he was having*
> *foot problems, maybe even an infection in a toe). Ran into Pippi and*
> *Baby Steps again at Road 39 (just before Lynchburg Reservoir). We*
> *snacked and talked there for a while.*
>
> *Mostly hiking in the slop today!*

An average day in a succession of average days. However, there weren't falls every day. It was interesting how the mental approach to falls changed as the hike progressed. There was enough naivety when first beginning to think that I would complete the entire hike without falling once. Ya right!

The average hiker is going to fall numerous times. Numerous times! The younger and more lithe hikers could navigate the rocks much better being more prone to jumping, some of that attributable to having lighter packs, needing less amenities than us older hikers. Most of that grace however just plain came from being more flexible and more daring. And actually, daring meant less falls. Those of us that were too cautious tended to muddle more and that caused falls. However, by about the twentieth or thirtieth fall, it just did not make any difference. A lot of the falls were simply when your feet slide out from beneath you while going down a steep hill, resulting in going down into sort of a sitting-down position; and that is where there is the most padding, the sleeping bag and tent were tied on the very bottom of the pack.

However, there were falls that did make a difference.

The night before at Greenwood Lake, New York, was so pleasant. A true zero day spent eating, reading, watching TV, eating, making phone calls, and later, more eating. The local folks were interesting and friendly. A motorcycle town where bikers took refuge and gathered at the local indoor/outdoor deli and shared good food and stories. I observed from a distance and didn't get involved. I wouldn't have fit in well anyway. Bikers were really not that interested in people that got around for great distances on their feet. They were born to ride, and ride they did. Not walk! However, they were distantly friendly to me, and I spent the day observing. As usual, being a thru-hiker meant not really being a part of society, more an outcast, which afforded a rather-unique unattached position of observation. An AT caste system of sorts.

The zero day prepared me well for the next day, and I was anxious to get going. Not, however, before enjoying some last-minute town amenities, one last stop at the Village Market. While munching on my delicious pancakes and ham, I considered asking patrons for a ride back to the Trail. But there were too many alternative routes out of town, and the chances of one going my way seemed slim. So I started to walk. After walking beyond all of the alternate routes, only Highway 17A lay between town and the Trail, and that was where I stuck my thumb out. It wasn't long before I had a ride—a pleasant young man who lived in New York and said that he usually picked up hikers being able to relate to hikers as he had done some hiking himself.

We exchanged some pleasant remarks at the trailhead, I thanked him again, and we said good-bye. There was some sense of urgency; my breakfast wasn't sitting too well in my stomach. I quickly made my way up the Trail enough to be out of sight of the highway, frantically dug the hole, and even much more frantically answered nature's call. It was always a point to ponder as to why these things don't happen while modern facilities are still available.

Soon I was back in regular hiking form and making good time on a fairly good part of the Trail. I hadn't gone far, however, when Impala went flying by; and in not too long, I heard voices behind me and turned to see Hare and Agile making tracks and rapidly catching up. We hadn't seen one another since before they had dropped off the Trail for a big birthday party for Agile. They had been off long enough to regain strength and were making very good time.

We exchanged the usual Trail news and acknowledged our progress, and with the usual "happy hiking," they went on by. I reflected, walking along, that it was best to maintain my sixty-two-year-old-body pace, content in the fact that slowly but surely, and with each passing moment, less distance existed between me and Mount Katahdin and my dreams and aspirations. However, subconsciously, I suppose there was a tendency to overextend somewhat with the lingering influence whenever I was passed on the Trail. I was probably hiking, at least for a little while, faster than normal pace.

That's when it happened!

Does one ever know just why such things happen? Can one later reiterate the minute details and tell the why and how it could have been avoided. I couldn't. I cannot, to this day, even know exactly what happened. I can only conjecture even after the fact.

I was lying on my nose. I picked my head up enough and mopped my hand across my face. Blood! Blood everywhere. I started to lay my head back down and was fairly convinced that I had broken my nose. I knew that staying there, any longer than absolutely necessary, would be detrimental, or probably disastrous, if the mind was allowed to linger on details and consequences. Trail doctrine.

"Ole Smoky, get up, get goin', don't stay here any longer than you have to. Get goin'. Don't think about it. Go go go go. Face your fears. Go go. GO!"

Which I did. As I walked, I started to assess the damage and pretty much stayed with accepting having broken my nose. I did not dwell on what might be and just kept my thoughts positive. However, I sorely needed to clean up and wash up. Nose bleeds as they are, there was blood on everything—my clothes, my pack, my fanny pack.

I walked about a quarter mile and stopped for an anguished five minutes or so, pondering over a water source. It could be described as a pond but would come closer to actually being an inundated swamp probably held back by a beaver dam. The water was stagnant and really didn't look too clean. It should be noted that this particular section of the Trail had a distinct shortage of good water sources, something that a hiker had grown accustomed to and had yet made the adjustment for using precaution in taking and using water. With trepidation, I started to bow down to the water to start the cleaning-up process and, upon seeing the dirty water closer, decided that this would be doing more harm than good.

I staggered to the next road, West Mombasha Road. Hare and Agile had stopped there for a break, with the latter sitting on a large cooler full of gallon jugs of water. As was the procedure along this area devoid of good water sources for hikers, the trail maintainers and volunteers provided water in containers and strategically placed these at road crossings, just out of sight of the road. Hare and Agile stared at me in disbelief. I assured them that I was okay, just in dire need of water for cleanup and rehydration as I had lost some blood.

There was a one-gallon jug that was three-quarters full which I adopted as my bottle, abandoning my usual practice of conservation. I drank as much as I could hold; and after about fifteen minutes, Hare and Agile, having left me with my misery as requested, was respectably clean enough to continue. The water was a godsend; and it wasn't long before, other than a very sore nose, I felt good again and was ready to resume my journey.

I shall ever be grateful to the trail angels or volunteers that had provided the water. For without it at the time, it would have been difficult to carry on. Yes, I probably should have hitchhiked and went into a doctor, something that I chose not to do; and with the exception of a dental visit in Gorham, New Hampshire, I managed to conclude the hike without medical assistance.

When I resumed hiking, it was with the same resolve and sense of purpose and maybe with more intensity as I had some time to make up and also the adrenaline flow was strong. I had survived a relatively serious fall with not too much damage; and as with many things in life, if we just take that first fall or defeat and continue on in spite of it, life will just seem to flow with a new perspective.

My journal entry for that day is rather nebulous, and somehow in my mind, the fall in my mind seemed to have occurred much earlier that morning. Possibly I had gone into a state of mild shock after the fall. I will never know.

> *THEN IT HAPPENED! Somewhere between Mombasha High Point and Prospect Mountain—back AT south from West Mombasha Road—took a very hard-front downhill fall (came down hard on my nose and right palm—bloody nose)—just kept going to road and Hare and Agile were there—Agile was sitting on a water cooler full of gallon jugs of water. Thank God.*

It was a journal entry that was rather unnecessary for the experience will never be forgotten. However, to this day, I question the exact location as entered in the journal. It really doesn't make that much of a difference for proximity is more important than actual location. So in this writing, graphic description can be afforded a dose of "writer's license" and it can be wherever I want it to be. The point being to make a case for journals and keeping records. What we remember too often is what we choose to remember. For the most part, that makes for good storytelling with ample embellishing; and hopefully, we never have to be held accountable.

# Chapter 31

## Fauna

*April 26—Day 22—Mile 308—(Journal entry)—saw a bright orange newt in the trail (near Highway 208)—moved him off trail so he wouldn't get squashed*

A lot of emphasis is placed on that part of the Trail experience concerning the living natural creatures that would be encountered. So much is made of the well-known larger animals that for the most part, the unseen creatures on and near the Trail are forgotten. Often those smaller creatures are as crucial to our existence as they represent the yardstick to measure the condition of our environment. Salamanders fall into that category to the point that basic conclusions about the health of our planet can be determined by their well-being and their numbers. There has been a steady decline of salamanders in the world, and that is not a good thing. Too often, human activities can be attributed to this reduction in salamander population. It is interesting to note that even the existence of the Trail itself is a barrier to some salamanders that spent their entire lives in a very small area. The Trail separates the leaf and humus cover necessary to retain ground moisture paramount to its existence and is a hardship for these little ground creatures.

Man's intervention never seems to enhance wildlife growth; therefore, as hikers, we have to do our part to not disturb nature any more than we have to. That is a concept that is well adhered to as the Trail is usually nothing more than a very narrow path and sometimes is difficult to discern that one could cross it walking perpendicular and never know it. A fact discovered a number of times when it went a different direction than did my feet, resulting in a lot of crossing and recrossing it before finally getting back on course. The number of newts and salamanders that I saw along the Trail could be counted on one hand. However, for the most part from my casual observation, wildlife health in general seemed relatively good.

Probably of the most interest to me was the drumming of the ruffed grouse that brought back fond memories of USGS field assignments in Northern Minnesota where I first heard this sound back in the midsixties. Back then, it reminded me of the small maintenance cars along railroad tracks whose distinctive small engines ran sporadically and then shut off while they coasted. Probably so that they could hear trains coming and get the cars (that could be lifted by two men) off the tracks before they were run over.

Northern Minnesota was very remote, and after hearing the ruffed grouse sounds, it occurred to me that there were no railroad tracks anywhere near where I was surveying. Our project leader, a much-loved man named Novie Hudson who died at a very young age in his late fifties, asked us one day if we had heard any grouse drumming. Being somewhat perplexed with the question, he elaborated and made a crude mimic of the sound; and instantly, the railroad maintenance car façade was dispelled.

The sound is heard only in the early spring in Minnesota when the grouse are going through their courtship rituals. The sound is accomplished by the grouse standing on a log and drumming the air with his wings. When I first heard the sound on the Trail, it was hard to believe that was the same exact thing that was heard so much farther north. For this was in the southern reaches of the Appalachian chain. I would realize later that with the elevation difference and the rainforestlike ecosystem, Northern Minnesota is somewhat emulated in climate with temperatures not quite indicative of such a southern latitude. Yes, ruffed grouse do inhabit these far southern reaches if the conditions are right.

Not unlikely my first animal encounter involved the one that the Trail is most noted for, the dreaded mouse. Usually a by-product of our sloven ways, they probably wouldn't be quite as prevalent if all hikers practiced good camping procedure, but who knows? Where in the world are there no mice? Ending my first week on the Trail, I had chosen a stealth campsite at Plumorchard Gap, not too far from Hiawassee, Georgia. I opted not to hike down to the shelter that was 0.2 mile to the right, and besides, the good water source was to the left. There was a very nice hemlock with totally bare ground underneath. I noticed some trash and a nasty-looking fire ring just on the other side of the tree. I picked up some of the trash and added it to mine. It took about an hour to get dried out before setting up, but it proved to be a waste of time for by the time I got set up, the rain had set in.

I managed to get my noodles cooked and took refuge inside to eat before settling in for the night. By the time I was through eating and cleaning up, the rain was doing a dance on my North Face tent. There was still enough light to do the journal and do some crossword puzzles. I listened to the rain as the drops gathered, and then rivulets would cascade down to again repeat the process. The water rolling down was a pleasant sound, and it was satisfying to be cozy and warm inside my small abode, more or less thumbing my nose to the elements.

The cascades went down and down. And then up and then down and up.

Wait awhile. Up?!

What is wrong with the picture here? Up? However, a little observation soon provided explanation. The Slickrock tent is designed where the support poles go through fabric grommets that are on the outside, allowing the poles to loop over the top of the structure. And a little mouse was doing laps up and down the pole. When we finally made eye contact, he was at the very top of the tent, looking at me through the mosquito netting. He was really not a problem, but the plethora of mouse horror stories stayed with me through the night, wondering if I would have holes gnawed in my home. However, the mouse must have known that anything that he was interested in was hanging out there in that plastic bag and left me alone.

Probably the most fascinating creatures on the Trail, however, are the coyotes. Being a light sleeper, I awoke many nights to hear the howling, some that seemed not too distant. That sound took the hiking experience to another level for unless heard in such proximity, it cannot quite be appreciated. It manifests that no matter what man has done to this planet and how "modern" we think we are in our self-importance, wildlife are still operating to the status quo and that their basic instincts are somewhat the same. The actions placed there in the millennium are still there, and though animals are probably refined in their thinking to deal with the intrusion of man, a lot of things just have not changed. What reassurance! Nature is after all the very base of life and our quality of living, and with man's mangling of its very core, it will continue to operate as it has before we started to "improve" things and try to throw Mother off balance. Those thoughts can be protracted further with intelligent assumptions that if man were removed from the planet, it wouldn't be long before nature would revert to what it was two thousand years ago in a very short time.

A lot of thought can be evoked from just the sounds of those wondrous creatures! A throwback to primal instincts and the grassroots from which living creatures all evolved.

The most frequently asked questions to the thru-hiker, of course, is "Did you see any bears?" Not really enough worthy of mention, but since that topic always comes up, it has to be addressed. Thirteen for almost 2,200 miles of hiking is not very many. Oddly, only seen in two places. The Shenandoah National Park in Virginia, seven of those, and the remainder within the state of New Jersey where there has been a resurgence and are considered a "problem."

It is important to note that the Shenandoah bears are probably the most dangerous. Because there are so many people in the park and with so many of them neophytes that do stupid things with food, those bears have lost their fear of man. When that happens as with any large creature capable of inflicting physical harm, a real danger exists. Ironically because there is such an acceptance and the bears get so close, a rather-casual attitude is assumed. And those close and "friendly" bears are the ones to watch.

It should be mentioned that it is hard to really concentrate on looking for shy animals, which bear are a prime example, for the trail surface for the most part does not allow one the luxury of casually looking around. There are just too many things to trip over to approach hiking the Trail as if it were a sidewalk or a smooth-level surface. Too many times forgetting this fact, I ended up looking facedown on the Trail at very close quarters. Rocks and root nubs have a way of returning one to the task at hand.

I was hiking with Blind Eagle one day through Shenandoah National Park, a devout section-hiker that was close to covering half the Trail in about five years. His "Look at the bear!" startled me out of my concentration. More because I was amazed that he was looking that close off the trail along a section with a constant array of obstructions. He was somewhat concerned with the proximity; however, I, in my ignorance and assurance from so many articles that bear just will not bother you, was not. We stopped much to Blind Eagle's discomfort and watched him for a while as he clicked his teeth and gave us the evil eye. I was told later that he was biting at flies. He seemed rather disinterested in us. However, we hikers knew, most of us, never to lay the pack down and walk away. Bear are intelligent animals and know where the goodies are. A note tied to a tree as a warning made mention of just that fact for some neophyte hiker had to learn the hard way. Hopefully resupply was not too far away for usually the bear will eat everything edible within the pack, including toothpaste and toiletries.

Deer were everywhere and had no fear of hikers or cameras. Prevalent mostly more in the southern states; by the time that the Mason-Dixon Line was crossed, they had thinned out some, still quite numerous through Pennsylvania and then above that rarely seen. Probably more because as the population decreases, so does the propensity of the animal to be comfortable in the proximity of man.

Hunting is allowed for the most part along the Trail, but apparently, the intelligent deer know the difference between hikers and hunters. Some stood within fifteen feet and posed very nicely for the numerous photos. One can only assume that they were smiling.

Rattlesnake! Just mention the name and one can envision the evil pit viper's eyes with the vertical slit, the flicking tongue and, of course, that eerie sound that so strikes terror into most human beings that know about them and have been close enough to invoke the warning. Arguably, the question most asked of the hiker regards how many snakes were seen, the assumption being that all snakes are evil and poisonous. Actually, a close count was never kept for there were a number of black racers through the Southern states and few garter snakes in the North. Of the poisonous varieties, there were only three snakes; however, I do not make a point of being silly-careful with such, so there might have been more.

The two rattlesnakes seen make good stories as do most incidents of snake sightings. A lot of the hiking in the vicinity of Knife's Edge in Pennsylvania follows tumble-down races of loosely stacked rocks that precariously lie on one another with usually a lot of space down through the rocks. Some are human-hand-placed in such a way for a more sure footing, but in most places, the rocks are in a natural state. There is a tendency for the rocks to clatter as the weight shift is made to the next rock. On one particular configuration, the rocks clattered just a little longer than normal. That made me stop long enough to realize—*whoops!*—that isn't a rock clattering.

I carefully stepped back to hear more rattling and to observe the long camouflaged body partially hidden down in the hollow between the rocks. The rattlesnakes along the Appalachian Trail most generally are timber rattlesnakes, and it's relatively sure this one was of that species. There was another rattling sound before seeking refuge farther down, and the snake disappeared. After that, I did make it standard practice to poke around some with the walking stick before placing my next step into hidden places in the rock crevices. One can be too careful in such endeavors, but also there was no need to take needless chances.

The other rattlesnake was also nearby in Pennsylvania and had been forewarned by a fellow hiker that was southbound. About 12 miles beyond

Port Clinton is a rather-unique monument (Tri-County Corner) that marks the common corner for Schuylkill, Lehigh, and Berks counties. Just the kind of stuff that surveyors love to see. There was a blue blazed trail of about four hundred feet left, leading to the monument. Just before the side trail, a hiker warned me that a rattlesnake was making his home right there in the rocks adjacent to the marker.

The vertical concrete monument was photo-worthy, but the light was not good from the angle approaching it. So after skipping over and around the large rocks, a relatively good shot was finally accepted. Prior to leaving, a search was made for the rattlesnake, not really believing that the snake would still be there. And just like the sobo had said, there it was down in the hollow of a rock group by the monument. All that was seen were the rattles still very much attached to the end of the Tri-County Rattler. The snake remained subdued, not feeling any reason for alarm, and I made my way back to the Trail to continue my hike for the day to near Knife's Edge.

The only other poisonous snake seen for the entire hike was also in Pennsylvania, about 6 miles before getting to Duncannon. A perfectly coiled copperhead lying on the left side of the Trail and about a foot off the beaten path. He (possibly a she) lay perfectly still and perfectly coiled while I took the picture, being careful not to get too close. The thought of leaving a note as warning crossed my mind; however, it remained as such for the paper was much too deeply packed. Justification for not doing so toyed with my mind somewhat in the context that these were the chances that hikers took and also that human knowledge of the snake's whereabouts was probably a death sentence for the copperhead, and as far as I was concerned, the snake hadn't done anything wrong to have to die. I could live with that. It was intriguing that just beyond the snake sighting was a porcupine waddling toward a tree before making a rapid accent. Possibly there was some truth to the symbiosis of wildlife, and that if one species were observed, there are probably other animals in proximity. A fact well documented in Aldo Leopold's book, *A Sand County Almanac.*

And one moose. A huge stereotypical bull with huge stereotypical antlers right out of a State of Maine tourist brochure. He was not afraid of me, and my curiosity allowed me to get too close. It has always amazed me how these fantastic animals navigate among the trees with that wingspan. Apparently their peripheral vision is something that we humans cannot appreciate. It makes wonderful mental diversion to imagine holding a pole about five feet long sideways and then plowing your way through the woods playing dodge-ball with the tree trunks. Maybe moose are just smarter or more nimble than we are.

But of course, as is usual in real life, the dangers in the woods come in small packages. The fear was constant of doing the body search and seeing the telltale ring indicating the most dreaded scenario from living in the wilds, a deer tick bite and Lyme disease. Pippi—a fellow hiker-ette, a great lady from Kansas City—supposedly contracted it as did Socrates, a young man who had taken a couple of weeks off to regain some strength. I saw Socrates at Upper Goose Pond in Massachusetts. He was drawn and lethargic and wondering what the long-term symptoms would be. Somehow I dodged the bullet on this one, possibly some immunities had been built up from years of tick bites, the nemesis of the surveyor.

So in nearly 2,200 miles of hiking, I had encountered three poisonous snakes, thirteen bears, and one moose. However, nonhiker/nonoutdoors people usually ask that first as if one were immersed in dangerous wildlife on a continuous basis. Our early influences sadly left their toll. The tales of the Big Bad Wolf and scenes from *Indiana Jones* certainly do leave an indelible and lasting impression, residue of hearsay and misinformation.

However, fear only came for this hiker from that most dangerous of animals, *Homo sapiens,* as unpredictable and cunning as any species in the woods. If only somebody would ask me about those dangers then there are truly some tales of derring-do to narrate.

# Chapter 32

## Purist

*April 18—Day 14—Mile 188 (Fontana Dam)—(Journal entry)—*NOTE: *did not hike from NC 28 to Fontana Shelter*

I am a fraud!

To be considered a true thru-hiker, one has to do the entire Trail. Every step of the way from Georgia to Maine. This claim is made on the honor system for nobody will monitor your hike closely enough to actually witness the hiking of every step for the entire length. The only way that this could be done would be if two or more hikers went the route together. This does happen, but not that often. And who could actually witness for another hiker if that hiker was also aspiring to being a thru-hiker? Also, numerous times, hikers that are hiking together separate for periods of time; and who is to say that shortcuts weren't taken during this time for there are sections of the Trail where that can happen, either "blue blazing" or following roads or highways. *Blue blazing* simply means to follow a blue blazed trail to a town or trail service and, instead of going back to the point of leaving the actual AT, to continue the blue blazed section the other way and reconnect with the white blazes farther along the Trail. Not in the true spirit of actually doing the entire Appalachian Trail.

A rather-strange term is applied to the honor of completion, *2,000 miler.* My wall currently is adorned with the tiny cloth emblem suitable for sewing on something that was awarded to me by the Appalachian Trail

214

Conference (now Conservancy). I am a 2,000-miler. Why not thru-hiker? That would better represent the accomplishment without getting into a lot of particulars. However, *2,000-miler* is probably used so that a section-hiker that eventually completes the hike can be awarded the same patch. And let's face it, a section-hike is very hard. The logistics are very difficult to work out, and maintaining the desire to complete the hike year after year is amazing.

And since there have been numerous trail changes through the year, the mileage has varied; and that may well explain the term, for to accurately maintain the current year's mileage would somehow weigh the system down and maybe it is rather moot anyway when one considers a hike of 2,000 miles. What is a hundred or more miles on top of that?

The honor system works well. The very highest percentage of hikers are religious about covering the Trail step for step. Nor'easter epitomized that concept as well as anybody. He was in our group when we rode back to the Trail from Waynesboro, Virginia, that fair morning of June 5. He was the first one out of the car. We were dropped off just beyond the overpass where he had left the Trail on this section that follows the highway for a short distance before reentering the woods. When Nor'easter got out of the car, he immediately walked back across the overpass, turned around, and walked back to where we were waiting before donning his pack and proceeding north on his venture. Nor'easter was what some would call a purist. And he, personally, obviously could never have made the claim of thru-hiker had he not covered the *entire* Trail.

Now back to me and my fiasco at Fontana Dam. Approaching Highway 28 and my first real forage into town and the intricacies of being back in the real world had left me in a daze. Motel or hostel? Eat at the buffet or go to a good restaurant? The realization of having the comforts of town were just too much for me to try work out and comprehend, let alone knowing just what to do while staying there. I stumbled through the rain, anticipating my night at Fontana Dam, making my way down from Walker Gap descending out of the Yellow Mountains. It was very good going down but gave my mind too much time for the details of a totally new experience, and there was no precedent to draw on to help make these decisions. For the most part, the rain was a deluge. I had donned my rain gear even though it was rather warm and uncomfortable doing so. Also I debated not taking the first route into town at Highway 28 and spending the night at the Fontana Hilton, a shelter beyond the highway that goes into town, almost an icon of the AT experience. Early plans before the hike had even started were to include this as one of the prime places to stop.

The waiting white van was catalyst for making up my mind. As the rain intensified and the comforts of the van beckoned, further thought processes were no longer necessary. I struggled with the pack and managed to wrangle it into the back and climbed in to meet Odyssey for the first time. I glanced at his gear and immediately mistook him for a day hiker. He had a tiny pack, tennis shoes, and cotton T-shirt and seemed young and impetuous. My estimation turned out to be totally incorrect. When I asked him if he was day hiking, he gave me a rather mischievous grin and said that no, indeed, he was a thru-hiker. I smiled and wondered how long that would last.

So I digress: Odyssey had attempted a thru-hike the year before. He had made it all the way to New Jersey, had some girl problems that distracted from his adventure, and had gotten off the Trail. This year he did, indeed, know what he was doing. With the exception of food, he had the bare necessities. He traveled light, moved like a banshee, and covered more ground than anybody. When I arrived at High Point Shelter in New Jersey on July 10 (mile 1,328), there was a note there from him with his telephone number. I later called him from the motel in Greenwood Lake, New York. He had completed his thru-hike, summiting Mount Katahdin on July 6. He must have averaged close to 30 miles a day. A truly amazing feat! I contacted him when I got back to Florida, and we have talked a few times since then. A truly amazing thru-hiker!

So in this case, serendipity created a situation that wouldn't quite develop until the next morning. After spending a wonderful night in Fontana Village—doing laundry for the first time in about a week, enjoying the amenities of town, overeating at the buffet for dinner and for breakfast the next morning—the morning meant it was time to get back to business. The shuttle runs back and forth to the Trail on somewhat of a schedule. Odyssey and I had decided to do laundry that morning and catch the next shuttle out of town. It all worked out as planned.

However, when we were about a half mile from the Trail, the van suddenly turned left off the highway on to a side road to the dam. Meaning that I would be advancing beyond where I had exited the Trail the night before. At first I objected and said that I wanted to go back on Highway 28 to the point where the Trail crosses. However, after looking at the six hikers that were in the van, it occurred to me that would create undue inconvenience. And the shuttle people had been so nice in providing these free rides. So the mile that I would miss just didn't seem that important when considering that I was the only one in the van that wanted to go the other way. So I abandoned that idealistic thought and just went along for the ride.

Therefore, instead of resuming my hike where I left off the night before, on North Carolina Highway 28, I picked up at the shelter (Fontana Hilton) at the east end of the dam, thence not doing 1.1 miles of the

Trail. When I got out of the van, I had a lot of mixed emotions. It seemed too early in the hike, 175 miles, to start getting sloppy about my rules for hiking the Trail. However, the first really challenging section of the Trail lay ahead, the Great Smoky Mountains National Park with all of the rules and restrictions that hadn't really applied prior to this point, one of those rules being that stealth camping away from shelters just was not acceptable. I was running rather late already, and my plans were to make Russell Field Shelter that night and a long climb of 2,600 feet in elevation lay ahead. With a 14-mile day planned, to reverse hike and then turn around, for it appeared that a ride was out of the question, and to add 2.2 miles to the day just didn't appeal to me at the time.

I opted to do it the easy way. So with great turmoil I started across the dam. At least this gave me the opportunity to meet Buffalo Bobby. We first spoke with those first steps of the day and then passed each other a number of times, concluding with camping side-by-side at Russell Field Shelter. Our first night in the national park. I liked his name, and it didn't take long to realize that he was my kind of guy. Friendships form easily when there is so much evident esoteric activity involved. It was the best thing that happened to me on this adventure.

The mind has a very nice way to justify just about anything. I later reflected that in human endeavors, rarely is anything perfect. Not hiking 1.1 miles made it more perfect. By not being mechanical and/or too rigid, a certain maligned credibility had been attached. A euphemism could be applied in my justification making it all okay—the mantra that this was your hike, leaving that interpretation for me to determine.

Most importantly, it gives me a reason to go back. Just to hike that 1.1 miles. What a day of celebration that will be. For then the thru-hike will truly be creditable. Hopefully Kris will come with me.

# Chapter 33

## Judas

*May 24—Day 50—Mile 708—(Journal entry)—I do not like this man!*

So much of the Appalachian Trail experience is pure emphasis on positive thoughts, on always accentuating the good and staying away from those areas of negativity that could undermine such a long and arduous venture. However, if the basis of Christianity could be based on the suffering and eventual death of Jesus then possibly all of life, no matter how pure an image it may portray, has an underlying source for conflict. A Judas, if that name can be used in this context, had to be waiting in the wings to provide contrast, to be the bad guy, to possibly even provide inspiration in a rather-convoluted manner. With those thoughts, we shall address the one character on the Trail that I did not like, no matter at first how hard I tried. The name of the hiker is not important.

In most everyone's childhood, there was a class or neighborhood bully. The obnoxious kid that always tried to maintain the upper hand with intimidation, insults, physical violence, or any means that worked to that end. Usually sometime just beyond puberty, this behavior seems to wane as experience brings on enlightenment and a semblance of maturity; and with that, some curtailing of these characteristics somewhat subside, possibly when one has run out of friends.

However, sometimes this behavior is carried into adulthood. Sadly such a person seems not to realize that there is some reason that people eventually avoid him. The Appalachian Trail did not seem to be the place for such a person. Just the mere sacrosanct quality of this most pristine of places and the aura of the concept and how such a pure and righteous activity as hiking and enjoying the best that nature has to offer would somehow serve as a culling process. However, sometimes life just doesn't work in predicted ways. Thus the word *oxymoron* was created for such things, and here, no other utterance could suffice. So there he was defying all that could be considered predictable and sane.

He almost made me get off the Trail!

He proved to be my nemesis. And I just could not like the man. However, he worked so hard at being liked that he actually succeeded for a while. I kept wondering what was wrong with me for it seemed that everybody liked him just fine, except me. And I normally can like almost anybody.

Having started my journey with my own adopted personal philosophy to be, "There would be no causes, no controversy, no getting out of line. That I was in a rather-delicate and vulnerable position and out of my element, and that I would for the most part be a compliant and subservient sort of soul." It was the mantra voiced to my son Will on the way to Amicalola Falls State Park in Georgia on the day that the hike started. Will, who is usually politically and socially correct, agreed, wholeheartedly agreed; and so it was established. My usual mode of operation would be abandoned for the duration of the hike.

This guise was totally out of character; however, being totally out of my element, it seemed like the way to play the percentages. That to succeed in this endeavor, causes and feelings would have to be set aside. Certainly for a while I could forget about my indulgences of self-proclaimed idealism and just accept things as they are. It would be difficult to do. I would also think of it as a survival instinct impulse. Possibly even turn within the energy that sticking up for conviction requires, and use it to my advantage for the physical and mental demands of the Trail.

So when he first hiked into my life in those early days of this venture, I accepted him as I accepted other hikers and, with my newly created trail philosophy, dealt with his idiosyncrasies as just that and not as a personality that seemed to have run somewhat amuck. He seemed okay to me early on.

However, he was an entirely unique sort of person, and eventually, a certain amount of trail weariness set in. My resolve and immunity were weakening, probably helped along considerably with his insensitivity that had thrown me so off guard. Slowly the realization set in that this was clearly a man who had some serious problems regardless of how well disguised these traits were. His was the classic case of a man that was always very threatened and always on his guard; he was hard feelings just waiting for manifestation.

For most hikers, the reasons for thru-hiking were rather subtle and rarely mentioned; however with him, the reasons were clearly worn on his sleeve: the AT was the proving ground for his derring-do and his variation of a hyper ego trip. Yes, there were other "strong" personalities for the Trail does not attract too many that are feint of heart, the types that are overachievers and come on rather strongly. However, the majority of hikers were pleasant and easy to converse with, and the exchange went both ways and good feelings came out of it. A sort of trail camaraderie was usually the ambiance that prevailed as we all dealt with the same problems and self-doubts. However, in his case, there was just too much to deal with. He obviously felt something to the effect that "I'm okay; it's the rest of the world that's screwed up."

About 700 miles into this venture it was necessary to do some serious soul-searching. This introspection resulted in a line of rationale that the concept of this being a growing experience should prevail and that dealing with idiosyncrasies in people was all part of it. However, just merely hiking the Trail was difficult enough. Additional growing experience was not needed. I was growing enough as it was.

I couldn't seem to avoid him and his constant criticism was wearing me down. The only conclusion conceivable and workable was that it was time to get off the Trail. The fun had gone out of the hike. Hiking the AT was important, but not important enough to completely destroy my self-esteem. However, fate turned out to not be so cruel, for after Connecticut I only saw him one more time. Possibly he had dropped off the Trail as he had been threatening to do that for quite some time.

It has to be noted that a number of times, my self-worth was heavily questioned along with my empathy for my fellow man and that my feelings toward another human being should have been better. I did not seek support in this venture. However, it eventually came to me. There were so many other hikers that I highly respected and admired and, yes, loved. We would see each other time and again, and eventually we became family of sorts. It was old-home week when a great deal of time would pass before seeing each other again. And reserve eventually gave way as familiarity being a part of this same adventure; we started to confide in each other, but, not a lot for that is not the ways of Appalachian Trail thru-hikers. However, enough opinions were voiced to lend some support. The general consensus was that others felt the same way. Factions within any group of people usually tend to be destructive but this exchange was not of that nature. These confiding statements only served as an aid in dealing with a difficult situation when just surviving on the AT was hard enough as it was.

This man had managed to alienate a number of other people. I am not sure how he could not have known this. He either was so totally oblivious that he couldn't identify it or just chose to evade issues. I really didn't care, but it was comforting to know that I was not alone. That even on the Trail, there was room for just feeling the way you feel. One sometimes just cannot control human behavior.

In retrospect, what a tragedy it would have been to have quit because of one fellow hiker. I could not see what was inside of this man or what made him what and who he was. Possibly I should have been more understanding. Possibly tried to walk a mile in his boots. We all have our demons, and apparently his were especially vindictive. In my defense laid the obvious. Hiking the Appalachian Trail is an extremely difficult venture. We were in a very wet year, arguably the wettest on record. Nature had thrown most everything she had at us; and it took every bit of energy, every bit of gumption, every bit of resilience, every bit of chutzpah to continue.

Every one of us has a nemesis to deal with from time to time. In good times, possibly one can take one under his/her wing in an attempt of making the life voyage somewhat kinder and gentler. However, the survival instinct is too strong; and when resources are spread very thin, one has to preserve oneself before trying to save somebody else. There are times on the Appalachian Trail when such priorities had to be addressed. The ills of the world would have to be taken on some other time.

The reasons for even mentioning this are rather nebulous and intended more as inspiration not only in such a venture as thru-hiking the AT, but as in all aspects of life, there are just times when we have to accept things as they are. As in life, one person should never constitute a reason for quitting an endeavor.

However, as life on the Trail seemed to always provide the contrast, human nature's other side would soon give cause for celebration.

# Chapter 34

## Good Samaritan

*July 24—Day 111—Mile 1514—(Journal entry)—hiking to Jug End Road was very tough (about 10 miles)—Race Mountain, Mount Everett, Mount Bushnell were poorly made trails (very steep—long wet slippery slopes)—had a number of controlled falls*

I had crossed Massachusetts Highway 41 and was somewhat confused as to what to do. This was one of those sections that had too many options for resupply. It hadn't taken long to determine that it was better by far having one choice about every 40 to 50 miles apart than to have too many resupply choices at short distances. Longer distances demanded better planning resulting in a clear-cut and standard mode of operation with resupply about every three to four days. Also, today with my distraction, other problems had arisen and had not been taken care of as usual.

Having hiked about a half mile beyond the highway, I realized that water resupply would also be a problem for this stretch was mostly low lying and streams that did cross the Trail were slow moving and the water quality was questionable at best. I stopped at the footbridge over Hubbard Brook and weighed my options. The thought occurred to me that the little gray Pur water filter in the little gray bag was being asked to do things that had to be eons beyond the scope of its intent. A smile slowly formed as the thoughts of pulling water from just any cess pool-looking collection of hydrogen and oxygen atoms that comprised water may be viewing that little pump filter as the panacea of all of our water supply problems. The Pur company would be proud. Or more likely, shuddering at the thought of giardia-based law suits at the hands of uninformed and overly confident users of their product.

So the little Pur filter went back in the bag, and continuing along the Trail, other options started weighing heavily on my mind. I knew that there were a number of secondary road crossings ahead and that there were houses shown on the map not too far from the Trail.

Maybe on another day and maybe being more desperate, Hubbard Brook would have looked good, but not today. It was a hot day but not that hot. It was time to put a good Samaritan into play. Maybe as a test also for I was now officially in the North and my curiosity needed to be allayed about the good people north of the Mason-Dixon Line. I continued to the nearby Sheffield Road. There were houses both ways. The houses to the west were a shorter distance, and I headed that way, passing the Shay's Rebellion Monument. I eventually knocked on a door but nobody responded. I wandered farther on the road and having noticed a spigot with a garden hose; I stepped up on the porch of the house and knocked on the door. I hadn't waited very long before a rather-gruff voice shattered the afternoon quiet, coming from the second-story window, "What do you want?!"

There was mostly animosity coming from the invisible voice. I wasn't sure whether to answer or just forget this idea but did manage. "Could I possibly get some water from your water spigot outside?"

"Water isn't any good." The answer came much too quickly from somebody that obviously wasn't too delighted about my interruption. A long pause and then some clarification. "Had to put in a filter inside the house so that I could drink the water."

A very long pause. I stood waiting for an eternal twenty or thirty seconds, and with that came the reality that this conversation was over. I slowly backed off the porch, keeping an eye on the upstairs window. Nobody there. No talking. Nothing. Slowly I walked to the road just knowing that the voice would say to come back. Nothing.

All of the good and warm and fuzzy thoughts of wonderful people along the Trail were dissolving as I made my way back east and past the monument, stopping halfheartedly to read some of the inscription. By this time my thoughts were somewhat cynical with some disparity and even anger. Asking for a little water seemed like a reasonable request and not one to cause such hostility and the unfriendly reply. I tentatively considered the houses to the east of the Trail and decided that even though those houses were farther away, this was not the time to totally give up on the good folks of Massachusetts.

However, my spirits were somewhat dampened and my confidence weakened; and when I stepped into the first yard, I proceeded at best quite hesitantly. I noticed the swimming pool along the back side of the house and to the west of it. There was laughter and the usual activity surrounding a pool on a warm and pleasant early-summer afternoon. In a more bold and brazen mood, I would not have hesitated. However, I balked; and with that, all of my resolve disappeared and I merely walked away back to the road and back to the Trail.

About five hundred feet up the Trail through a cornfield was a bend, and looking back, it afforded a rather-nice view. It seemed like a good place to drop the pack, take a break, and turn to food for consolation. I sat on the mowed path and ate beef jerky and raisins and contemplated people and goodness and decided that the things that I had read about being north of the Mason-Dixon Line might turn out to be true. Attitudes were different, voice inflection was harsher, there was a crispness to the ends of the words. North and South. Always a conflict. Whether these thoughts and concepts were conscious thoughts or valid ideas, one had to admit that there was a vague nondescript and nebulous existence, something. A rather-hard pill to swallow for a truly dyed-in-the-wool Yankee with strong opinions about Northern versus Southern hospitality. Obviously I had been wrong all of these years. Or was it the Northeast?

Eventually, having not come to definite conclusions about the next day's stop in Great Barrington and for the sake of rationing, the beef jerky and raisins had to be put away and the day's walk had to be continued. Hoisting the pack, I slowly made my way along the edge of the field toward a bend in the Trail and hadn't walked too far when I noticed a driveway, a dirt road that paralleled the Trail along my left side. A feature that was rather hard to read on my map. It was rather confusing wondering if the Trail had taken a bend and was supposed to have crossed the road. However, after seeing a white blaze it was evident that I hadn't wandered off the Trail.

A car was approaching along the road and came to more or less opposite where I was walking and stopped. The driver's door opened, and a person was stepping out. It seemed more than circumstance that this should happen right where I was walking.

The mystery person came walking toward the Trail with conviction and purpose. It was difficult to come to conclusions—was this going to be another confrontation for some unexplained reason? My mind quickly reviewed the past half hour or so; however, no tangible thoughts could be put together. Only questions. What was going on here?

It didn't take long to realize that the mystery person was a cop. A cop! The thoughts of the swimming pool scene quickly clouded my reasoning. My hesitant actions may have been misconstrued more as clandestine. Somebody called the cops! I wasn't sure what to do. Panic told me that he probably couldn't catch me were I to retreat back down the Trail; however, those ideas quickly dissolved, thinking of running and trying to get away from somebody carrying forty-five pounds on my back and running with it was close to impossible. He had a gun for goodness' sake.

I took my chances. He approached the edge of the woods with obvious intentions of getting my attention. That he already had and obviously didn't know it. He appeared to be carrying something in his right hand. Soon he was reaching out with the object and said something. I stopped and walked over to the edge of the field just off the Trail.

He handed me a bottle of Dasani spring water. A nice new bottle. I reached for it, and when it brushed my hand, I could feel the coldness. Ice-cold! I took it into my hand and was starting to thank him, totally confused as to just what was happening; the scene begged for explanation.

As he turned and walked away, he said as much to the trees and surroundings as me, "By god, when a man asks for a drink of water, he should be able to get a drink of water." And he was instantly in his car and gone.

I could never ascertain who the person was and why he had brought me the gift. I had been up and down the road a number of times passing a number of houses and will always wonder. Was there communication between the residents that had observed my curious activity and had that information spread from one house to another? Was he the voice in the window? A safe assumption would be that I will never know.

I stood there with my ice-cold bottle of Dasani. I was delirious with joy and celebration. Brass bands played songs of patriotism. Warm and unctuous voices in the recesses of my being rejoiced of apple pie and motherhood. Twenty-one guns blazed away in a stupendous salute. American flags flew in their glorious red-white-and-blue splendor. There was laughter. There was crying in my head. My mind was numb, my mind was happy, my mind was glad that life was what it was and people were what they were. Life was again good.

One ice-cold bottle of water hand-delivered by a good Samaritan answering to a person in need. My faith in all of mankind was again rock solid and good. All the other troubles that may have been haunting me had went away, and all that was left was this bone-weary thru-hiking fool deliriously holding his bottle of water, enjoying a solemn moment, paying homage to the goodness that was man and his ability to be there when another man needed—really needed—something. I would never doubt or question that concept ever again.

The remainder of the day went well, very well, indeed. However, the very next day would prove to be about as perplexing and in the same way somewhat redeeming. It seemed that the goodness of man for some reason was being put to the test. However, this time I was on the other end of the stick, it was my turn for good deeds.

That evening, I reflected on the water miracle, and it was a pleasurable time of feasting on pasta and ramen and about anything else that was available in the food bag, knowing that I was resupplying the next day. I had made the town decision the instant that the water miracle took place, needing again to be with people. The "feast" was followed with relaxation and reading and a leisurely journal entry. Followed by a peaceful night's sleep in spite of the traffic along busy U.S. Highway 7 that was just across the railroad tracks from where I was illegally stealth camping. I preferred to call it *maverick camping*, but the accepted term, or jargon, along the Trail was *stealth camping*. It was just something that worked for me. I followed all of the rules of Leave No Trace camping—being kind to the vegetation as much as possible, burying my human waste, and leaving the area as natural as the state that it was found in.

My hiking boots were grinding the Trail early the next day, and—after some indecision, thinking about the 2-mile walk into town—decided with finality that, indeed, going into Great Barrington was a good idea. U.S. Highways were usually the toughest to catch rides on for, too often, the drivers were from somewhere else and didn't know about the Trail and the needs of hikers. And my big problem with the Northbounder boots had to be resolved. The boots had developed "air scoops" with the fronts of the soles now lying back at times almost to the heel. Duct tape and glue could only do so much, the Trail was notorious for destroying even the best of boots.

So somewhat reluctantly, I did a left (north) and started my walk along the highway and soon was looking forward to whatever treasures were awaiting me. Strolling along the highway was enjoyable experiencing an even surface and allowed a chance to again regain some of my pace and rhythm. Not something that happens too often along the irregular and rocky surface of the Trail.

I was almost into town doing my blacktop shoulder dance when a bright object caught my attention, glaring in the bright morning sun and screaming, "Pick me up, pick me up." A key chain holding just one key. The type that the used-car dealerships hand out for test-drives. The tag read that it was for a 2000 Volvo. Impressed with Volvo, I shoved it in my pocket and proceeded to town.

Around the first bend, I could see promising things, and it wasn't long before Bagel Shop could easily be read. Joy and happiness were again a part of life. The Bagel Shop proved to truly be a thru-hiker oasis. A place that made its own cream cheese flavored with about every flavor available, from blueberry to strawberry. I opted for plain bagels and plain cream cheese and was soon in a bagel-and-fresh-hot-coffee daze.

I lingered with my coffee and debated more feasting and finally made my way out with a supply for the Trail. I made my way across the highway only to find the outfitter store closed until ten. Too late for this thru-hiker who was just a few grocery items away from heading back down the highway. I managed to make my way through the grocery store maze with just simply what I needed. Then next door to the hardware store for a fresh roll of duct tape. A nearby bench at the corner of the strip mall provided a comfortable place to retape the boot toes and add some glue.

A bus stopped about the time I was well into this job. I asked the driver how far south he went on the highway. Not close enough as the driver told me that the farthest stop was about a mile out or only about halfway back to the Trail. And maybe that was omen. The 2000 Volvo key was still in my pocket.

Soon I was heading back south on the highway. Just a short way beyond the city limits was a small car dealership. I didn't see any Volvos in the lot but decided that I would stop anyway. The two car-wash jocks seemed confused when I mentioned the key and was advised to go inside the office. There a man heard my story and accepted the key. Soon I was back on the highway heading back to the Trail. It seemed like the end of story, one that just sort of ended with no sense of accomplishment, lost in the maze of incidents in this saga of unending proportions.

About a half mile short of the Trail was another car dealership. This lot was full of Volvos, something that I hadn't noticed on the way into town. A Volvo was just another Volvo until you happen to know the whereabouts for a key for one. I briskly stepped into the office and was face-to-face with a lady sitting at the desk. She seemed rather distressed.

I was just in midsentence about why I was there when the man from the first dealership stepped in and handed her the key. She was delighted. No, she was in a riotous state of celebration. Relief and happiness erupted, her face radiated stupendous joy. She had been working on the whereabouts of the key apparently for quite some time. It was the one and only key that the lot had for the car. She accepted the key; and after standing there for just a few moments, I realized that more than ample payment had been received merely by being witness to this scene, and I stepped outside and started making my way back south. As I walked by the car driven by the man from the first dealership, he stuck his head out the window and said, "It seems like they should have given you something."

My reply was all too apparent, "I think I've already gotten payment enough seeing how happy she was."

I waltzed my way down the highway and soon was back on the Trail doing what I do. The late-afternoon sun had heated up the thick vegetation; and the muggy, humid air engulfed me as I skirted the Housatonic River, preparing for some level river-hiking along the edges of farms and civilization. A Robin Hood sort of aura came over me, a good deed done, no monetary payment was ever mentioned—the sort of human experience that is truly meaningful. The recipients of this good deed didn't even know the name of the person involved, kind of like the Lone Ranger. A story that would be told and retold and maybe even embellished somewhat as the years go by.

# Chapter 35

## Canons Questioned

*December 8, 2002 (Ocala, Florida)—(Journal entry)—put in an order for the total coverage of maps—then asked about the boots, sure enough, they were there*

There is too much information on boots: the selection of, the buying of, the various brands and the virtues of each, and so on. Too much, for nobody seems to agree on anything, and after getting on the Trail, it was even worse.

The long-held theory seems to be that boots are selected based on the length of the hike and the amount of weight that the hiker is going to carry. The longer the distance and the more weight that is carried, the heavier the boot should be. Somehow for the neophyte that seemed intelligent even if adding weight to your feet defied good logic. So armed with such information had greatly influenced a very important decision.

Also a major obstacle in this critical purchase was the buy-American thing. American-made products we are all led to believe are the best, the only way to go. If one has a choice! However, it doesn't take long at a shoe store or outfitters to realize that is a pretty tall order. Look at the label Made In on the insides of almost all footwear, and you will find Philippines, Taiwan, China—rarely the United States of America. Maybe the shoe laces, never the actual shoes.

However, there was an exception and that was the boot that I sought. One American company was well noted for boots and for the purposes of this dissertation I shall simply refer to them as my Northbounders. Once the decision was made to go American-made, the brand name never again was questioned. And where in the United States they were made was never questioned. Or so I thought. So early on and busting with my American pride, the decision was made that Northbounders would be my boots for the Appalachian Trail. There would be no substitute. My visit to the outfitters in Ocala, Florida, on the hallowed boot-buying day was short and sweet. Soon my coveted Northbounders and I left the store, and there were no second thoughts. Yes, the other brands were noted on the shelf but were never considered. Northbounder, how I loved to repeat the name. A worldly name. A thru-hiker name.

The boots were heavy! And expensive! Made entirely of leather and, again following the accepted rules of the people that know about these things, with very few seams. One big piece of leather for the entire boot. Nothing to tear apart or come loose, with just rugged cowhide in-between. However, being leather, one big piece of leather, does require a break-in period of serious duration, at least a couple of hundred miles seemed to be the minimum. Now let's kind of keep that fact in the back of our minds as we embark on this very serious acquisition, arguably the most important piece of equipment on the Trail.

So this purchase occurred way back in December of 2002, four months before my hike departure date. The boots were a Christmas gift from my daughter, Tammy; but I brought my precious Northbounders home way before Christmas, the break-in period being the justification not to wait. They were just awesome. So smooth, real-man-looking boots with that deep and satisfying real leather sheen. I actually held them up to my face and sucked in that wondrous aroma. It seemed so sad that these wonderful creations of the American craftsman would soon have to be scratched up and defaced and abused, for the AT is not kind to equipment.

The boots were put into action the very same day that the purchase took place. Abandoning my work surveying boots for the Northbounders, I embarked on another one of those dreaded training hikes donning my forty-seven-pound yoke of sand and old backpack. However, those first steps made me wonder about my capabilities. I felt like Frankenstein! *Clump, clump, clump, clump.* Good grief, was I going to have to learn how to walk all over again? Walking was something that I really prided myself in, being able to pick 'um up and lay 'um down. Years of surveying and mapping had required such skills. Good powerful legs, ankles that had never once been sprained, never a break of any kind in the lower extremities. However my being had been relegated to spastic, one going constantly uphill.

However, I endured this initiation and eventually the leather started to give a little and there seemed to be more pliancy. Within a few days, not knowing if it was a mental ploy or actual physiological effect, I was convinced that these were the right boots for me. My loyalty to the American worker was intact.

In retrospect, it would seem that in the process of putting on the boots, this discovery could have been made sooner. A moot point at this juncture. However, about the second week with the boots and yet again lovingly caressing the smoothness and admiring the workmanship, the label jumped at me. There inside the tongue flap laid the awful truth: Made in China—good grief!

Made in China! How could it be? Was this another home product that had fallen victim to outsourcing? I wrestled with it subconsciously and pretended that it didn't make a difference. But it did. I had been violated. I should have been smarter and had checked these things more closely, but at that time of innocence and in that aura of new purchase, was enamored by it all. I was entering a world of the well-informed, the world of expensive well-made gear. In a store that sold expensive and well-made gear. Why would I check something like that? I knew that Northbounders were made in the United States. My patriotic quest need not question a long-held fact. They had always been made in America.

So my new pair of Northbounders had hardly been broken in and already doubts of their service and quality were invading my confidence. I walked a little more humbly after that in my nightly excursions into hiker-wannabe land and tried to rationalize this new world where we Americans tried to wring every ounce of profit that we could. Somehow this provided very little reassurance. So with only time could I accept this notion of justification being the bottom line. So my initial pride, though somewhat tainted, remained at a little bit lower level.

The Northbounders survived the initiation and probably had about the required break-in of 200 or so miles by the time the date of departure, April 5, rolled around. I felt confident with my leather beauties and always went out of the way to tell people that these boots would make contact with the rocks of Mount Katahdin. Yup, these suckers were going to go all the way. Made right, even if not in the right country—well, our standards were imposed on foreign workers and these were the best that money could buy. Made for the long haul and able to carry the forty to fifty pounds of backpack, plus my weight, for the distance.

The early parts of the hike went pretty good for I really didn't know any better; the boots seemed like the ultimate in hiking gear. To add to my enthusiasm, my hiking partner, Buffalo Bobby, had the very same boots.

We were twins, and we swore by our choice as we *clump, clumped* along. Neither one of us could have envisioned what lay ahead.

It wasn't too long, probably within the first 150 miles, that I noticed the toe-construction belied common sense and wasn't doing too well. Prior to the first steps on the Appalachian Trail, one cannot imagine how rough it is and how rigorous boot field testing could be. For some reason, the designers of the boot had decided that where the sole comes around the toe of the boot, it was best to stop the sole material about 3/4 inches up. The soles just sort of wrapped around the toe and stopped right there where one tends to kick things. It appeared to be well attached; however, had the toe material went up and over back to the laces and not had a seam at the kicking point; the construction may well have survived.

By Hot Springs, North Carolina, 275 miles of hiking, the soles were flapping. Granted, just a little bit, but flapping nevertheless. Possibly the boots were not intended to kick things on a regular basis, but the Appalachian Trail is not like walking down a sidewalk. And kicking things became the norm for there are lots of things just made for kicking. Rocks, roots, irregular places in the surface—the Appalachian Trail is rarely level and smooth. And with the joint of sole to leather upper right there at the kicking place, there was a tendency for separation, a peeling back sort of effect.

By the 460-mile point of Damascus, Virginia, the flapping had become a problem. More like air scoops. I worked on my technique trying to walk just a little differently to make sure my feet went over those little killer nubs of roots that were constantly lying in ambush and camouflaged from hiker boots. And if you were walking too fast, you too often found yourself checking out the ground at very close range. Common occurrences on the Trail.

At Damascus, I bought my first tube of boot-repair glue, convinced that would take care of the problem. Of course, a small roll of duct tape was added to the pack, the quintessential "tool of the thru-hiker." Some of the tape was in the original gear, but the tremendous demand for the stuff could not have been anticipated early in the hike.

So for the next thousand miles, I glued and taped and hoped for the best. Sometimes the repairs were "roadside," taking a break from the hiking; and other times, they were "fireside" while in camp making all the correct preparations (dry leather and proper removal of debris). Of course, fireside lasted longer but not too much longer. It was about this time that I realized just how very long this wonderful and heavy leather retained water. Days! Sometimes hiking for almost a week without once experiencing the wonderful feeling of dry boots. And with wet came weight.

But these were my Northbounders that were going to Katahdin with me and ever loyal and ever perseverant, on we trudged. Maybe it was the same stuff that makes one reluctant to quit hiking. These boots were from the charter group of gear, intelligently and carefully purchased and all part of the master plan. The rest of the gear was making it fine. Possibly, as far as the attitude toward the boots was concerned, the proper word was *stubborn*, stemming from that mental image of standing atop Katahdin with those Northbounders on as originally planned. However, Katahdin was a long way off, and this process of duct tape and glue had started way too early. Only time would tell.

# Chapter 36

## Enough!

*August 28—Day 115—Mile 1563—(Journal entry)—after much confusion—finally decided on EMS boots (at Eastern Mountain Sports)—had photo taken and posted in window of store*

I was not a good bus man. I didn't know that before this day began, but by early afternoon, it was clearly evident that this was just not a skill that I possessed.

It was one of the most demeaning experiences on the Trail! It was the simplest of tasks, and here it had come down to admitting that I did not know what to do. And also to admit that I was not a good bus man. How hard could this be, for goodness' sake! Catch a bus, sit comfortably, and leave the driving to the good and professional bus driver and if need be ask other riders that were knowledgeable about such things and follow instructions.

It's well-known that real men don't ask directions. But on the Trail, real men were of a somewhat different mettle; and after all, most real men wouldn't tackle something like the Appalachian Trail anyway. Concerning myself with the "real men" issue actually has been this reckless flirtation with the facetious, and the genuine real men issue just never was a problem. However, for this dissertation, it has to be addressed for the reader may wonder. Readers may wonder anyway, but that is not the point. Now the record is straight, and the reader can do what readers do—analyze and come to armchair conclusions with suggestions of questionable worth.

I had gotten on the bus a stone's throw from the motel. Easy enough. Then ride to the central terminal point that buses have had in metropolitan areas for eons, and then change buses for the one that would take me to my final destination. Nothing to it. However, living in suburbia or something akin to suburbia and owning multiple family-automobiles for the better part of my life, the need to deal with buses just had never come up. So here was this rebel on the Trail with a self-imposed demonstration against suburbia and the American obsession with convenience, and being a self-professed conservationist, it was difficult to admit that one of the most basic of skills of being not one of them just did not exist. I was not a good bus man. It hurt.

It is noteworthy to mention that in my now-hometown, Ocala, Florida, the advent of bus service is a rather-recent occurrence. It pulls at me to get on and ride to the mall, maybe do a little shopping while there and then ride back and, while doing so, scorn the profusion of cars that is becoming the trademark of our growing community. It should have been a part of my training for the Appalachian Trail. Then I would have know what to do. It is just hard to cover all the bases when preparing for such a massive venture and some things just were overlooked.

It has to be clarified that the area that includes Dalton, Massachusetts, is more like country than a large city; but after months on the Trail, almost anything seems metropolitan. There are numerous towns in proximity, and a bus system had been installed to get from town to town. A godsend for the thru-hiker coming through town with only feet to get around.

I was trying to get to Berkshire Mall. My obsession and loyalty to the Northbounder boots had finally run the course. It was time for replacement, and the mall seemed to be the only place to do that from the information that I had gleaned from the local people. Besides Dalton, there were numerous villages and towns loosely connected: Adams Junction, Coltsville, North Adams, Cheshire, Williamstown, Berkshire, and so on, the latter being the namesake of the mall itself. I might as well have been in New York City, for 115 days of hiking had changed me to basically a trail bum, even in spite of the worldly aura of GoreTex. This variety of stores and shopping centers was in complete contradiction to the lack of the metropolitan in the sparse world of the AT.

Not too long after getting on the second bus, it started occurring to me that we were pretty much heading back what seemed like east, and that was pretty much where I had come from. Cardinal directions are embedded within my mind from years of mapping and are usually a point of reference almost all of the time, even inside buildings if there is a reason for that. So here I am riding back east, and in not too long, go back by the motel and even farther to the east. My trail savvy was useless in this situation despite knowing that bus riding was not serving me too well. In not too long, I was farther from my intended destination than when I had started. The only consolation I could come up with was that I had just been on the Trail too long and was more accustomed to walking to get somewhere. Possibly my riding skills had become somewhat rusty. Nothing to get too excited about. It would work out.

We made the big circle east of Dalton and started back west, with landmarks starting to become familiar. About the time that we got back past the motel again, as inconspicuously as possible, I slouched up to the driver. I explained my situation without referring to my lack of experience with these sorts of things. He was sympathetic and was well aware of my AT thru-hiker status that was exuded by my scroungy clothes and emaciated body.

My timing for starting this conversation was perfect for as I finished, he stopped at a street intersection where we were about to make a left turn. He advised me to get off the bus and just walk straight ahead and that "the mall was right straight through there not too far." So I was back in my element doing what came so naturally, propelling my body via my own power. I whistled making my way up the street and just figured bus skills could be worked on at some later date should the need arise.

It was a welcome surprise to see a white blaze on a power pole after just a couple of hundred feet of walking. I was actually on the Appalachian Trail, for the street and the Trail were coincident, wending its way through this particular part of town. So it was turning out to be kind of a rehearsal for tomorrow, assuming that I would be ready to continue in so short a time with what had to be accomplished yet today. Shortly the Trail took a severe right, exiting the street to return to its natural state of single path through the woods. However, for today, I continued walking west to the mall.

The mall provided a mecca of stores; and one in particular, Eastern Mountain Sports, more than filled my needs and wants. But the latter would have to be answered to at some other time, needs having taken the priority. Here were all of the brand names, and after many questions, some understanding was ascertained concerning breaking one of the canons of hiking boots, that being that one never took a brand-new pair of boots right out in a continuance of a thru-hike. The nice lady assured me that the lighter models would not require a break-in period. After much debate and soul-searching and test-driving around the mall, getting the okay from the store people to venture out of the store, I chose a pair of spiffy-looking EMS boots (yes, I suppose it was their brand); and when leaving, they were proudly on my feet. I literally lived in them for the ensuing short hours that were now deemed the break-in period. Ninety-five dollars seemed like a heck of a deal after spending $175 on the Northbounders. Allow me the luxury to use the term, I again was a happy camper.

It was amusing noticing my reflection in the store windows as my new boots contrasted severely with the rest of my trail-grubby attire. Being from out of town, it was of no concern, so I exaggerated my strut as my boots glided over the smooth marble floors. It was time to enjoy some mall food, and while so doing, I engaged in some nontrail conversation with a local lady. I then attempted to exit the mall, taking the long way when suddenly stronger forces pulled me into Walden Books. The cheerful girl inside asked if there was a need for assistance. I told her that I wasn't sure just what I was doing in there and that a greater power was guiding my way more than I was. She pretty much left me alone.

Within about a minute, I was in the inspirational section and holding *All I Really Need to Know I Learned in Kindergarten,* by Robert Fulghum. Soon after, the book was mine in exchange for seven dollars; and the girl was left in a somewhat-befuddled state, wondering about such a quick purchase that had started with such uncertainty. After all, bookstores are for browsing and killing time, a place where shoppers normally spend hours.

This was my second copy, the first residing somewhere on my home bookshelf. I gleefully was looking forward to the rereading. This book should be mandatory reading and probably should have a regal position within households throughout the world right next to the family Bible or Book of Mormon or Koran or whatever the case might be. This Fulghum masterpiece holds within its few pages more wisdom, more savvy, more peace, and more advice than a library full of lesser works. His approach to the mundane business of living and dealing with life's situations lend an attitude that makes even tying your shoes an exciting event. Mr. Fulghum has led life in such a way with such a positive approach that were we all to adopt these simple rules in our lives, there would be no wars, strife would be virtually nonexistent and life would just simply be fun again.

It was perfect for the Trail. It turned out to be the most looked-forward-to event of the day until I finished it and left it for others, for it is too good to just lie somewhere and not be experienced. The book was casually left on the bookshelf at Lake of the Clouds Hut and, hopefully, is not merely gathering dust. Its presence in my life was just another one of those unexplainable events in the course of the hike that elicited the now-common utterance of "thank you, God."

The day ended with more food, a lot more food. While eating, my mind pondered the fact that I was not a good bus man. I later talked to fellow thru-hiker Aussie who—of course, as his name indicates—is from Australia. He appeared perplexed with my revelation, so it was rather embarrassing telling him about the bus fiasco. He had navigated the labyrinth of bus-hood, had traveled as far as North Adams and had visited the museum, all without a bit of trouble. Possibly, I rationalized, real bus men came from foreign countries where there was a need to know about these things. Where people actually lived not owning a fleet of automobiles in their oversized garages and traveling by foot and alternate means of transportation were a way of life. A certain amount of appeasement came about, emphasizing to myself that probably most Americans were not good bus people. Oh well, tomorrow, it really wouldn't make any difference.

Most importantly, tomorrow would tell me if I had the made the correct choice with my boot purchase resuming my trek north. And a correct choice it was. So correct in fact that it elicited this entry in the journal the next day: *Probably the best day-hiking yet! Could it be I hiked 1,560 miles in the wrong boots? The new boots are wonderful! No blisters, light, nice.*

A final note about the Northbounders. Looking at them now, the 1,560 miles of rough AT terrain hardly did anything to the rest of the boots. The soles look virtually new, the leather is perfect, but those darn toes. Sigh. It would have been so nice had we completed the trip and stood on top of Katahdin together. They hold a regal place in the AT corner in our home and now merely serve are a small part of the déjà vu all over again.

# Chapter 37

## Insight

*August 10—Day 128—Mile 1737 ( just across the Connecticut River from Hanover, New Hampshire)—(Journal entry)—zero day—probably didn't walk 1/2 mile today—cleaned water filter—shaved my beard off and cut my hair some—water-proofed my tent bottom, backpack, and fanny pack (did that in the parking lot)*

It was satisfying to say that New Hampshire was another state that had been added to my list, albeit for such a tiny, tiny distance. Hanover is just over the Connecticut River from Vermont. But it, too, was now in my repertoire of conquered cities and towns and places; and now, hard as it could be to believe, only one state remained—Maine! I could look in what appeared to be the correct direction and wonder if those blue hills there in the impossible distance could actually be the ever-illusive Maine. An exciting butterfly feeling would erupt within my insides while gazing to the north and realizing that maybe, just maybe, I could be a 2,000-miler, a thru-hiker that had done it, an Appalachian Trail thru-hiker. It just did not seem possible when I thought back to those early days struggling uphill to make six steps at a time and wonder if I was merely dreaming and that it was attainable only by those worthy of such lofty goals.

But there was a long way left, and the very hardest of the hard climbing and hiking remained. As throughout the hike, what should have been there all along was missing—the confidence, the assurance, the cocksure-strutting attitude. It just did not happen. My being still was permeated with self-doubt, and I was just certain that one day, my body and mind would just break down and somebody would have to rescue this blubbering and exhausted miscreant, this now-outcast from society—that a helicopter would have to lower a line and somehow lift this useless poundage of depraved humanity and airlift it back to someplace where relatives or friends would claim it and have to haul it away in a state of defeat and humiliation.

But that could all be set aside for a while. I could, if only for a short time, bask in my victory and aura of self-accomplishment. I had made it to New Hampshire, and celebration that involved gluttony was in order. Buffets and convenience stores laden with overabundance beckoned and only that need be addressed at the moment.

He was black. A large and smiling black man. Possibly I should have suspected ulterior motive in his friendliness; however, in this new role of AT hiker, it just didn't make any difference for I usually talked to everybody and anybody regardless of whether they wanted something specifically or just needed friendship.

However, having made it to New Hampshire, I was back in Vermont for that is where the motel was situated. Back across the Connecticut River from Hanover was a small complex of motels and restaurants and amenities of humankind, the little village of White River Junction. I was seeking refuge from the pricey-ness of Hanover and the Ivy School-ness of Dartmouth College, trying to save a few dollars even though I had allowed the extravagance of a cab to take me there. With the motel being a mere $71 a night—well, with all of the money I was saving as compared to Hanover—a cab just seemed okay. My prevailing mood, though one of some apprehension thinking about the White Mountains and of what lay ahead, was of rather headiness and giddiness, of being just one state away from the ultimate. One state away laid glory and a tiny light at the end of the tunnel to this endless condition of masochism and depravation and abuse.

His question just sort of oozed out. Caught me unaware and slightly off guard. Yes, my being reeks of gullible, and he must have sensed it. Or possibly he just could see that I was a fairly decent human being.

"Was won'erin' if ya'll cou hep me out a bit?"

He had out-of-state plates, his older vintage car was visible in the parking lot. It was my drying-out time, and that always meant a good feeling of accomplishment of getting gear back in order. Life was good. My tent was erected and lying on its side so that the bottom was catching the sun rays and breeze in the parking lot, the rain fly lay nearby. It was sunny, though rain was threatening. Meanwhile, things were drying out nicely.

I suppose it was a cut-to-the-chase sort of reply. Or maybe just wondering if the "help" came in the monetary form. It didn't really sound like my voice. A disconnected sort of utterance from somebody.

"How much you need?" It really was my voice. It quivered just ever so slightly.

No answer. Possibly I had caught him unaware also, and possibly my trail grubbiness had suggested to him that there wasn't too much money there to spare. Unsuspectingly, we both had been placed in positions of cat and mouse warily eyeing each other as to intent and purpose. His brought on by a question that must have required courage to ask and mine by my directness.

Having left him open for possibly too much and wanting to maintain the upper hand in what could become a situation that could get out of hand, I felt compelled to set a limit. My intentions would have to be questioned later. However, this state of Robinhood-ness that had prevailed for the past four months of my life had altered my thinking with regard to the human condition and our state of symbiosis. Too many good deeds had been flowing my way as trail angels and simply good people had helped me in my mission. It seemed like the correct time to pay back some. The gods that controlled this aura needed appeasing from time to time, or these good deeds would surely end. It was payback time, indeed. Or maybe I was merely trying to maintain good relationships with the gods, a sort of guarantee of good karma.

"Hundred be enough?" Again the strange quivering voice. A hundred! What was I thinking!

His reaction was more like a lack of such. Again nothing. A long silence. Possibly he was thinking he had not heard me quite correctly. Or worse, was he vying for position to barter for more, of envisioning having stumbled on a really good thing. Or again possibly, maybe he was thinking that he had a big-enough fish on the line, that he better make sure the line was set before reeling it in. His reply eventually came.

"Ya, da be fine."

My mind was reeling just a bit, thinking that after being so careful to avoid the expense of Hanover, I had just spent one hundred dollars in a moment of reckless abandon. For a fleeting moment of recoil, a ploy of hesitation wanted my being to renege, that after further thought, I just did not have the money. Silence. Another silence. However, I knew that the trail gods were there with us, witnessing this scene. There was no turning back.

"I don't have the cash on me right now. Give me some time and I'll get some from an ATM machine and I'll get it to you. What room you in?"

He gave me the room number and then went on to tell me that he had come here for work from the South and that his family was with him and that the job he was promised didn't quite pan out. It appeared as if my money had been well spent and had been placed with a human being struggling as was I. The good feelings returned, and the doubt of the sanity of this transaction was merely reaction to somebody in need, a situation that I had been in for almost the past half year of my life.

The Trail does something to people that is not witnessed in quite this pure form in "civilian life." I did not know this man's name. I really did not want to know this man's name! For with that would come encumbrance and obligation. He only knew me as Ole Smoky Lonesome that was evidenced as being written on the brim of my hat, if he noticed; and that was a good thing. The only problem that would occur to me later was that, possibly, he could never relate this story to friends or relatives.

The ATM was at a convenience store across the highway from the motel, and I didn't want to abandon my drying project, so I told him that I would get the money to him as soon as possible. He seemed satisfied with that, and a state of trepidation based on trust seemed to ensue.

The tent was eventually dry, and I made my way across the highway and soon had the money in my wallet. When I knocked on the door of his room, there was a long delay, nothing happened; and I realized that there was nobody there. The money would have to stay burning in my pocket for a while longer, a situation that was uncomfortable wondering if I somehow would justify not going through with this, coming to some sort of justified conclusion that I had been hit at a weak moment. However, that conclusion never was reached before I again found myself at the same door; and this time, there was somebody there. He answered the door and took the money and thanked me. The exchange was brief and to the point; he might have felt a little embarrassed by it all.

The story would have been better had it ended there, but fate has ways of intervening and casting different perspectives on experiences just when one is convinced of being in total understanding. Coincidence could be the culprit, but attributing too many things to that removes mystique and that is just not the nature of the human beast.

Mere proximity could support the coincidence theory, and with pricey Hanover our only option, it really required little thought beyond that. He and his family were seeking food as was I, and while walking to the nearby Chinese buffet, it was hard not to notice the entire throng behind me. There were other places to eat along the way, but they too chose the buffet. My seat inside made it hard to avoid my presence; and as we made our numerous trips to the cornucopia of culinary delights, he could not thank me enough, to the point of making the kids stop and thank me. Then it was my turn to be embarrassed.

I suppose that a feeling of self-virtue could have filled my ego with pompous ideas of goodness and self-importance. The Trail does not allow for such deception. Over the past months, I had been at the other end enough times to know that giving and receiving were synonymous dependent only on status at that particular moment. Humility came easy on the Trail and might possibly be its greatest attribute and virtue.

Too often in our world of materialism and abundance, we forget about our numerous blessings, thinking that everything existed in such excess as the norm. We have become so galvanized from those that have nothing, that rational thought of doing without is impossible. And if that abundance is not shared from time to time, there can be no joy in living. The Appalachian Trail had manifested what a thousand sermons could not. Those meek shall, indeed, inherit the earth. Not because they had earned it, which they had, but because it is just the natural progression of this complication that we call life. Those times when we are the closest to something or somebody a lot of times is when we are the farthest away, and all of those things that we learned in kindergarten were forgotten when we went from the innocence of youth to adulthood.

Again my thoughts drifted to the little note so thoughtfully taped into my first journal back cover, my fortune cookie message before leaving for the Trail. A phrase that had been repeated many times and waited to be repeated again. "Your path is arduous but will be amply rewarding." I only felt humbled to be so regally treated just because I had taken some time to take a little walk.

# Chapter 38

## Humility

*August 16—Day 134—Mile 1819—(Journal entry)—got to Galehead Hut about 2:00 p.m. (maybe slightly later)—was intent on staying one night in a hut in a work-for-stay status—checked with the Croo, and it was okay*

Writer's note: This hiker/writer has nothing but deep respect for the AMC (Appalachian Mountain Club) and what they do. Maintaining the huts in the severe climate and high elevations of the White Mountains requires superhuman effort for all involved. Just hiking into these places is a major job in itself. And bringing in supplies that have to be packed in is beyond comprehension. The huts are wonderful, clean, and neat; and the availability of cheap or free food was the difference between making it or not.

It should be added that when staying in the campsites operated by AMC, the treatment of thru-hikers was world-class. I loved my stay at the Liberty Springs tent site, and the setup on a wooden tent platform was definitely downtown. The caretaker there was a previous thru-hiker and we had a heart-to-heart about the joys of watching the movie *The Wizard of Oz* while listening to *The Dark Side of the Moon* album by Pink Floyd.

I did not understand the system at the huts. And quite frankly, I was one beat-up hiker by this time. I probably was not the best of company and certainly was not pretty to look at. So, take the following dissertation as strictly my opinion and as a rather tongue-in-cheek observation from the trail-weary view point of a thru-hiker observing the other world that had long been left behind.

So hats off to the Croo and thank-you to the AMC. You guys do one heck of a good job!

As we sat on the little bench situated between the men's and the women's "restrooms," the thought slowly percolated that we, of our choosing, had become outcasts of this rather-elite, as they chose to be considered, and closed society. The caste system had been quickly established. We being Draco and me, the only thru-hikers in the lot and the only nonpaying customers. This particular society was of the intermittent sort as the clientele wandered in and out, changing nightly. Galehead Hut, one of the AMC "huts" in the White Mountains chain and at 3,820 feet above sea level, was proving to be a rather-heady array of folks, most of whom hardly gave Draco and me the acknowledgment of our presence or the consideration that our thru-hiking endeavor could possibly be of interest.

The possibility, of course, might just have been a reaction to our rather-deplorable state of personal hygiene as Draco and I hadn't had a recent shower. Also, our 1,800-mile-old thru-hiker grungies were rather offensive when compared to the brilliantly colored and virtually new designer attire of the jet-setter hikers. Also, the two holes in the back of my shirt caused by the pack riding there for the past four months made me look somewhat like a homeless person that had somehow wandered into this place and appeared more in need of a handout than just some human contact.

The little bench was just room enough for the two of us and for all practical purposes was the only place left to sit in the building. It should be noted that the "bathrooms" are the fancy version of the same pit toilets along the Trail and not of the flush-water type that we are all familiar with. For after all, we were still in the wilds out in the White Mountains and not back home. So sitting here basically between two outhouses, we were exiled; and desperately in need of identification, I chose to think of Draco and me as just—the Untouchables.

We were waiting for some leftovers that hopefully would remain after the feasting was over, that being our payment for the "work" that we had done or were waiting to do. We watched and listened and laughed as the Croo provided the entertainment for the evening, ranging from skits to standup comedy. We sat quietly. There was no questioning the credentials of the Croo, being a group that had tons of credibility being a truly elite collection of people from virtually all over the world that chose to spend their summers working the huts in the employ of the AMC either between careers, between university stints, or various other ambitious endeavors. A Croo member had to be somebody to be there, and they were courteous and considerate and empathized with thru-hikers, having seen the straggle of us over the past month or so as the northbounders made their way through. The Croo could, indeed, relate to the rigors of months on the Appalachian Trail.

As the evening progressed and the various courses of the feast continued, Draco and I were becoming rather concerned about just what would remain, the food was going fast. We were in dire need of nourishment. My body fat bottomed out to near nothing two months before, and I had long since quit looking at myself too closely in a mirror, if one should ever afford itself for my service. Observing the proceedings, I could relate to those in society who had to face this inequity on a daily basis as a way of life. My views of the roles in the human condition were changing drastically.

The AMC rules concerning the huts were rather hard for me to understand. This was my first night in a hut, and I had no idea of how to act or what I should be doing. So we more or less sat in subservience and waited for whatever was going to happen, it was the easiest attitude to assume. A difficult role after four months of derring-do on the Trail and approaching life as if anything was possible.

The large problem with the segment of the Appalachian Trail that goes through the White Mountains is that there really are very few options to not utilizing the huts. For a large part, the hiker is above tree line; and the regulations clearly state that camping is allowed only in designated places. So with the huts about the correct distance for a good daily mileage, and with no camping in between, the thru-hiker ends up utilizing the only resources available. Granted no thru-hike is complete without experiencing this rather-humbling experience for it would not truly be a thru-hike. However, as a thru-hiker, this attitude is unique only to this portion; contrary to the curiosity that most persons along the Trail have toward anybody that was attempting a thru-hike.

I had been asked to scrape out a freezer that was heavily caked with ice. Yes, the huts do have electricity; acquiescence to at least some of the amenities of modern man. The job only took about thirty minutes. However, with that, I seemed to have qualified for the night's free room and board. I would have done more if asked; however, it appeared that Croo members pretty well had it covered. Draco was also a willing helper, so the two of us exuded this aura of a much-too-eager willingness for our privilege of sleeping on the floor in the dining room and any food that may have been left over.

The party finally ended about nine. Amazingly, there was some food left over, and Draco and I dove in. Mostly there was roast turkey, and that was fine for I was probably more in need of protein than anything. There was a sprinkling of mashed potatoes of which I took my reasonable portion in the spirit of sharing, an unusual dressing and a few spikes of pumpkin pie. Not really enough for a thru-hiker appetite, but it was enough as it represented more than the usual nightly trail fare would have been. We then were assigned some more work resulting in the cleaning of some huge and greasy pans and the stove. Draco worked like a trooper. It wasn't long before we were done.

Our allotted sleeping spaces were in the dining area more or less between the tables. I chose a spot close to the outside wall and soon had my teeth brushed and lay in the sleeping bag, making the comments in my journal that were used in the writing of these past few pages. Possibly I had waited until then for the true perspective to manifest itself. And to assess the situation and with that came the much-needed amusement thinking about the paradox and how the human condition is merely a matter of perspective. That the station in life at any one time can usually be rationalized or dealt with if the sense of humor can be incorporated in the process. I went to sleep with the usual anticipation for the coming day, and all was again well with the world. It could not have been more perfect had I been one of the paying guests for then it would not have been worth writing about.

I left Galehead early the next morning, August 17. The first 0.8 mile was very steep and rock strewn leading to the top of South Twin. It was a difficult climb; but by that time, the adrenaline flow was going good, the lactic acid lag ABOUT disappeared, and my strength was starting to come back. The remainder of the day went quite well, and I found myself at Zealand Falls Hut shortly before noon. I had a bowl of the soup-of-the-day and contemplated my arrangements for that night. The most daunting part of the Trail in the planning stages was this stretch through the White Mountains. It was difficult to discern how to go about it for the information was rather nebulous concerning the limitations above tree line, the restrictions on camping, and the lack of camping facilities at the correct mileages.

While eating, it was difficult not to overhear the plans of a couple of serious slackpackers who were discussing their strategy. From what I could ascertain, they had slackpacked both ways down from Mount Washington that is accessible by automobile, doing this under the guise of a thru-hike, thus doing a serious climb *downhill.* My mind was in a state of turmoil as

I left there, wasting as little time as possible leaving. My thoughts would eventually make their way into my journal that night with: *When is some slackpacking genius going to rent a helicopter, fly to the top of Mount Katahdin, and hike down to complete his thru-hike!* My ideas of a thru-hike just seemed to clash with too many that were also involved in a similar endeavor: Start from point A (Springer Mountain) and hike to point B (Mount Katahdin), or in the case of southbounders, the reverse of that. Period. Otherwise it is just not a thru-hike.

The next day, while leaving the Mizpah Spring Hut with the intention of getting to Lake of the Clouds Hut that evening, I used the phone there and called for a reservation, having justified in my mind the $68 nightly fee. That was about 11:00 a.m., and I was told that they did not take reservations until 1:00 p.m. Reflecting on that conversation while hiking; it seemed hard to believe that I accepted that information without questioning it as it was truly a catch-22. There were no other phones available before getting to my destination. I chose not to pursue the matter upon getting there about 3:00; being happy to have made it and attaining my goal for the day. I checked in with one of the Croo and soon was happily washing huge pots and pans and feeling my usual subservient White Mountains self.

My duties were more clearly defined at the Lake of the Clouds Hut and soon my confidence had somewhat returned; and with it, the notion that this was all part of the thru-hike and dealing with the inequities could only work to enhance my experience, this approach was much more interesting than trying to be one of the people that I was not. A role that I had played in other locations and towns as I progressed north.

For some undetermined reason, an older Croo member, and obviously one who had spent considerable time in the Whites gave me some serious advice. He told me that I needed to consider "giving back." Later I wondered why I hadn't told him that maybe we all "pay back" society in our own manner and if not trail-related possibly in other ways. I failed to mention working with kids for eight summers in Missouri, teaching them to play tennis strictly as a volunteer through the Optimist Club or having donated ten gallons of blood over the years or picking up trash along the roadways in my hometown or singing in the church choir.

The Lake of the Clouds experience was somewhat similar to Galehead. However, there was some thru-hiker camaraderie provided by three brothers from Mesquite, Texas who were heading south on an attempted thru-hike. They kept our spirits high; and being again with my brethren, a warm and fuzzy feeling ensued. They were in the early stages of their southbound thru-hike, they were young, and theirs was the attitude of the potential successful thru-hiker. All three seemed to have perpetual smiles on their faces. They were enjoying the experience as much as anybody that I had encountered on the Trail.

The partying and carrying on and stories and jokes continued until late for this seems to be standard operating procedure. The food had more or less disappeared, leaving mostly bread; however, having taken care of protein on the first hut experience, this was a good night for a carbohydrate overload. And so the AMC thru-hiker experience was drawing to a close for in two more days, I would be out of the Whites and addressing the daunting fact of Maine and the Mahoosucs. To most of the hikers encountered that were in the know, "the hard stuff was just beginning."

After 1,800 miles of hiking, the hard stuff was just beginning. Scary, but then nobody said that it would be easy. The Appalachian Trail has ways of reminding you of that on a fairly regular basis.

# Chapter 39

## Dufus

*August 20—Day 138—Mile 1869 (Journal entry)—into Pinkham Notch Visitor Center by 9:00 a.m.—had coffee, cereal with milk, and three ice cream bars—also bought six large cookies and minestrone soup mix*

He came out of nowhere.

I had left my hat sitting on the ground at Carter Dome having taken a picture of what was left there of the old fire tower. The hat usually never left my head, but for some reason, I had changed my routine. The hat was an absolute must to hide the rat's nest of hair that I had grown back by this time. I would later refer to that profusion of tangled mass as the Kosmo Kramer cut made famous by the wily character from the television series *Seinfeld*. So when I discovered the hat was missing, there was no question as to whether I would go back.

After taking the photo, a sublime sense of accomplishment had permeated my being, knowing that my view to the northeast looking up the Trail was, indeed, Maine. The mountains of Maine. My spirits ran very high, and I virtually was skipping along, feeling like some kind of a world-beater with supreme confidence and derring-do. Maine! Finally Maine!

What a downer to discover the hat missing. It cannot be stressed enough how walking backward on the Trail went against every fiber in my body, where adding needless distance to such a prodigious hike just simply pissed me off. I dealt with the detour as best as possible but finally could no longer do so gracefully and had to resort to my usual stress reliever.

A resounding expletive that was screamed at the top of my lungs.

For some reason, this usually worked. I really tried to not do this on the Trail, but necessity prevailed this day and there was no stopping the urge and impulse once I had worked myself into such a state. However, my mood quickly improved as I observed the amazing fact that walking the other way was an entirely new experience. How different the scenery appeared with light on the other sides of the foliage and rocks.

In about ten minutes, I made it back to the old fire tower, straining to see if the hat was there. It was. And that pretty well corrected the inconvenience. However, life was about to change dramatically—again. He must have heard my earlier exclamation and possibly even thought that I was calling him.

A bluetick hound. A gorgeous and sweet-dispositioned animal, and it didn't take long to realize that this wasn't just another mutt. This was a cherished and loved and cared-for creature. He had tags and was robust and muscular and was gorgeous and full of vitality and life.

However, I just did not want to complicate my already-complicated life. A dog on the Trail when thru-hiking just simply added too many logistic problems. I tried to shoo him away. He simply would not leave. I could only ignore the responsibility that was so suddenly foisted on me for so long. It was obvious within about a half hour that the owner was nowhere around. I now had a dog to care for.

I reversed my direction and again enjoyed the views of Maine and noted that the day was rapidly waning, and a certain sense of urgency set in. For a few moments, I toyed with just camping at the top of Carter Dome but decided that I needed to make a few more miles. My good mood again resumed, and the additional burden didn't seem that bad. We made our way north. However, before the Trail dropped off the ridge, the marking was quite nebulous; and it took some backtracking to finally find the blazes among the rocks leading downward.

By this time, I had named him Rufus, not knowing any better and not bothering to check gender. I needed a name as he wandered off from time to time and there were a number of trail junctions where I would call him and it wasn't long before he would appear. He was covering about three times the distance that I was. I finally arrived at Zeta Pass by about six and was disappointed that there was really not an acceptable spot for setting up camp. I decided that this was far enough and that it was stealth camping time again. With some mental improvisation, the Trail itself would have to do for at its junction with Carter Dome Trail seemed to be the only place level enough, an absolute priority in this business of being comfortable in a tent. The nearby water source was adequate at best, but the day was too far gone to be choosey.

Rufus would wander off from time to time but would always come wandering back, and I knew that I had a companion, at least for a little while. I hadn't bothered to look at the tags and was envisioning a long and complicated process of locating the owner who I had prematurely assumed would be a thru-hiker from heaven knows where and probably not anywhere near the area.

Earlier in the day at the AMC Pinkham Notch Visitor Center, I had bought six huge cookies. They just looked too good to pass up, and the price was very reasonable. I hadn't really needed the food but was in one of the constant hunger stages which was most of the time and could have sat down then and ate all six in one setting. It was now designated dog food, albeit its contents. Chocolate chips or not, Rufus would just have to bear with me. I really didn't have anything else that could be considered nutritious and filling for a dog. Chocolate chip cookies it was. He gobbled one down like it was nothing and, of course, was looking for more. I assured him that was all there was, and he seemed satisfied and had already more or less secured his place next to the tent.

A married couple from a Deep South state had drifted into the area about the time I started to set up; and they decided that this was a suitable, if not quite perfect, place to camp and chose their magical place about seventy-five feet from where I was. They didn't seem quite as concerned about tramping down vegetation, probably having thrown the Leave No Trace concept to the wind. Rufus wandered close by; but the lady wanted no part of taking care of a dog and, with a certain amount of success, managed to shoo him out of their area. So we fairly well cohabitated and shared some trail lore and stories of woe while eating our evening meal. They had peanut butter and bread, and I had my usual noodles with ramen. She seemed like a lady on a mission, but then weren't we all, and her intentions to complete the hike were very strong in spite of having a chronic knee problem as did a number of the thru-hiking ladies on the Trail. It pained me to watch her hobbling around gingerly on her heavily Ace-bandaged legs and carefully choosing her steps. As with most hikers, it seemed that everything came home to roost at camp. Once back hiking and warmed up and away from camp, hikers were back striding out and making time.

They had been on the Trail somewhat longer than me, having left Springer Mountain about the middle of March. It always amazed me that for the most part, except for those young and strong hikers, I was making better time than most. So even with my extra burden of Rufus, I now felt more assured that somehow things would work out.

I fed Rufus another cookie in the morning and he seemed satisfied with that and we were out of camp by about six forty-five. However, my energy level was very low, and I struggled for the most part and having the dog just seemed to be weighing heavily on me as we slowly made our way through the thick and large boulder fields. There just were no breaks. I caught up with two male hikers with dogs of their own and relayed the story of Rufus and, as with everybody that I encountered along this stretch, wondered if they knew of anybody that had inquired about a dog and got the usual negative answer. They, being more knowledgeable about such things, also informed me that the name Rufus being of a somewhat male gender just would not accommodate the plumbing; and immediately *she* became Dufus, a name that seemed more appropriate and nongender.

Also it had finally occurred to me to take the time to check her tags, and it was such a relief to see NH Dog—Gorham imprinted. Suddenly what had seemed to be complicated beyond comprehension dissolved back to a fairly simply solution. I just had to get her down the mountain; and hopefully, a scraggly hiker with a dog could actually get a ride into Gorham, and hopefully, the owner would welcome me with open arms and maybe possibly even offer a reward, though it would be something that I wouldn't take anyway.

By this time, I had become rather attached to Dufus as she provided entertainment, wondering at the trail junctions if she had chosen the correct route, which amazingly she usually did. She would have been the perfect dog to own; she was obedient, intelligent, good-natured, and just fun to be around.

It seemed strategic to detour to Imp Shelter and leave a message in the trail register. The side trail seemed forever, and arriving there, I found the caretaker mucking the privy. I underestimated the physical effort of this compacting process; he was perspiring heavily in his labors. However, after standing there for about three minutes with no response, I started to leave. He stopped me.

"What do you want?" His chest was heaving from the extreme exertion.

It finally occurred to me in my rather-agitated mood of dealing with my encumbrance that mucking the privy probably was not a lot of fun. I mellowed somewhat while explaining as succinctly as possible the situation with Dufus. He told me that he wasn't aware of anybody looking for a dog. I told him of my intentions of leaving a note in the register, and he told me to make myself at home. I sort of apologized for my curt attitude and left on good terms. It was difficult wording the message in a vein of "to whom it may concern," but eventually, it was done as well as could be and soon we were heading back to the main trail.

The section of the Trail dropping, literally, down to U.S. Highway 2 was rugged. A number of places, Dufus had to be encouraged to make the jumps; and it required some tricky rock scrambling, this being one of those sections where you spent more time on your butt sliding than on your feet. She obviously had done this quite a lot before and did well. I was impressed and wondered what she was thinking about all of this. She had plenty to drink as water was available almost continuously as we were paralleling a stream; the Trail actually was the stream for the most part. The name Rattle River Trail was aptly named.

A short stop at Rattle River Shelter allowed us to catch our breath somewhat and for me to make plans for Highway 2. I decided that using the bear line as a leash for her was about the only safe way of doing this. The leash worked well. However, where she had been drinking water along the Trail, no amount of persuasion could get her to do it along the highway. Having found a Styrofoam cup along the highway and adding water from my bottle, she just would not drink very much of it.

I had envisioned that some kind soul would actually pick the two of us up. I am convinced that had they known the circumstances, drivers would have been empathetic and helped me out. However, it just appeared that I was a hiker with enough chutzpah to have a dog companion and ballsy enough to attempt hitchhiking. A large dog at that. No rides.

We had made it about halfway into town, having covered about 2 1/2 miles, and I was becoming quite concerned about my companion. She had done so well trail hiking but the leash was alien, and not taking water, she was clearly overheating. The temperature was about eighty, and for most of the time along the highway, we were in direct sunlight. This just was not working good. I started to go by the White Birches Camp Park, a RV park on the south side of the highway, and decided that this was just far enough. The lady named Janet inside the office listened to my story intently and, clearly a bearer of Northern hospitality, soon was on the phone. She got a rather-disturbing piece of news at first, being that the rightful owner of the dog was shown on record as "living out of the country." However, Janet was the type that was not to be denied. She pursued the ownership issue further; and after about six phone calls, she found the current owner, apparently there had been some dispute over ownership that was now resolved.

However, in the interim, Dufus had to be provided for. A veterinarian, known for being the last stop before animals that had been abandoned were to meet their demise, came to pick her up. It was with great sadness that we—for Janet had become very involved in this in a short time—watched as the vet truck drove away, wondering if that was the end of my wonderful short-time companion. I managed to wrangle a ride to town with one of the RV camp residents and was soon checking into the Royalty Inn in Gorham. I made it to my room and scattered my belongings around for drying, for inventory, and for general maintenance. I delayed the shower for some reason and hadn't gotten around to that before the phone rang. A woman's voice asked me to come to the lobby.

Lori proved to be a very attractive woman and the rightful owner of Dufus, actually Cally, though the exact spelling remained nebulous at best. She was ecstatic! She had pretty much given up on ever seeing her beloved dog again and could not believe that Cally was back. We talked for a long time. Lori handed me a white envelope and said, "This is for you." I didn't need to look inside and at the look in Lori's eyes to know what was inside, though the amount was never known. However, my idea earlier of a reward had already been taken care of, money would just taint my good feelings.

"No, I'm not taking your money. If I would have had to pay for everything for the help that I have had along the Trail, I could not have afforded the hike."

She implored. I declined a number of times, and finally she put the white envelope away. A warmth evolved, and an instant friendship was formed. We talked for a while, and finally Lori said, "Do you want to see her?" Of course I did.

She was in the back of Lori's SUV. She told me that Cally had never been this exhausted before. Cally did raise her head just a little to acknowledge me; and it was so very good to see her there, safe, in loving care, the world was again very okay. Trail magic, though this time in reverse. What a wonderful feeling knowing that I could have actually helped somebody else, quite contrary to what a thru-hiker normally experiences.

Lori insisted on hugging me. My smelly, scroungy self was somewhat reluctant, but she insisted. Even in my deplorable state, I would not have declined being hugged by an attractive and grateful young woman. A hug that I will remember forever.

The story probably should have ended there. However, this was the North, and people just are not like that. Besides, my arrival in town was about to be good for the local economy, to the tune of about $600.

The next night, I had an appointment at North Country Dental with a Dr. D to attend to the filling that had fallen out at Lake of the Clouds Hut. That day I toyed with the idea of replacing my boots yet again. The pair that I had purchased at Eastern Mountain Sports in Dalton, Massachusetts, had developed a tear along one seam of my left boot; and in spite of my love of these light boots, the idea of them holding up through Maine didn't seem too likely.

The people at Gorham Hardware & Sports Center were happy to oblige to my wishes for a new pair for a mere $100. I left there knowing that I had made the right decision and the Merrell boots would serve me well for the duration of the hike and are still going strong to this day, having also spent a lot of time surveying and doing yard work.

My visit to the good dentist also proved to be a nice experience, something not always associated with dental work. No pain, but more so was the caring of Dr. D. I didn't realize until late into the appointment that he was the only one left in the office, having scheduled my appointment much beyond the normal hours. He worked without an assistant and spent probably more time with me than he would have with one of his regular patients, or so it seemed. About seven that evening, he had finally replaced my lost tooth with a "temporary" filling, more like a total rebuilding of a tooth. He then had to do the billing thing. We eventually had everything squared away, and I left that dental office knowing that Dr. D had gone above and beyond his normal call of duty. Gorham had a special place in their hearts for hikers, especially thru-hikers. I can still remember the remark of the receptionist as she left about six. "Take good care of that hiker now."

The night was to continue somewhat in a chaotic state. I knew that in the morning, I would be ready to make my way to Maine, only about a day and a half away. So I wanted everything ready to go in the morning. I made a quick trip to a local pharmacy that had everything and stocked up on some food, a new camera card, and sundry items. In my haste, I left my Olympus at the drug store, and when I got back to the motel room made this discovery. I rushed back to find the camera in the good care of the woman there that had waited on me. One had to wonder at this city, a place that I would have loved to live in.

My stop back at the motel room after the dental appointment and pharmacy run is a moment that will stay with me for a long time. As I walked into the dark room, I almost tripped over a large decorative bag of stuff. Inside, carefully packed with loving attention were more goodies than thought imaginable, even for a thru-hiker. It was full of homemade cookies, Snickers bars, wonderful gourmet chocolates, granola bars—all of the things near and dear to a thru-hiker's heart. Inside was a note from Lori thanking me again for rescuing her dog. So Cally, in her innocent way, had been catalyst between two people to form a bond that will last a lifetime.

Gorham, New Hampshire, will always hold a special place in my heart. A wondrous city of warm and caring people, a microcosm of America as we wished all places should be.

# Chapter 40

## Priorities

*August 25—Day 143—Mile 1,913—(Journal entry)—made it through the Mahoosuc Notch (to east end) by 9:00 a.m.—that's about 2.6 miles from camp!—and to the top of Mahoosuc Arm (1,500' climb) by about 11:00 a.m.*

Backpacks aren't supposed to be just lying there all by themselves. In the middle of virtually nowhere. It just did not make sense! And when items that are normally in the backpack are scattered around, one is led to make assumptions, intelligent or not. And when those items indicate that the section of the backpack delved into was where the first aid stuff is kept and Band-Aids and related items are there lying on the ground, very huge metaphoric flares are blazing into the sky, telling somebody else that something is not quite right here.

However, there is reason to digress. For it was Monday, August 25, and my first entire day in Maine, having spent the previous night at Full Goose Shelter enjoying a very comfortable night on a tent platform, my favorite place to set up and camp, when such is available. This had allowed for a good solid early-morning start for "the most difficult mile on the Appalachian Trail," the Mahoosuc Notch. Perhaps being fully prepared had spared me the anticipated trauma for this day. So many scenarios had been played out during that mental preparation. I imagined everything that could go wrong happening as I struggled with the myriad of strewn large house-sized boulders stacked upon one another and getting caught in the rocks with my large backpack. Nightmare tales of hikers actually turning back because of the Notch and other stories of hikers taking a day to get through just didn't pan out that way for me.

My initial steps were somewhat hesitant but facing up to the challenge soon found me treating the experience more as play than work. My adrenaline flow was about perfect. Too many times when there is too much of the stuff, there is a tendency to overdo. That was not the case here. A skip and a slide here, a pull up and over there, a squeeze here and there, I navigated with a sense of confidence. The mental anguish was serving me well as the adrenaline flowed with my fine-tuned preparation.

Most of the navigating was done in a stooped or sitting-down position as an entirely different mode of operation takes over. Instead of thinking hiking upright, one just assumes somewhat alien positions—the rock-scrambling mode, more or less on all-fours, and sitting and sliding and bending and stooping. By nine I was through it, amazed with that fact, and facing the climbing of Mahoosuc Arm and summiting Old Speck Mountain. The latter probably presented more of a challenge than did the Notch.

Now, back to the mysterious backpack.

What was probably most amazing about the entire setting was that this was not a place that somebody would intentionally pick as a place to stop. There was no view to speak of, and the location was pretty much along a downhill run (for a northbounder), and there were no quaint little places to sit and observe. The foliage along the Trail was quite thick—it was difficult to break through it to get off. So the only assumption that I could make was that a hiker was making a potty call, might possibly be a woman; and it would be gentlemanly to just continue, not holler if all was okay, causing embarrassment. If she was out there, an answer to the beckoning would probably not come anyway, there would be no response. It would be most prudent to just quietly continue on my way.

So that was what I did. That approach worked out for a while, for about a half mile, replaying the notion that there were just times when things are left well enough alone. However, slowly my mind went into turmoil; and with each few steps, the urge to go back to check became stronger. And stronger. A realization started creeping into my consciousness that I had chosen not to get involved simply for convenience. Those initial thoughts were that it would be inconvenient to get involved, the day was wearing on, I had some more miles to cover that day, the overcast sky appeared to be getting heavier as the afternoon progressed. I had to look out for number one. And so on.

However, that train of thought would soon lose credibility when the entire dog-rescue scene of a mere four days before went through my mind. A sense of priorities and the values attached to different living things evolved, and mine seemed way out of whack. I had spent the better part of a day rescuing a dog, bringing the beast into town and then going through the process of finding the owner. My thinking started to get somewhat radical. What kind of a maniac was I to place more value on a dog than a human being? A person that might be lying out there bleeding, possibly a life-or-death situation was unfolding and I had done absolutely nothing about it.

The entire hike was suddenly being placed on trial. My pure intentions were undergoing a scrutiny that was hard to ignore. I had managed to do this thing to this point untainted, without slackpacking, hauling my entire needs with me at all times; had stayed in only three shelters, a minimum of motels; had sworn off creature comforts for five months, an almost angelic mission with proper motivation—and here I was with a maligned sense of priorities to totally ignore the needs of another human being.

Meanwhile with my mind in a state of turmoil, my downhill trek was progressing at a torrid pace. Unconsciously I had covered almost two miles without hardly realizing it. With each step going back lay a little closer to not happening merely through processes of procrastination, an amazing mental tool in such a situation. Going back meant hard climbing. And there was no way that I would leave my pack. That is just not the way that things are done as all hikers know that was breaking one of the cardinal rules of hiking. A bear would find the abandoned pack. A fighter pilot never leaves his wingman as Tom so poignantly observed, a hiker never leaves his pack. Down and down, I continued in this mental anguish.

The outcome had been written beforehand. The previous hour or so had been a façade, merely mental trickery where the sleight of hand was already known. I could hear the traffic along State Highway 26 at Grafton Notch when I stopped but could go no farther. I could bear it no more as the realization set in that for all intents, the hike would no longer be pure, my feelings about my accomplishments would forever be tainted. Probably mental elaboration would create a monster within me that would plague me the rest of my life.

The matter at hand could not be ignored.

Back up Old Speck Mountain I went. About two thousand vertical feet back uphill. What was I thinking! Knowing the answer to such hypothetical, irrational thought could not remove the guilt, for there just was no way out of this mental dilemma. To continue without at least making the effort would mean dealing with a conscience that would not leave me alone. And somehow, more-than-enough energy was there for the climb. Judy and Libby, who I had passed before, eventually reappeared working their way down. Their recognition of me required little explanation. They shook their heads knowingly with my stuttering and weak excuses. They were understanding and thanked me for doing it and said that they would call the ranger that covered this section of trail. Just beyond them, the lady that was passed just beyond the summit coming down, who turned out to be a self-styled ridge runner, also came along; and we went through the same conversation. She also agreed to call the regional office for rangers on this part of the Trail. A lot of bases were being covered, and the abandoned backpack was still a long way back up. Turning back was turning out better than expected.

I finally arrived back at the pack. Nothing had changed. I spent the next twenty minutes hollering at the wind. There was nothing. No signs. No feeble voice answering my calls. No voice at all. After assuring myself that if somebody was nearby in distress, there was no way to find that person. In a nutshell, everything that could be done had been done. I started back down only to realize that somebody else might go through the same ordeal if my efforts weren't known. So I hauled out the only paper available, my trail journal; tore out a sheet; and wrote a succinct note, assuring another concerned hiker that if someone were nearby and needing help, they did not respond. I attached the note to the pack, picked up the strewn items, and placed them back in the pack, securing things so that pending rain would do little damage.

The awful weight had been removed. My mental albatross immediately flew away. My mind soared in its newfound freedom, an elation abounded that would carry me for days. The encumbrance of just a few minutes before was gone, replaced with virtue and goodness. Life was good again. The joys of the Trail prevailed. I skipped downhill even faster than the first time in my joy. Deep down inside, within the deepest recesses of my psyche, a miracle had been performed. Manifestation of these days on the Trail and payment for the good deeds that had been bestowed upon me. The Trail works its wonders, and those of us that seek it out shall be rewarded much beyond anything that we could imagine.

# Chapter 41

## Maine

*August 26—Day 144—Mile 1,929—(Journal entry)—the climb to Baldpate Mountain went real good (lean-to trail) by 7:40 a.m. and West Peak by about 9:15 a.m.—stopped at Frye Notch Lean-to (wrote in register)*

Maine holds a magic on the Appalachian Trail that the other thirteen states can only envy. And after walking 1,875 miles to get there, it was hoped that it could support a theory that had been gnawing at me for the entire hike. My Yankee tendencies are much too prevalent, and being such, my opinions are much too strong and often brutally voiced. However, a concept that is based solely on opinion has been eating away at me for years and years. That conflict concerned the business merely referred to as Southern hospitality and that the South was superior in its approach to the treatment of fellow human beings. However, I had experienced enough Northern hospitality to know better. And numerous cases of the so-called Southern hospitality reeked of façade. Realizing that my roots run much too deep and that I was somewhat of a bigot, it just seemed to me that for the most part, Northern hospitality seemed more genuine. Maine was the ultimate North state on the AT and was my panacea to prove or disprove my theory.

Just the term *North* brings back fond memories, and stories come back that support my wild and reckless claims. Years ago, the summer of 1970 to be exact, moving into a place called the Parkinson House in Northern

Wisconsin, near the uptown of the small village of Phillips, manifested my theory. Yet another one of those field assignments and yet another one of those places of residence in the long list of places that we lived while moving around the United States in the quest for cartographic information for U.S. Geological Survey maps. We had found this place quite by accident with a simple question at the bank on the main drag and one employee's remark to another, "Well, there is always the Parkinson House."

A house with an actual name did get my attention.

The house was wonderful, and after looking for three days, we were ready for anything, let alone a mansion. It turned out to be a doctor's luxurious home from years ago that had recently been renovated. In the meantime, it had served many purposes, including being a "maternity house"—about half of the residents of Price County had been born there. The building at one time was set up for midwives and doctors to temporarily come in and perform the duties of bringing new human beings into the world. Usually finding homes as a USGS fieldman were mini-miracles, this was another one of those cases. Soon the necessary arrangements had been made and we were gleefully moving in.

It was late in the day, and in my exhausted state, I was struggling with the refrigerator, trying to get it through the front entrance. About that time, a man and his family came by, a part of the constant flow of pedestrian traffic. He was quick to offer help. We soon had the refrigerator inside. A handshake and an offer of a beer later and we were on our way to becoming friends.

His name was Bill Ding which, apparently, could not go without comment; and soon we had found things to laugh about. His wife, Marilyn, and my wife, Kris, seemed to find common ground almost instantly. Just in a few minutes, a small miracle had taken place as two couples became what eventually proved to be a longtime friendship.

However as a Yankee with Southern habits, a manifestation was about to take place, somewhat of a slip in accepted protocol. I heard my voice say, "Why don't you guys come over sometime." That being more rotelike than actually thinking about it, a hard and fast reply was not really expected. Or maybe not even desired.

His reply caught me totally off guard, "When do you want us to come?"

This was the North. Bill was from the North. An invitation to him was not just idle vibrations of the airwaves as compliance to social expectations. An invitation demanded a viable reply.

I had breached an area where there is a great disparity between the cultures of North and South, inferences were not to be confused with casual utterances. And in my Southern background, again as a transplanted Yankee, I could still hear the woman in the recesses of my memory making the comment that she had invited somebody over but really did not want that person in her house. And possibly that is why a lot of Southern people find Northerners to be somewhat caustic when in all probability, the correct adjectives should be *direct* and *to the point.*

I managed to recover somewhat but still stammered before setting the following weekend as a good time. It was the start of a beautiful and lasting friendship. And the good-byes when we left for our next six-month assignment were emotional and genuine. Many years followed with exchanges of cards and letters and phone calls.

Without being too crass, it should be noted that had this scene taken place south of the Mason-Dixon Line, the outcome and answer would have been quite different. "Ya, we'll have to do that sometime." And in all probability, it would have never happened. This is not a scientific conclusion. Probably more like a slanted belief developed years before real input to know the difference had taken place. However, now it is based on numerous observations through the years of going back and forth. North was usually our summer home, and South was usually our winter home for nearly twenty-four years. So my conclusions may be based on some semblance of science and not just pure prejudice.

Over the years, the Parkinson House story has been told and retold. Possibly the actual story now is not quite accurate because of embellishment. And possibly too much weight and too many conclusions were reached from that one incident. We had as many friends in the South as the North. However, rarely did instant friendships occur as did this one; and therefore, the reasons for the lasting impression. Worthiness assessments had occurred a number of times in the South in these kinds of situations. And this incident of instant total acceptance in the North always stayed with me as proof, albeit slanted proof, of my theory.

When I was nine years old, I lived within a stone's throw of the 49th Parallel and knew nothing of Southern hospitality. People around me were all friendly, and maybe that was just because there were no strangers. Who in their right mind would move to Northern Minnesota? And if everybody knows everybody, there is always some tendency to think that just anybody was accepted into the fold.

When the term *Southern hospitality* first came to my attention, it was my early conclusion that statement seemed to exclude the peoples of the North; that hospitality did not exist there. So this attitude has been worn somewhat on my sleeve in defense of these friendly souls that were a part of my childhood.

The North has a strong propensity toward hospitality, and it seems to be of a much more genuine variety. Maybe it is simply because of practicality. It has always been my opinion that severe weather has a way of making people come together. Just go to a blizzard sometime when one presents itself to see the very best come out in people dealing with the uncertainty. The sanctity of our structured and comfortable lives is suddenly in real jeopardy, and the need for other people becomes real and not just trivial matters of inconvenience.

Also a correlation can be drawn here to explain the values of the proximity of human contact from years ago when there were not so many people crowding our space. The general migration is toward the South. And let's face it, there are places now where there are just too many people.

So now being in Maine, the most northern state on the Appalachian Trail, my narrow-minded theory was about to be put to the test.

It should be noted that there is some misconception of the north-ness of Maine. The belief being that Maine is the north state and that there is no part of the United States that has larger latitude numbers. However, a perceptive look at the map and taking earth curvature into account reveals that Maine is actually south of a great deal of the United States. The very tip-top of the state is about 47 degrees, 30 minutes north latitude. So that leaves a lot of Minnesota, North Dakota, Montana, Idaho, and Washington north of even the very top of Maine. It is noted here that, actually, the honor of being the northernmost point in the United States, excluding Alaska, actually belongs to a small portion of Minnesota known as the Northwest Angle, a peninsula completely surrounded by Canada that protrudes into Lake of the Woods and Ontario and connected to the Canadian province of Manitoba on the west side.

It was August 26 and the aura of actually being in Maine was still holding me in a rather transfixed state of mind. The morning had been a workout of massive proportions, and I was more than ready for the road and getting to town. However, the morning hike had also provided some of the most unique scenery along the Trail so far. Waterfalls and massive boulder formations and gorgeous forests of conifers and deciduous woods, the best that the North had to offer. Dunn Notch Falls had provided some respite from the difficulty of the Trail. It was clearly a Snickers break opportunity as I succumbed into my chocolate trance with a symphony of roaring water coming from the falls below me from my overlook spot on the Trail. However, my digression was short-lived for town was beckoning, and I had some trepidation as to whether a ride would be readily available on East B Hill Road. Andover was 8 miles to the east and too far to consider walking.

I was now at the mercy of Northern hospitality and was eagerly awaiting the outcome.

I finally got to the road just before 1:00 p.m., fairly positive that every step that I had taken that morning had been uphill with legs laden with lactic acid that just would not respond properly. I was ready for some town food and level streets and resupply. The road was gravel and crooked and backwoods. I set the pack down and prepared for a long wait. However, it wasn't long before a man driving a pickup truck slowly came toward me. It really came as no surprise that the pickup came to a halt even though I hadn't stuck my thumb out.

The truck was well lived in, not a lot of time was wasted tidying things up, evidently a truck used for working. I did manage to find room in the bed, so threw my pack in among some rather-strange-looking containers and climbed in the cab after he had done some serious reshuffling inside. As we drove, he told me that he had to make a stop before we got to town and provided explanation.

He had a bear bait site located just off the road, about a mile from where he had picked me up. Two of the containers in the bed were full of day-old donuts from a local bakery that saved them for him when the donuts were beyond saleable. It was hard not to look at this huge supply of what I viewed as food without considering eating some of them. He told me that a number of other hikers in the past that he had picked up had the same thoughts. However, fresh food lay ahead, so I controlled my impulses.

It was an alien act for me to help him with this errand, knowing that by association, I was helping him kill an unsuspecting bear. Not being a hunter, the entire process ran contrary to my thinking, but I was not in a position to voice my opinion with a good person that apparently had no problem killing animals. He went into great depth telling a story about his son having "bagged" his first bear sometime in the immediate past and told the story with great pride. I listened and smiled and played my part in the scenario and kept my opinions to myself.

Soon we arrived in my first Maine town, Andover, and my first phone call to Kris from the state that I had been plodding toward for the past five months, Maine. Maine! I kept saying the word over and over and metaphorically pinched myself with the concept. I ate pizza and ice cream and pecan pies and had some store coffee and immensely enjoyed sitting among friendly, inquiring people. I resupplied with the usual Snickers and trail food, refilled my Coleman fuel bottle, and soon was ready to get back to the Trail.

The ride back came just as quickly. I had walked about the equivalent of a block when a car went by and, apparently answering to second thoughts, stopped and backed up and made their humble offer. The driver and passenger apologized for the small backseat in their compact car. However, there was plenty of room for the pack and me. They talked about going fishing that day and were inquiring whether I knew of a good place, and after some explanation that I was from Florida, the talk drifted to other subjects.

Amazingly, I was back on the Trail before any thought had been given about time elapsed. In less than two hours of leaving it, and this being on a remote rural road, I had eaten in a restaurant setting, resupplied, refilled with Coleman, called my wife, repacked my backpack, went to the restroom, and had tended to some hungry and maybe soon-to-be-dead bears.

The North, specifically Maine, had lived up to its reputation of treating people courteously, efficiently—direct and to the point. I reveled in this fact as I made my way up Wyman Mountain. Still happy to be basically a Yankee, even if I had spent more than half of my life south of the Mason-Dixon Line.

And as I progressed north through some of the most beautiful scenery on the Trail, my thoughts turned to the ever-pressing matter of reaching the base of Katahdin on my target date. As I met the sobos (southbound hikers), I had been asking, for about the previous three weeks, their dates of departure. Every night I did the math trying to come up with a date that I could make it to the Katahdin Stream Campground at the base of the mountain. However, dealing with the difficult terrain, hiking in Maine made for the estimated mileage each day being somewhat unpredictable. I grew ever more anxious as the first days of September were melting away.

There is so much talk of the rocks of Pennsylvania that it would appear that the Trail in other states is smooth and rock free. Maine was probably the worst with the mix of rocks and roots. The roots actually are worse than rocks for there is always a tendency to slip about any direction when stepping on top of them. An interesting journal entry was made on September 4, referring to the stretch before crossing the Kennebec River: *This was one of those slippin', slidin', trippin', stubbin', bitchin', pissin', moanin' sort of hiking days [rocks, roots, PUDS].*

However, I progressed north as rapidly as possible, still worrying about getting to Katahdin in time. The crossing of the Kennebec River could only be described as routine, though I had obsessed about the canoe ride not being available when needed. That proved to be yet another case of needless worry, and now Monson wasn't that far.

There was no way that I was going to shortchange Monson and the ever-anticipated stay at Shaw's Boarding House. Always the highlight of any thru-hike of the Appalachian Trail, the two names were synonymous. Monson also meant the start of the 100-Mile Wilderness that would require more time for extra rest and preparation.

Shaw's will usually bring a smile when mentioned. I luxuriated in the abundant wonderful food for two days and got to know Mr. Shaw a little (may he rest in peace—his passing came after my hike) and knew that this was a special place. When I got ready to get back on the Trail after a relaxing, refreshing, and well-earned zero day, he was there with the old Chevy Caprice and gave me a ride back in royal fashion. I took some photos of him and was on my way. Having spent time with the icon of the Trail left me with good feelings and well prepared for what lay ahead.

I smiled, taking my first steps that morning, thinking about the "system" at Shaw's: all breakfast orders come in multiples of one, two, three—you cannot, say, order two eggs, one piece of toast, and four donuts—nope, one of everything (one around), two of everything (two around), and so on.

# Chapter 42

## Preamble

*September 8—Day 157—Mile 2064 (Shaw's Boarding House)—(Journal entry)—up at 5:45 a.m.—showered and dressed—across for breakfast by 6:15 a.m.—had two around (two French toast; two scrambled eggs with cheese, bacon, ham, sausage; and two donuts)—lots of coffee*

The 100-Mile Wilderness falls somewhat into the same category as the Mahoosuc Notch. A thru-hiker is so psyched up for it that there is tendency to overprepare. I left State Highway 15 heavily laden with food, probably weighing close to sixty pounds for the first time since the early days of the hike, before sending unneeded items back home from Fontana Dam. My largest fear was running out of food. And with the purist approach, I had opted not to go to the White House Landing Wilderness Camp for food or resupply. The 100-Mile Wilderness was an entity and would be treated as such. I would go all the way.

And with all of that preparation came the worry of the fords. Those proved to be nothing more than just drawing on some of my past experience as a government mapmaker and some common sense. The following journal entry pretty much sums it up: *ended up getting my feet wet fording West Branch Pleasant River—so took off gaiters, boots, and socks (wringing them out)—left rain pants off.*

The Wilderness was challenging because of the distance, but the camping was the best on the Trail. The fifth night out and with still plenty of food, I stealth camped at the perfect campsite, flat and open with mostly spruce needles and seventy-five feet from a stream with very pure water.

By the sixth night, I was through. Tired and satisfied, having averaged 16.5 miles per day with a high of 17.5. I arrived at Abol Bridge camp store at four that evening. It was a night that proved to be one of the most truly satisfying of the entire hike. And for the first time, though distant glimpses had availed themselves for the past nearly 100 miles, I was looking across the West Branch Penobscot River at the prettiest site that any thru-hiker would ever want to see, the sun starting to set on Mount Katahdin.

After checking in at the camp store, I was free to select my campsite. As I walked in on the road checking out things, I saw Horizon, Lacey, MzRouge, Cakalaki, and others setting up for the night. There was a consensus from the group in the form of advice to me to "avoid the lady at the end of the road in the camper." Well, the most suitable campsite by far, one that overlooked the wonders of Mount Katahdin, was right across the road from the camper. There was no need to look any farther.

She soon poked her head out as I was setting up my tent, and she said hello. It was getting dark fast, and I hurried to get my food bag suspended. I then drifted over in the gathering dusk after getting everything arranged in the tent. Her name was Marcia. And she was from a place in Indiana that has one of the most intriguing names in the history of place-names in this great country, French Lick.

She told me about her adventures. She operated on a sort of theme basis, this was her year to do Maine. She had been all over in her little camper. This was my kind of person—full of adventure, full of optimism, full of information, opinionated, and full of ideas about life and the human condition. We immediately and forever became friends.

The next morning after a number of trips back to the camp store and bathroom, the first wisps of diffused sunlight started to filter through the crisp and moist morning air. The picnic table next to my tent was the obvious point to convene, and the gathering started way before any real sunlight actually appeared. We could just barely see but realized that a cow moose was in the little lake adjoining the camping area with moose calves there too.

It was partly chemistry but mostly magic. Chemistry that prevails when circumstances bring people together to view the wonders of nature. A nature that was catalyst to bond together this ragged and varied and somewhat motley group of hikers and a person totally alien to the hiker-world who had just become a part of this esoteric group simply by association. As Marcia and the thru-hikers all gathered on and around the picnic table, we watched with wonder the moose and slowly realized that a rare thing was about to happen. We were about to witness the very first light to settle on Mount Katahdin and the United States for this day, September 14, 2003. That point can be argued, but that would not be in the spirit of this dissertation for sometimes the poet in us just simply preempts all logic and reasoning and math.

There were very few dry eyes. There was a lot of hugging and shaking of hands and congratulations. A group that came together as entities had, indeed, become an entity. It would have been appropriate had "The Star-Spangled Banner" been playing somewhat subdued in the background. But that would not have been necessary for in our hearts it was already playing.

The walk to Katahdin Stream Campground was anticlimactic. Ten leisurely miles with a stop for photos around each bend in the West Branch Penobscot River, the morning light playing with each nuance as the leaves and rocks and water combined in an ever-dazzling display.

I left about seven thirty that morning and had stopped at Big Niagara Falls and visited with Horizon for about a half hour before reflectively continuing for the last few miles. Horizon was sad. He did not want it to end. Of course, I had to stop at Daicey Pond Campground and took the postcard photos with Mount Katahdin in the background even though I could have bought the same at any drug store in Millinocket. However, one of the photos had me in it, compliments of a ranger helping me out and taking the photo. Yes, the walking stick, my one-pod could have served the same purpose with the removable knob exposing the camera mount; but the ranger insisted. It was a nice touch.

Katahdin Steam Campground came into view about midafternoon. I stopped at the park ranger office, and the nice man filled out the official form witnessing to the completion of my hike. It was September 14. I had made it with a week to spare. A Baxter Park employee gave me a ride for about 6 miles where another employee picked me up. I rode in the bed of his pickup to Millinocket, what proved to be my last hitchhike.

I had made it. A week lay ahead for rest. For relaxation. For reflection.

# Chapter 43

## Points to Ponder

Even at the risk of redundancy, a few points have to be reiterated. Being a purist, I had made a pact as to my intents in this venture, subsequently, my canons read,

I will thru-hike the AT with a total purist approach. If the Trail is to be my conquest, it will be at its terms, not mine. Every mile of the AT will be hiked. I will not slackpack. I will hike the entire Trail in the direction that I chose to thru-hike it (in my case, northbound). I will camp in the truest spirit of a natural setting, that being in a tent as much as possible. If the Trail decides to go the hard way when an easier route is clearly available then that is where I will go. I will respect its integrity to the best of my abilities.

So this chapter is merely venting, for my mantra was adhered to religiously, and that self-imposed discipline may have created difficulties that a more-relaxed approach might have avoided. I respect the Trail completely. The concept and the dedication of so many people to make it possible make it one of the true treasures in the United States. I, as a mere hiker, have no right to question the overall spirit of what the Appalachian Trail stands for. I merely take it upon myself to voice what a lot of other hikers may or may not feel. Consider this merely a foisting of my opinions upon others involved in the posterity of the Trail.

Hiking the Appalachian Trail was the hardest thing that I ever did. In my active and diverse life, there have been numerous challenges. None even came close in difficulty to doing the Trail. I have read firsthand accounts by thru-hikers saying that the Trail really wasn't that difficult. These hikers must have done a different Appalachian Trail for I found that thru-hiking was, indeed, quite difficult and could find affirmation for this from numerous fellow hikers that were going through the same type of ordeal that I was.

Another point to consider is that the general consensus is that the Trail has become more difficult as the years have went by since the beginning of time for the Trail. With the evolution that the Trail goes through as it is being rerouted and miles are added, there has been a tendency to make it more difficult. More challenging. As the cliché goes for the ones of us that have done the entire thing at one time, just how challenging does it have to be?

There are numerous locations along the Trail corridor where the route selection just wasn't necessary. There are places that the Trail went out of the way to follow a more difficult route. For whatever reason, route selection took hikers through and over difficult rock formations for no apparent reason other than to make it more difficult to hike. Usually it appeared that an easier path could have been built adjacent to the route selected and made the hiking more enjoyable.

A woman who gave me a ride near Lehigh Gap in Pennsylvania beamed as she told me that stretch was the hardest on the Trail. Of course when I was there, a lot of the Trail remained for me to hike, and no conclusions could be concurred as to which was the most difficult. However, to the south in Virginia, North Carolina, and Georgia were a number of difficult sections and maybe not as difficult as Lehigh Gap; but there was not really enough difference to ascertain that this was the most difficult on the Trail. In fairness for lack of a better term, there are some huge boulders going up from Lehigh Gap that were difficult to surmount, and it was somewhat scary looking down. But for the most part, this didn't last long, and the long flat stretch after the Gap through the desolate downed trees and zinc-damaged area was some of the easiest hiking on the Trail; so that took away some of the difficulty from this very short section.

It is common knowledge that mile for mile, there is nothing to compare in difficulty with most sections in Maine or New Hampshire. It should be noted that Maine and New Hampshire routing would not affect the difficulty for there just are no easy places available. The Trail is just inherently difficult to negotiate because of the rugged terrain and any extra efforts to make it more difficult would be a waste of time. Or impossible to hike, for there have to be limitations to still be able to call it a trail. Some sections required a lot of imagination to apply that term to just simply because white blazes had been added to the natural landscape.

I asked a maintainer one time if efforts were made to make the Trail difficult on purpose. She really didn't answer the question and seemed somewhat irritated with the implication. However, later upon thinking about the conversation, I realized that for the most part, she seemed rather proud that if efforts were made to make the Trail more difficult, she would not shirk her duty to contribute to that cause.

And of course everybody has read about the hardest mile on the Trail, the Mahoosuc Notch in Maine. Kind of a slap-in-the-face introduction and welcome wagon greeting to Maine. It is an age-old debate as to whether Maine is more difficult than New Hampshire or vice versa. And usually with that discussion, opinions flourish and a comparison is made between the White Mountains in New Hampshire to the Mahoosuc Range in Maine.

I was severely nonplused having reached the summit of Webster Cliffs and well through the Franconia Range, having attained above tree line and over 1,800 miles into my adventure to be almost attacked by an "experienced" woman hiker. I was feeling pretty good about myself until she more than assured me, "You haven't done anything yet." She went into a long dissertation about the difficulty of the Mahoosuc Range and how the hard stuff lay ahead. It was with some difficulty that I continued from this point being so amply put down. She must have felt quite smug in letting me know of my frailty and lack of accomplishment.

The section from Gorham, New Hampshire, to Stratton, Maine, is usually proclaimed as the most difficult on the Trail. The route is very rocky and steep most of the time and includes Mahoosuc Notch itself. The comparison in my mind is rather moot as there just isn't any difference, for even though the Whites have higher elevations and is above tree line, a lot of the time the Mahoosucs are generally a little rockier and there are sections that are difficult during rainy weather. Too alike to compare and unequivocally say that one is harder than the other. Both are rugged and require a lot of stamina and perseverance to get through. And usually by the time that a northbounder gets to these parts the hiker is usually just happy to be nearing the completion of the hike. That elation alone keeps one going through this section, and the difficulty just isn't that much of a factor. It is the land of promise for the northbound thru-hiker, and that keeps one going, much stronger than having easy sections to hike as is the case in a lot of the southern parts of the Trail.

However, back to the issue of built-in challenge factor. A 2,200-mile hike is challenge enough! The thru-hiker sometimes feel that maybe sections are made tougher that would better serve day hikers or short-distance hikers that welcome the additional difficulty. And even the thru-hiker can relate to added difficulty in a lot of the cases for what would an AT experience be without the Mahoosuc Notch or the Lemon

Squeezer or the summiting of Mount Washington. Those are not the issues that this diatribe is addressing. The thinking here is just to try to make some sections a little easier to give the bone-weary thru-hiker a break from time to time.

It is interesting to note that the state with the worst reputation for rocks is Pennsylvania. It is hard to specifically pinpoint where this notion came from. The last forty or so miles coming into Delaware Water Gap do have a lot of rocks. However, there are sections in Virginia just as rocky, and it seems like the stretches without any breaks last longer. Also, Pennsylvania had long sections that were very smooth and followed old logging roads that gave the hiker alternate places to step when a lot boulders and rocks were encountered. I found Pennsylvania quite pleasant to hike.

The hiking of the Trail has been equated to climbing Mount Everest about seventeen times if that were figured from sea level to the top of the mountain, minus, of course, dealing with technical climbing and the lack of air. The average upward elevation change for each mile of the Trail is 224 feet. There just are not too many places where one is just cruising. It actually is easier this way, for in some ways after one acclimates to the climbing part and once the summits are reached, then the long cruise downhill always was a treat and time to enjoy the surroundings and make up time if that were necessary to make mileage allotments for the day.

One of the places that I found totally different than expected was Shenandoah National Park where my understanding was the Trail was "manicured." Not true. There is a stretch through the area in proximity of Mary's Rock that was rocky throughout. It was better to expect the worst in trail conditions, that made it easier to deal with. I had been brainwashed into thinking that the stretch through the park would be an easy walk. It was somewhat easier on a few short sections, but for the most part, there really wasn't that much difference.

Of course, it was fun hiking Shenandoah because of the park stores that were just a stone's throw off the Trail and were a treasure trove of the kind of things that a hiker was looking for—ice cream bars, pizza, and most generally, a lot of the trail food for resupplying—though that wasn't too necessary through the park as most generally there was too much food. A nice break.

And of course, the business of slackpacking has to be addressed. Early on in my hike I ran into Sloop hiking *south* on the Trail. He was slackpacking. When we made eye contact, he looked down and very softly said, "You caught me."

That was manifestation of the way that a lot of hikers felt about this practice. The world of thru-hiking allows us to forsake that most imposing and restricting of factors in our modern lives, the automobile.

Slackpacking puts us back in the grip of this most abused so-called convenience. Thru-hiking with all of our needs on our back gives us freedom. Everyday living is mired down with cars and it is so nice to thumb our nose when hiking and be totally free.

In our lives of convenience and amenities there is always a tendency to find the easier way; the modern way of thinking. However, thru-hiking is not about doing it the easy way. Thru-hiking is a world devoid of convenience, a time and a place when we chose to forsake all of that and proclaim our independence. And, what a wonderful feeling that is.

I sat on the overpass overlooking the Pennsylvania Turnpike for about a half-hour and knew that for awhile I was part of the solution and not a part of the problem. And, for awhile in my life, my humble being without wheels actually felt somewhat aloof, being self-sufficient, even if for only a short time. Slackpacking to me just seemed to run totally contrary to all of those concepts and all of those feelings and ideas. It brought me back to a vague kinship with the charter member of all of this, Earl Shaffer.

Mr. Shaffer was the consummate purist, and if there is any similarity to what he did and what we do as thru-hikers, it seems like there should be some effort made to emulate how he did it as well as what he did—hike the entire length of the Trail, fully loaded, heading the correct direction at all times.

Probably the worst-case scenario was two gentlemen from Great Britain that were slackpacking through most of the White Mountains in New Hampshire. When I heard that they were slackpacking down from Mount Washington in both directions, I was disgusted.

And could console myself only with what my ideas and efforts were and to hold to that mantra. No apologies or explanations were necessary to anybody, especially to myself. Hike the Trail completely, no shortcuts, no blue blazing, always came back to the same place that I left the Trail and carried everything for each and every step.

The subject of the Mahoosuc Notch needs more elaboration. For it is one of those places that has a hiker so hyped that by the time you get there, your plans are so well laid and extra time has been allotted and this extra preparation gets you through in fine form. If it were to catch somebody totally by surprise, it could impose quite a hardship. However, that is quite unlikely for every hiker knows about the Notch ahead of time; most hikers do their research quite thoroughly.

For me, well, it just didn't seem that hard even though it does present a number of very tough scrambles with impossible rock formations and gaps in the rocks. I left camp earlier than usual that day, having spent a restful night at Full Goose Shelter on a tent platform and was surprised to find myself through the Notch by about 9:00 a.m., already about 2 1/2 miles of hiking. Getting through the Notch took about an hour. I didn't hurry because I didn't have to, and that is very positive thing, for patience is the best approach going for you through something like this. Of course there are all of the Notch stories to deal with and how some hikers just gave up here because it was just too difficult. And also stories of taking five hours to negotiate the labyrinth which mystifies me completely. Most of this stuff just boils down to hype and stories that have grown, well, out of proportion; and maybe some of it is just untrue. It should be noted that for a northbounder, the Notch appears to be easier than for a southbounder as the general trend is downhill. Whether that is a factor or not doesn't ever seem to be mentioned in any of the books and information on the Appalachian Trail.

If anything, the section after the Notch caught me somewhat unprepared. There is so much written about the Notch that anything afterward just isn't going to register. However, the Mahoosuc Arm was harder and more challenging, that being probably in part due to the fact that there is a two-thousand-foot climb involved. And because all of this should be anticlimactic after all of the hype about the Notch. So, future hikers, beware of the Arm, for it is steep, requiring the same rock scrambling as the Notch. I was exhausted when I finally got to the top.

Yes, the Trail is a challenge and is very difficult to thru-hike. The context of its difficulty doesn't get fully addressed too often for the distance much overshadows that factor. However, sections of the Trail are really not hiking as much as they are rock scrambling. More emphasis should be placed on this fact. Distance aside, there are sections all by themselves that comprise challenge and, at times, even danger if one gets in too much of a hurry always trying to maintain a certain mileage for the day. Preparation for allowance for difficulty is critical for a lot of the Trail. Too much distance ambition can lead to a lot of frustration and possibly injury.

As a thru-hiker, it took awhile to realize that the distance was not as much the factor that had to be prevailed upon as the extreme difficulty of sections. And being a northbounder meant that those conquests would have to come very late in the hike where the most difficult sections are. So the true challenges come when one's body is totally exhausted and beat-up. That led to the ultimate challenge of the Trail: dealing with the mental anguish of wondering if one were up to the task. It seemed so daunting to think that after all that one had invested in this venture, New Hampshire and Maine would prove to be the nemesis and that a thru-hike could not be completed.

I worried about the Whites and the Mahoosucs continuously and rightly so. No amount of preparation, even the 1,730 miles of hiking to get to the New Hampshire line, is sufficient preparation for what lay ahead. So when one is making plans to thru-hike, it is mental torture when you are about a thousand miles into this overachievement knowing that what lay ahead in New Hampshire and Maine was so much harder, a hiker found himself wondering just how to make it the next mile. And in these early sections, there are places where the Trail has been made difficult just simply because some rock formation provided challenge.

The AT is not supposed to be easy. Of that we are constantly reminded. However, in retrospect, one has to wonder just why sections are made more difficult to provide challenge when the mere completion in itself is challenge enough. My Ole Smoky Lonesome hat is off to all of the trail maintainers for they all do one heck of a job, and to them, I will be eternally grateful. However, if there is a section where some debate is being made between maintainers about routing, why not just make it the easier route. Take the entire Trail into consideration. Not just that half mile or whatever, give the thru-hiker a break. I realize that the extreme bulk of the Trail users are day hikers and persons that just enjoy it in little doses. However, the notoriety of the Trail has come about because of those rugged souls that take it on in its entirety and are probably the ones that truly come back as maintainers and support it with money and their valuable time.

# Chapter 44

## Family Values

Hiking the Appalachian Trail evokes emotions usually associated with the works of great artists and musicians. Bach in his creations of sounds could only be envious that this inconspicuous narrow path in the woods could sing such metaphoric songs that create illusions and ideas, concepts and epiphanies beyond the scope of anything the masters could come up with. Rembrandt could only be frustrated in attempting to depict scenes with mere oils or similar artistic mediums when comparing such with the manifestations of the mind in the medium of human sacrifice and endurance of hiking the Appalachian Trail. For the Trail is so much more than the physical aspects and the tangibles, its main reason for being deal more with imagination than reality, more with abstract than with rocks and trees and mountains and the beauty of nature. This creation of Benton MacKaye and Myron Avery went way beyond the scope of its original intent.

The Appalachian Trail for me meant rebirthing and refurbishing, an approach best described as the "first day of the rest of my life." And as the case with many hikers, the Trail was being asked to perform miracles. Simply by being. And I was asking it, by taking the liberty of enduring the test, to make me a new person. Somewhat akin to the flight of the Phoenix, the ashes would simply be left behind out there somewhere in that long and arduous journey. With completion, I would fly away, pure and clean and pristine.

The Sandul family had endured some intense trials throughout its short history as do most families. Many conflicting ideas and thoughts and opinions abound within this family, maybe even more so than others for there has been exposure beyond what could be considered the norm. This family thrives on independent thought, pulling as one only in crisis, otherwise drifting in every direction each to his own thinking. Possibly products of a nomadic life, or possibly the reasoning goes much deeper than that, back into the millennium of genetics and heredity.

Environments were unique in that home never meant one place, one state, or one town. The U.S. Geological Survey and its influence was home, that being where we happened to be. A mapmaker for the government does not stay in one place too long. No one locale could ever be given a chance to soak in. A comment by a Missourian manifested this concept with regard to longevity and acceptance. Speaking of a man wanting to run for a local political office that was regarded not to possess the credentials in that he was a newcomer that had only been in the area for a mere "ten to twelve years."

So as neophytes to the local traditions, we had to rely more on our views based on all the places that we had lived. Consequently, there was little room for narrow thinking. There was no room for racism for we did not belong to any one group to allow such a luxury, if such a word can be used for such human deception. As outsiders, we were relegated to be observers and acceptors of the colloquial conversation or traditions, not in a position to criticize and beyond camaraderie to participate. As observers, we were at a loss of trying to make changes if wrongs were being practiced. This abstract view, however, allowed for the ability to see things more clearly and to not get ill-conceived concepts too permanently ingrained.

My daughter, Tammy, had to endure always being the outsider as the numbers mounted; and eventually, she attended sixteen different schools. Curt attended eleven schools. Will, the youngest, avoided being a Survey brat in that the moving stopped by the time he started school. However, the influences of nomadism were still a part of his young life. In the twenty-four years that I spent in the field, nineteen different states were home, about as many in the South as the North. With one exception, every one of us was born in a different state: me in Minnesota as was Curt, Kris in Wisconsin, Tammy in Illinois, and Will in Arkansas for a family simply must have one Arkie in the bunch.

Tammy, who as a child had almost white-blonde hair with blue eyes and very white skin, simply reeked of Caucasian. She attended a public school in Marigold, Mississippi, in the second grade. She was a minority in that her class was mostly black. We were advised to place her in a private school replete with the racism and prejudice that would imply. We chose a public school for two reasons. We could not afford a private school. Secondly, and most importantly, being a part of society as it presented itself was worth more in education from the school of life than anything that could have been gained from a higher "quality" of education. Imposing superiority would have been damaging. She learned a lot that year in school. She learned that our paths in life are shared with the masses, that exclusivity narrows the mind, leading to a shallow form of happiness. She learned that there is much more to learning than reading and writing and arithmetic.

So we were exposed to the prejudices that exist and the narrow-mindedness that prevail in each region. The South against blacks, the North against whoever: Mexicans or Native Americans or Irish or Scandinavians or Lutherans or Methodists or people that read *USA Today*. For the South does not hold the patent on racial injustices, that fault seems to go with the territory of being human. The beauty of living in different locales and observing from a distance makes one more empathetic but not immune. The nomadic condition seems to imply that possibly, we were not meant to merely stay in one place, for moving about seems to broaden one's thinking enough to at least consider the other person merely as that and not as belonging to some narrow group.

An incident has stayed with me, simply too radical to ever be forgotten. I was strongly corrected for calling a black lady ma'am. This happened in Arkansas, and my tormentor was one of the locals who was the product of his environment. In his mind, we were white and better than blacks. There was no room in his myopia for thinking to the contrary. Typically, the situation became rather inflamed; but I stayed cool enough to tell him that I considered myself a creation of God and that in His eyes, there really was no difference and that just possibly, that black lady was, indeed, better than me for living more in a godlike manner in her life of abstinence and need.

Evolution is much too controversial a subject to foist upon the reader, but a point has to be made. Mutations as studied and related to DNA have proven beyond any doubts that we all are quite similar. Even if that is uncomfortable to accept. Those mutations have created different races that have evolved through time, and only because of our propensity to eventually inner-breed have we managed to maintain an almost-startling similarity that DNA comparisons reveal. If a race of people could totally isolate themselves for a very long time, longer than any precedent in the history of man, could we ultimately say that we are different? Probably not for we are merely *Homo sapiens*—all the same, all with different characteristics, but none that could imply superiority by any faction.

This life of roaming made for a family that spent a lot of time together, and an intense love developed because in our isolated roles, we really needed each other. Nomadism creates problems in that we were not a part of society; however, those shortcomings created an attitude, placing a unique value on individuals. More simply phrased, life was good for we just simply were not going to accept it any other way. Material things more than took a backseat for "stuff" just got in the way and simplicity and frugality were necessary. There just was not room for extraneous things. It was always amusing and sometimes stressful accounting for the new acquisitions on a field assignment and making decisions as to what had to go to compensate for those additions. A remarkable tool for inventory control. Garage sales were the norm usually just prior to the next move.

Embarking on the Trail was cause to reflect on things that had gone wrong with our family. We are no different than any other family, and this reflection was one of the reasons for doing the hike as a milestone: a time for healing and a time for reestablishing validity. The youth of idealism gave way to middle age, and with that came rebellion and family crisis and doing things that should not have been done. It is not the intent of this book to reveal deep Sandul secrets. However, it shall be simply stated here that my own behavior went well beyond what this remarkable family should have had to endure. However, those events had been far enough back in the past that a certain amount of forgetting and forgiveness had taken place. However, a residue seemed to just hang there. The human propensity to "remember" needed catalyst, something tangible, for exoneration. A profound happening, a turning point from whence reference could be drawn. Kind of a BC-AD sort of thing—Before the Trail, After the Trail.

So this narrow path in the woods of dirt and rocks and roots and natural things was being asked to be the panacea, the magical thing that brought us all back together, to restructure some of the past. To place so much emphasis on my one act, albeit a rather-long and enduring one, was rather haughty. However, it was just time for something profound. To regain viability. To regain respect. To have my family members say, "Hey, Dad is okay."

So walk I did. I walked those first miles laden with guilt to some extent but more so with idealism and virtue, knowing that there was intent here way beyond the scope of such activity. A sometimes-hackneyed term for other books on thru-hiking seems to establish a subculture of reprobates, taking a sabbatical from society. Character was being tested, abilities were being put on the line, commitments were tested to the breaking point. A healing process was about to take place unprecedented within the confines of our little family unit, that forgiveness on a grand scale was about to manifest itself and could only come about with walking the walk, for talking the talk had went way beyond the intent as the preparation process went way beyond promises that I was comfortable with. Shoot, I had never carried forty pounds up one mountain, let alone over 2,000 miles of mountains! And of course, thoughts soon drifted to thinking that, possibly exoneration, could have come about in an easier way!

So my heart and entire being reeked of emotion those first days. I repeatedly kept saying, "Face your fears," and I nodded and kept going. For in doing this thing came about this self-awarded feeling of being a hero. I envisioned great speeches and standing on Mount Katahdin to wild and tumultuous fanfare as bands played and people of renown were there to present me with honors and plaques and trophies. I wandered along in this narcissistic trance full of goodness and mercy and self-praise, not even knowing if I would make it through the day, let alone tomorrow. Mount Katahdin was over 2,000 miles away, and no small part of me had been put to the test. However—a very important however—the impetus, the stimulation, the inspiration was so very strong there just did not seem to be room for failure. Failure just could not even be in the picture. Too much was riding on this endeavor.

Yes, I wanted good reason to hold my head high and know that I deserved to be an important part of this group of people that I simply called my family.

Even at sixty-two years old, I still have a lot of life ahead of me. It should be noted here as it will be noted in other places that I expect to live to be a one-hundred-year-old. On that birthday, I have a tennis match scheduled with my old tennis nemesis that I haven't beaten in years, my old friend and world-class finger-style guitarist, Bob Dillon. He will be a mere eighty-three-year-old on that day, and I hope to whip his butt.

So walk I did. Every day another tiny milestone in this task that had to be taken in small chunks for the whole was just too mind-boggling to accept. Walk I did in hopes of reaching a goal that held so much promise. That beyond this endeavor laid a quality of life that had too long been forgotten and that I yearned to get back with such intensity. That the true manifestation of the value of family and the true value of people sticking it out together was about to be contested and that the frailty of the human condition only lay within the mind. With numbers came strength, and when those numbers concern family members, that strength is second to absolutely nothing. Family and goodness and virtue—all of that was being put on the line along this narrow little clearing in the woods adorned with white blazes that were leading me to my new life and to happiness and fulfillment.

Early on, the manifestation haunted me that a little bit of doing the Trail did not count for anything. Equated to being second. Second was nothing. Not finishing was nothing. The only acceptable conclusion to this mission was to stand on Mount Katahdin and say that I had done the entire thing. Way back when Corsican (near Hiawassee, Georgia) had told me, "Don't quit, whatever you do, don't quit." I didn't understand then just what he was saying if one were to look for deeper meaning in the statement for it sounds pretty simple. However, eventually the manifestation would come about. Quitting is just too easy on the Trail for one can justify that in so many ways, usually some sort of contrived physical ailment is the most prevalent. To be reminded that there are no options or it meant failure could only come in those simple words, "Don't quit."

Even getting to within a stone's throw didn't count. The sum total of the individual parts did not come close to equaling the whole part of which they were comprised. If 2,175 miles is accepted as the total mileage, 2,100 miles was still nothing. Kind of like climbing a major mountain and dying on the way back down. That doesn't count either. For if one doesn't return, there is no conquest for the mountain climber. A concept much debated in that elite circle of mountaineers that I have not even the slightest iota of knowledge about. Just something that I had read. For hiking the Trail is in the mountains but should not be confused with "mountain climbing."

So walk I did. And with the walking came healing and with the healing came forgiveness and with forgiveness a sense of family unity prevailed that had no precedent. The Trail did something that all those years of living could not. A true panacea for the long-past forgotten ills of the Sandul family. Yes, the Appalachian Trail runs very deep. Probably within the scope of its original intent for the reasons for its being are truly more complicated than the surface would imply.

Nothing in the contrivance of accepted human ways of dealing with pain could have compared to the therapeutic massage of the thru-hiking of the Trail. Not a church. Not a group therapy program. Not money. Not possessions. The hiking of the Appalachian Trail was worth every ounce of energy that was expended, every minute where doubt and worries existed, every dollar that was spent to make it happen. As the fortune cookie message so aptly and succinctly stated, "Your path is arduous but will be amply rewarding." The Appalachian Trail was all of these things and more and will be for the rest of my life.

# Chapter 45

## Katahdin

Son, Will—half-way up Katahdin—a lot of moral support

This was the Day. Rehearsed. Planned. Hoped for. Dreamed about.

Early impressions that are purely conjecture and formulated from reading and various other forms of information are so much different than the actual thing. Mount Katahdin should have been the stereotypical mountain from information gathered over the past few years. Reality proved otherwise, for here we were near that ultimate peak, and it was nothing like those preconceived concepts. However, it really wasn't clear what it was supposed to look like or smell like or feel like.

Five months ago, there had been so much doubt; but now that it was actually happening, a surrealistic shock had set in as I approached the infamous summit. My son Will, who had led the way up, had very gracefully deferred the lead to me, for he was always the gentleman and knew that it was the proper thing to do. This changing of places had been done without a word spoken, merely an understanding after making eye contact.

For Will, this had been a serious matter of priorities, for by rights he should have been back in Salt Lake City doing his master's degree thing. However, he had made a point of being there regardless and would have to do some serious making up when he got back to Utah. Yes, Will did have a good sense of priorities.

Kris was supposed to have been at Millinocket to see Will and me off for the completion of the hike, but Hurricane Isabel had other ideas. AmTrak, which was to have been her conveyance to the Washington DC area, hauling her Honda Accord on the train, had canceled for that week because of damage caused by the storm. She was to have driven from there to Millinocket, and then we were to leisurely drive back to Florida, basking in accomplishment. However, back in Ocala, she had to settle for just a phone call from the motel after we were done.

There was a throng at the summit that provided some weak applause. A number of them had passed us on the way up and knew that I was a thru-hiker about to culminate my odyssey. My haggard looks seemed to demand at least some semblance of recognition. The rock cairn beckoned and seemed to be the most obvious thing to touch first, but then the sign came into view, the most famous sign on the Appalachian Trail. It turned out to be a decision based more on common sense than sentimentality. There was more room around the cairn to stand as the crowd had all clustered around the infamous sign.

After paying homage to the cairn, I slowly moved over to the sign for the stereotypical photos (hero shots) and rituals. I hugged the sign as all of us that have embarked on this mission must do, maybe more out of tradition than joy. The hugging part was expected of thru-hikers.

Emotion is a funny thing. I felt more subdued than anything and really didn't know if I should be doing metaphoric cartwheels or just quietly enjoying the moment. With Will being there, the moment took on a sense of reverence. With him as witness to the culmination by being a part of these final miles, the moment had taken on ceremonial overtones. Not to take away from the other two Sandul offspring for their priorities were also well entrenched, and obligations can't always be just put away. Will was the representative Sandul, the others were there in spirit, and that was all that was necessary.

My mind was full of Kris, my wife. Almost to the hour forty years before, I had stood beside her in her long flowing white gown, had looked into those impossibly blue eyes, and had made some reckless promises that only a twenty-two-year-old could make. Those promises, uttered in a small Lutheran church in central Wisconsin, had been made on September 21, 1963.

Forty years ago, I had hugged Kris in that small church. Today I hugged the old board sign and remembered our anniversary. Both of these important milestones had come about because of dedication and perseverance. The hike, however, was only a commitment of 170 days and paled in comparison with the other.

We had grown up together, brought three human beings into the world and cared for them together. For twenty-four years, we had been on the move constantly, having lived in thirty-five different towns. Then with moving behind us, we had settled into a totally different lifestyle as she pursued her long-held dream to be a nurse and I became Mr. Mom while finishing the remaining eleven years of my career with USGS. She earned her degree as the dream came true after such a long time, eventually leading to working in operating rooms in three different hospitals in three different states.

We had survived the death of our parents and her sister and had wallowed in the uncertainty of what we so succinctly call life. For in life, as on the Trail, our finest hour came not at the zenith but rather at the nadir, when we blundered with mistakes and failures, when commitment to each other had grown rather thin, when it would have been easier to have just given up. And as on the Trail, we had dug deep to answer to that commitment and to press on and live life as God had intended. And I knew that those youthful first years of frolic and unbridled passion, as sweet as that was, could not hold a candle to this—the good stuff, the manifestation of the deepest relationship between two human beings. Life had thrown all the crap at us that it could, and somehow, we were still the best of friends and knew that we would grow old together and were still deeply in love with each other.

The accomplishment of thru-hiking the Appalachian Trail severely paled to our marriage, of that I was very sure about standing on Mount Katahdin that day.

Except for a tiny ritual and the long hike back to the car, it was over. I dug into my fanny pack where it had been conveniently placed—a tiny pebble that I had picked up back in Virginia, not too far from Bland, along a creek that was one of the places that Jack Agee had taken Buffalo Bobby and me on his local tour, a rock-strewn, bubbling shallow brook that Jack frequently visited. It had seemed appropriate to pick my memento from that place to commemorate this man in this small way. Adhering to the longtime tradition, I carefully reached into the rock cairn and placed it there and remembered this man that had helped me so much. For he had by far been the most inspirational person of all of the numerous people that I had encountered along the Appalachian Trail.

Done—finally done
Sept 21
Mt Katahdin, Maine

# Epilogue

It occurred to me in the process of writing this book that I was trying to write it for too many people. That concept was leading me away from the original intent, that being an account of my thru-hike of the Appalachian Trail for posterity, for neighbors and friends, for those that supported me in my effort, for my family, and just possibly for somebody that doesn't know me and would like to know what it is like for a sixty-two-year-old man with no particularly outstanding abilities, with no particularly outstanding accomplishments to do something that at the outset was considered impossible for me to do. But mostly, I was writing the book for me so that years from now, I can reread it and remember the turmoil, the sweetness, the friends, and the memories.

This book is not the panacea for Appalachian Trail information and does not pretend to be things that it wasn't intended to be. This book was not intended to provide everything that you may want to know about the Trail's flora and fauna and geography and geology and history. The research for that information would have been detrimental to its original intent, that being to provide insight and personal information and possibly some human-interest stories and humor.

If the book does have a genre, it is rather subtle, placed somewhere between unadulterated stories of the human spirit and adventure. However, there is an intent to provide practical information more or less aimed at the "older" hiker. I made mistakes as would anybody engaged in something new. As we all know, the most useful lessons in life are the trial-and-error lessons. Possibly most hikers would rather make their own mistakes for within that methodology lies true learning. However, sometimes it's better to know what to expect ahead of time and possibly make adjustments where expense and convenience can be better controlled instead of trying to make corrections away from home.

There are excellent publications on the subject. Possibly there is redundancy; however, it seems that each publication has something to offer that other ones don't. Also, the Appalachian Trail is not static. For in spite of its long history and its long list of traditions, the Trail seems to be like the rest of our society, subject to change whether that is necessitated by nature or the efforts of man. A listing of current publications and a very brief summary of what to expect in each is made below. Please refer to that list for the types of information that you may be seeking. Also, excellent Web sites exist out there with almost every conceivable bit of information and stories that one could want.

Probably the best information comes from the ones that are doing. Trail journals are accessible on trailsjournal.com and provide so much insight for these are rather succinct entries of what is happening currently with little regard to literary style or clever writing. The type of information provided candidly, honestly, and from the heart.

Suggested Appalachian Trail reading and a brief synopsis of each:

* *A Walk in the Woods* by Bill Bryson—A delightful read with humorous accounts of his attempt at a thru-hike (only about 850 miles), part of it with a friend, Stephen Katz, who turns into a sort of antihero. The book also is well researched with a lot of information about the Trail's history, geology, and evolution.

* *On the Beaten Path* by Robert Alden Rubin—A well-thought-out account of Mr. Rubin's successful thru-hike that is beautifully written, sometimes almost reading like poetry. Mr. Rubin was the editor of the *Appalachian Trailway News* in 2003. I stopped and talked to him and complimented him on his book.

* *A Journey North* by Adrienne Hall—Again about a successful thru-hike but by two people, Ms. (to become Mrs.) Hall and her fiancé. He proposed to her on Saddleback Mountain in Maine near the completion of their journey. She talks a lot about the physical difficulty in hiking the Trail. The book is well researched with a lot of information about the effects of man upon the ecology along the Trail corridor.

* *As Far as the Eye Can See* by David Brill—Another successful thru-hike with a number of companions. The book touches on the simple life of the Trail and how amazingly little is needed in Trail life when compared to our so-called needs (wants) in our real society.

* *A Woman's Journey on the Apalachian Trail* by Cindy Ross—A wonderfully written (in longhand) and illustrated book (in pencil sketches) that turned out to have poignant prose while still being packed with information. Ms. Ross and her companion only make half of the Trail the first year, and she comes back to complete it the following year. The artwork is superb, and the narrative is heartwarming.

* *Walking with Spring* by Earl V. Shaffer—A must read for anybody interested in the Trail. The original thru-hiker and his story. No precedent had been set. The information that would be gained from his experiences was invaluable to future thru-hikers and would set the bar, for it was always thought that a one-season thru-hike was impossible. Mr. Shaffer proved the naysayers totally wrong.

* *The Thru-Hiker's Handbook: Georgia to Maine* (these are published yearly, my issue was for 2002) by Dan "Wingfoot" Bruce—The guru of the Trail. Invaluable information for the thru-hiker or section-hiker or whatever capacity the Trail is encountered. Not only does the book provide logistics (shelters, mileages, towns, services available) but also is choked full of information about the geology, flora and fauna, and other pertinent historical and amusing information. Not really intended to be read from cover to cover, I did anyway to be aware of just what all was in the book and out there on the Trail.

* (1) *Advanced Backpacking: A Trailside Guide* by Karen Berger—A must read for new hikers. Very informative and well written with vital information for the long distance hiker. The book is well illustrated and full of wonderful photographs.

There are numerous other books about the Appalachian Trail. These eight to me were the most noteworthy. A full listing is available on either Amazon.com or on the Appalachian Trail Web site.

Writer's final notes: Without having another chapter that deals with omissions or oversights, a few points have to be noted.

Concerning the term *the Mahoosucs*: I have used the term as all-inclusive for the parts of the Longfellow Mountains that comprise the mountains and ranges of the Appalachian Trail in Maine (primarily on the western side of the state). It was easier to make the reference that way instead of complicating the issue with other range names that may apply.

All of my toes on both feet will probably never be the same. There is numbness and contradictory severe pain when stubbed on hard objects when barefooted. A small price to pay. However, in fairness to hiking and boots, these toes have been abused from childhood on. Surveyor's toes take a beating in the wilds. And those hundreds of hours on the ice rinks in Fargo in ten-degree weather took their toll.

One glaring omission concerns equipment that a thru-hiker should not be without: a pair of gaiters.

Gaiters are the best thing since sliced bread. The purposes are at least trifold: (1) it keeps the rocks and debris out of the boots, (2) the socks stay relatively clean, and (3) the shoelaces stay tied when foliage is encountered. I made it 460 miles to Damascus before male ego had to be ignored, for gaiters did have a sort of feminine aura, and purchased a pair there. It took much less time to clean feet when showering, and socks were in good condition from then on.

Lost photos: My Olympus Camedia served me well. However, it was somewhat ancient by camera/computer standards. The disks (SmartMedia) became harder and harder to find, and eventually the only size available were the 128 mb. These proved to pose a problem never anticipated. Probably just too much for the ancient camera. However, the tragic part is that two of the disks fouled after getting home while in the process of trying to make prints. A number of different companies were contacted to try a recovery process, and all were unsuccessful. Result: about seven hundred photos were lost forever. And ironically, these were from the last half of the hike. Only because of Will being there with his camera are Katahdin photos available now.

So advice. This is not rocket science. Transfer the disks to CDs or whatever as soon as possible and certainly before trying to make prints.

And there are those things that appear to be omissions:

My Dad. It would be difficult to write about a man that I did not know. Mom left him when I was nine years old. From the time that I was twenty until the day I was forty, we did not speak to each other. We made our peace two years later at a Sandul family reunion, and when he died eleven years later, I attended the funeral. He was a good man that had simply made some mistakes early in life. Soon enough that he could more than exonerate himself and left the world at peace with himself and with me.

Duncannon, Pennsylvania, and the Doyle Hotel should be a book in itself. So I just left it alone. Possibly that can be the sequel.

Delaware Water Gap. I just want to go back and visit and eat one more time at the Water Gap Diner. However, that is only one of the approximately fifty awesome restaurants along and near the Trail that a replay is definitely a must.

However, as Ole Smoky Lonesome, it was a disappointment that fried green tomatoes were not available at the Whistle Stop Restaurant near Clarendon, Vermont.

Trash along the Trail when crossing highways or going through towns. This only happened in about a dozen places, but it was bad. However, conversely, thru-hikers are to be commended, for trash away from the thoroughfares is virtually nonexistent. However, within comfortable distances of roads and towns, there was trash carelessly discarded, leading to the safe assumption that it did not come from thru-hikers. I packed EVERYTHING out, including those things that I found (if there was room for the additional stuff).

I finally found Buffalo Bobby in the *ATN* publication (May–June 2004), showing that he had completed his thru-hike. In the course of making the final changes in the book, I finally talked to Buffalo Bobby on the phone. It had been six years. What a wonderful phone reunion! I was delighted to hear that he had thru-hiked again in 2007. And, also during this time of obtaining permissions during the wrap-up of the book, what a pleasure it was to again talk to Pippi, but was saddened to hear that she had, indeed, contracted Lyme Disease. However, that was not stopping her as she continued her hiking adventures.

Lastly, if there is some confusion about my references to living in Florida. While in the process of writing this book, my wife and I moved to Wisconsin.

Some explanation—it would seem logical that the reader is somewhat confused with a book published in 2009 when the story dates way back to 2003. The original writing was more in short story form but slowly evolved over a number of years into a book. Those stories resided in my computers for about three years, having been submitted to a number of publishers who were not interested.

So, staying with the main theme of commitment, the ultimate in that endeavor came in the writing of the story and the eventual publication. I had never written a book before, and, like the hiking of the Trail, it too evolved into a series of ups and downs and, eventually—success.

The publication process was an eye-opener trying to find people for permissions; people who went with various trail names and who were very hard to find. So, creative methods had to be devised to make the book right and if there are oversights, please accept my apologies. There are so many more trail names and hikers that should have been included in the book, but that was not to be done without permission. For those beautiful and well thought out trail names that are not included, please excuse my inadequate substitutes.

List of equipment and costs (listed more or less in sequence that these items were purchased):

Backpack (Dana Design) $223.20
Rain cover 40.00
Gloves 27.00
Long-sleeve shirt (2) 72.00
Pur water filter 59.95
Water bottles (Nalgene, 48 oz: 2) 15.98
Convertible pants (2) 75.00 (about)
Sleeping bag (North Face Cat's Meow) 179.00
Tent (North Face Slickrock) 239.00
Therm-a-Rest 75.00
Boots 175.00
T-shirts (3) 102.00
Briefs (3) 54.00
Stove (MSR) 69.95
Cook set 33.95
Fuel Bottle (MSR) 9.95
Hiking socks (2 pairs) 29.98
Leatherman all-purpose tool and knife 19.99
Repair kit 12.00
*The Thru-Hiker's Handbook* 15.95
Turtleneck shirt (L.L.Bean) 32.00
Long johns 34.00
Rain jacket (L.L.Bean) 169.00
Rain pants (L.L.Bean) 149.00

Maps (topo and profile, complete set) 225.90
Tarp (groundcover) 4.00
Digging tool (for, well, you know) 3.00
Boots (EMS, bought at 1,560 miles) 95.00
Boots (Merrel, bought at 1,737 miles) 100.00
Tennis (camp) shoes (bought in Damascus) 40.00 (about)
Gaiters (bought in Damascus) 20.00 (about)
Watch (kid's, bought at 700 miles) 23.00

In addition, there were a number of odds and ends (boot laces, glue and repair kits, poster maps and sales tax). My grand total for equipment and gear amounted to $2,757; and except for the boots (the Northbounders are part of my AT shrine), all of this stuff is still being used and will be for years to come.

Lodging (and camping) costs (number of nights) and places stayed:

(1) Rainbow Springs Campground (Franklin, NC—04-13-03) $15.00
(1) Fontana Inn (04-17-03) 20.00
(1) Mountain Moma's Bunkhouse ( Waterville, NC—04-22-03) 25.00
(1) Uncle Johnny's Hostel (Erwin, TN—camping—04-29-03) 6.00
(2) The Place (Damascus, VA—camping—05-07/08-03)) 10.00
(1) Holiday Motor Lodge (Pearisburg, VA—05-18-03) 50.74
(2) Econo Lodge (Troutville, VA—05-25/26-03) 109.50
(2) Quality Inn (Waynesboro, VA—06-03/04-03) 109.40
(1) Big Meadows Campground (Shenandoah National Park—06-08-03) 19.00
(1) Bears Den Hostel (06-13-03) 13.00
(4) Hilltop House (Harpers Ferry, WV—06-15/18-03) 174.40
(1) Doyle Hotel (Duncannon, PA—06-27-03) 16.00
(2) Presbyterian Church (Delaware Water Gap—camping—07-06/07-03) 6.50
(2) Greenwood Motel (Greenwood Lake, NY—07-12/13-03) 85.00
(1) Fife n' Drum (Kent, CT—07-20-03) 55.88
(1) Shamrock Village Inn (Dalton, MA—07-28-03) 60.25
(1) Inn at Long Trail (Killington, VT—08-05-03) 51.88
(2) Super 8 (White River Junction, VT—08-09-03) 155.00
(1) Hikers Welcome Hostel (Glencliff, NH—camping—08-13-03) 6.00
(1) Liberty Springs Campground (White Mountains—08-15-03) 6.00
(2) Royalty Inn (Gorham, NH—08-21/22-03) 140.40
(2) Stratton Motel (Stratton, ME—08-31/09-01-03) 85.60
(2) Shaw's Boarding House (Monson, ME—09/06 & 07-03) 50.00

(1) Abol Bridge Campground (09-13-03) 5.00
(1) Katahdin Inn (Millinocket, ME—09-14-03) 79.18
(7) Hotel Terrace (Millinocket, ME—09-15/21-03) 379.85
   (this last motel includes Will's room also)

Total $1,709.58

# Trail Jargon

**Thru-hiker**—Old definition: A complete one-way hike (either north or south from Springer Mountain, Georgia, to Mount Katahdin, Maine, or vice versa) of the entire (white blazed) Appalachian Trail in the same direction in one season unassisted and carrying all one's needs in a backpack—generally either tenting or staying in trail shelters with occasional town stays in motels, hostels, or other rooming accommodations.

New definition: Hiking (more or less) the entire distance not necessarily in the same direction and not necessarily carrying a backpack—the only requirement being to cover the entire distance in one season.

**Section-hiker**—One who hikes relatively short sections of the Appalachian Trail a season at a time in an attempt to eventually cover the entire distance.

**Slackpacker**—A hiker who has his/her backpack hauled ahead by vehicle to a predetermined meeting point, usually a paid service, thus eliminating having to carry anything other than daily needs of food and water.

**Sobo**—Southbound thru-hiker.

**Nobo**—Northbound thru-hiker.

**Zero Day**—A day off the trail with no hiking—usually in towns.

**Getting off the Trail**—Quitting. Discontinuing a thru-hike attempt.

**PUDS**—Pointless ups and downs along the trail route. Most generally applies to sections of trail with approximately two hundred to five hundred feet elevation changes with the scenery staying essentially the same. These types of elevation changes seem to be more tiring than major changes of one thousand feet or more where there is at least a view to look forward to upon reaching the ridge or mountain summits.

**MUDS**—Same definition as above, but using *mindless.*

**Blue Blazing**—Blue blaze sections (versus white-blazes along the AT proper) are side trails to towns, vistas, or points of interest. Occasionally, the blue-blazed sections could be used as a shortcut when a triangle is created with reconnections farther along the AT. True thru-hikers return to the point of leaving the white blazes to continue and thus maintain the integrity of the hike.

**Maintainer**—Volunteers working with the Appalachian Trail Conservancy to maintain trail conditions conducive to good hiking—cutting down trees and brush, marking stubs that can be tripped on, relocating rocks, clearing and creating drainage chutes for water, and generally making trail conditions better.

**Stealth Camping**—Also occasionally called *maverick camping.* To camp in other than designated or approved places along the Appalachian Trail corridor. A problem often occurs at the shelters where tent camping sites are available that too often are not on level ground (a must when setting up a tent). The important issue when stealth camping is to be conscientious about Leave No Trace procedures.

**Leave No Trace**—Applies to all human activities in nature. The objective being to not disturb anything—foliage or fauna—or to the very least degree that is possible.

**Trail Angel**—Any person along the Trail that provides transportation and food to thru-hikers or helps out in various ways to facilitate the hiking endeavor.

**Trail Magic**—Any of a number of types of good deeds along the Trail where good feelings occur between thru-hikers and the local people (occasionally past thru-hikers); usually in the forms of providing food and drinks or transportation to towns.

Printed in the United States
154372LV00001B/152/P